Sovereignty in Dispute

Also of Interest

Military Lessons of the Falkland Islands War: Views from the United States, edited by Bruce W. Watson and Peter M. Dunn

The Exclusive Economic Zone: A Latin American Perspective, edited by Francisco Orrego Vicuña

†*Latin American Foreign Policies: Global and Regional Dimensions,* edited by Elizabeth G. Ferris and Jennie K. Lincoln

†*Latin America, Its Problems and Its Promise: A Multidisciplinary Introduction,* edited by Jan Knippers Black

†*Latin America and the U.S. National Interest: A Basis for U.S. Foreign Policy,* Margaret Daly Hayes

†*FOREIGN POLICY on Latin America, 1970–1980,* edited by the staff of *Foreign Policy*

†*The Caribbean Challenge: U.S. Policy in a Volatile Region,* edited by H. Michael Erisman

Controlling Latin American Conflicts: Ten Approaches, edited by Michael A. Morris and Victor Millán

†Available in hardcover and paperback.

Westview Special Studies on Latin America and the Caribbean

Sovereignty in Dispute:
The Falklands/Malvinas, 1493-1982
Fritz L. Hoffmann and Olga Mingo Hoffmann

The Falkland (or Malvinas) Islands—a peaceful haven for land and sea birds and once a profitable paradise for whalers and seal hunters—erupted into the headlines on April 2, 1982. The armed conflict between Britain and Argentina that continued during the following two months was but one more stage in a long-standing struggle over the sovereignty of the islands, a conflict dating back to colonial times. The issues, much discussed, remain unresolved.

In this book, the Hoffmanns present the background to the confrontation between Argentina and Britain, as well as an analysis of the present situation. Clarifying the importance of the seemingly insignificant, remote islands in the South Atlantic, over which European nations nearly went to war several times and which Britain wrested from Argentina in the 1830s, the authors trace the history of the dispute, the involvement of the United States, and the impact of the recent war on inter-American relations.

Fritz L. Hoffmann is professor emeritus, University of Colorado, Boulder, where he taught Latin American history from 1937 to 1975. **Olga Mingo Hoffmann** has taught Spanish language and literature and Latin American history.

To
the young men who died in a
senseless war over the islands

Sovereignty in Dispute:
The Falklands/Malvinas,
1493–1982

Fritz L. Hoffmann and
Olga Mingo Hoffmann

Westview Press / Boulder and London

Westview Special Studies on Latin America and the Caribbean

Published in 1984 in the United States of America by Westview Press, Inc., 5500 Central Avenue, Boulder, Colorado 80301; Frederick A. Praeger, President and Publisher

Library of Congress Cataloging in Publication Data
Hoffmann, Fritz L. (Fritz Leo), 1907–
  Sovereignty in dispute.
  (Westview special studies on Latin America and the
Caribbean)
  Bibliography: p.
  Includes index.
  1. Falkland Islands—History. 2. Falkland Islands—
International status. I. Hoffmann, Olga Mingo.
II. Title. III. Series.
F3031.H57 1984   997'.11   83-23446
ISBN 0-86531-605-8

Printed and bound in the United States of America

5   4   3   2   1

Contents

Illustrations

Preface

This study centers on the history of the dispute over the Falkland Islands (Las Islas Malvinas), a remote, windswept archipelago in the far reaches of the South Atlantic off the coast of Argentina. They are held by Great Britain and claimed by Argentina. Few people know anything about them, and when the war over them broke out in April 1982, many Britons had to run to a map to see where they were. But not the Argentines, who are taught from the cradle that "las Malvinas son argentinas" (the Malvinas are Argentine).

But even the Argentines don't know how complex the whole question of ownership of the islands is. They do know that for 150 years, during the last quarter century through negotiations, their country has been trying to recover land taken from them by force in 1833. When negotiations proved futile, Argentine patience ran out. Argentina tried to take the islands back by force in the Seventy-Four-Day War of April–June 1982. This book is an attempt to relate the long and complex story of what led to that tragic event.

Besides secondary sources, our story is based mainly on official documents and on contemporary periodicals, including newspapers, many of them collected during extended stays in Argentina. As would be expected, much has been written on the islands by Argentines, who through years of frustrating attempts to get the islands back have developed a kind of collective mania about the Malvinas, something the outside world has failed to understand. Few people have even tried to go through the flood of materials printed in Argentina on the islands. This we have tried to do, we hope with some degree of success.

Many people, far too many to mention them all, have assisted us in our work. However, a few of them must be singled out for their eagerness to help and the unusual and remarkable assistance rendered. In the University of Colorado Libraries they were Marie L. Campbell of the Serials Department; Benedict LoBue and R. Carol Cushman of the Reference Department; and Catherine J. Reynolds, Martha S. Campbell, and Marcia L. Epelbaum of the Government Publications Department. Martha Campbell's enthusiasm in finding materials for us was exceeded only by ours in receiving them.

In Argentina we found other generous people ready to help and encourage us. We are most grateful to Marta and Nelly Aphalo, whose assistance and encouragement were unending; Lavinia M. de Baumann-Fonay and Claudio Baumann-Fonay, whose eagerness to send materials was heart-warming; Juan Carlos Moreno, noted authority on the Malvinas, who took time from his busy schedule to make useful scholarly suggestions; and Pedro García Rueda, director general of the prestigious publishing house Librería y Editorial El Ateneo, whose answer to our request to use some materials from one of that company's books was graciously given by return mail (possibly a world record), together with offers to help in other ways if he could.

We wish to express our special gratitude to Señora Marta Maldonado de García, who generously gave us all the materials on the Falklands/Malvinas collected over many years by her late husband, Doctor Eduardo Augusto García, distinguished writer, lawyer, publicist, diplomat, and professor of international law as well as champion of Argentine democracy.

Fritz L. Hoffmann
Olga Mingo Hoffmann

1
Introduction

The Falkland Archipelago: Las Islas Malvinas

In the South Atlantic, between 52° and 53° south latitude and 57° and 62° west longitude, lies the Falkland Archipelago, 7,500 miles (12,068 kilometers) from Great Britain and 300 miles (483 kilometers) from the Argentine coast. The total area of the archipelago is over 6,000 square miles (over 15,500 square kilometers). The archipelago consists of two large islands, East and West Falkland, and over 200 small islands and islets. Of these a few are inhabited by people, some by sheep, and all by birds at one time or another. Falkland Sound separates the two major islands. It was so named by its discoverer, John Strong, in 1690, in honor of Viscount Falkland, then treasurer of the Royal Navy. From it the islands ultimately got their English name. The Spanish name, Las Islas Malvinas, is derived from the French name, Les Iles Malouines, given them by Louis Antoine de Bougainville, who established the first settlement on the islands in 1764. The islands were very well known and frequented by Malouines, French sailors from St. Malo on the northwest coast of France. This familiarity gave Bougainville, also from St. Malo, the idea of settling them for France.

Land and Coastline

For most visitors the islands seem bleak and windy, gloomy and inhospitable, but for some they have special charm. There are no trees in sight except for a tiny park in Stanley, three acres of wooded land in Hill Cove, and a few trees in some of the rural establishments where human care has succeeded in overcoming adverse nature.

The soil of the islands ranges from clay-slate to peat. There is much peat in the islands, dug for fuel purposes. The soil holds many ponds, lakes, and marshes, and in the peat bogs a rider who has lost his way may disappear. In the more rolling terrain there are hills of white granular quartz, some reaching over 2,000 feet (600 meters) in height. The strata of quartz are frequently arched with a symmetry that gives them a peculiar appearance. Valley bottoms are often covered by unusual

2

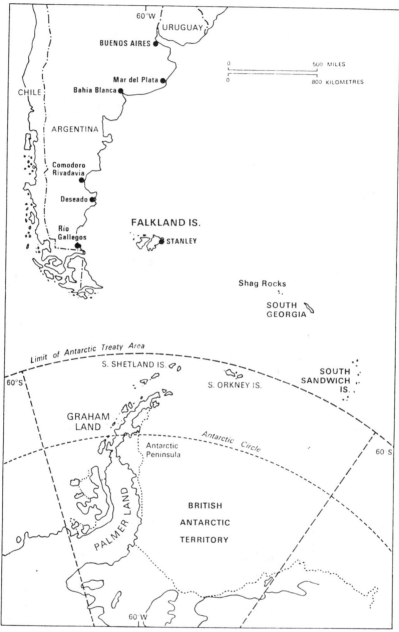

FIGURE 1.1. Map of the South Atlantic and part of Antarctica showing the Argentine coast and the Falkland Islands.

Source: British Information Services, *Survey of Current Affairs* 12, no. 5 (May 1982), p. 150.

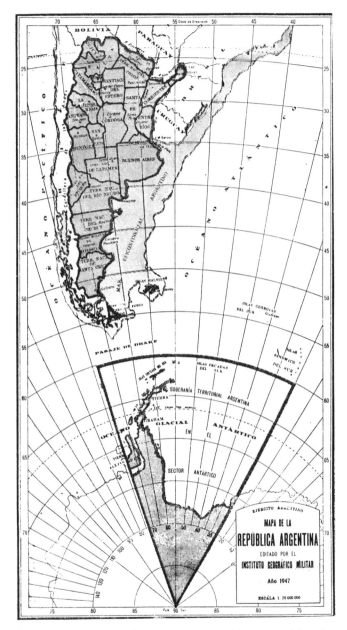

FIGURE 1.2. Map of the Argentine Republic printed by the
Military Geographical Institute in 1947 in Buenos Aires.

Source: Juan Carlos Moreno, *Nuestras Malvinas*, 6th ed. (Buenos Aires:
El Ateneo, 1950).

rock formations called "streams of stone," which are formed by myriads of loose, angular fragments of quartz, their edges barely blunted and their size varying from two to twenty feet or more in diameter. They are spread out in almost level sheets. The depths of these formations are very great. In many places the trickling of water can be heard, suggesting underground streams. These "streams" range in width from several hundred feet to a mile or so, and are closely packed in irregular forms, giving the impression of stone rivers. The southern part of East Falkland, where Stanley, the capital, is located, is an extended plain.

Treeless banks flank the creeks of clear water descending lazily from the hills in search of the sea. The most characteristic contour of the land as it approaches the sea is a series of descending terraces covered by huge quantities of loose rocks. In other places the grasslands descend gradually to meet the line of high tide. And there are still other places where the land plunges into the sea in imposing cliffs.

The profile of the coastline presents deep, fjord-like indentations, forming all sorts of harbors, bays, and inlets. The beaches are often covered with an extraordinary variety of pebbles of all sizes and colors. There are also beaches of very fine white sand alternating with rocky points and cliffs lashed by the sea. The coastline of the islands exhibits a picture that is both beautiful and fierce.

Climate

The archipelago lies in the path of a deep, cold current moving northward from Cape Horn, which accounts for the cold—a mean annual temperature of 43°F (6°C)—and for the zone of persistent stormy weather in which the islands lie, a characteristic first registered by Amerigo Vespucci in 1501. Tempered by the surrounding sea, the year-round median temperature varies an insignificant 12°F between seasons, from 27°F during July, the coldest month, to 49°F for January, the warmest. These averages, however, can be misleading. In January the thermometer can reach a high of 73° and in July drop to a low of 22°. If we add to the mercury indicator the humidity and the winds, the chill factor may become something to be reckoned with.

Vegetation

The variety of vegetation on the islands is severely limited by the short growing season, the wind, the very low temperature and high acidity (pH 4.5) of the soil, the very little potassium and phosphorus, and the near absence of nitrogen. Moreover, the islands are always wet.

A so-called white grass covers most of the land and gives it a creamy color during all seasons, because the dead blades remain erect for over a year, hiding the new green growth. It is not very nutritious, but good enough for sheep. In the well-drained areas a small berry-bearing plant

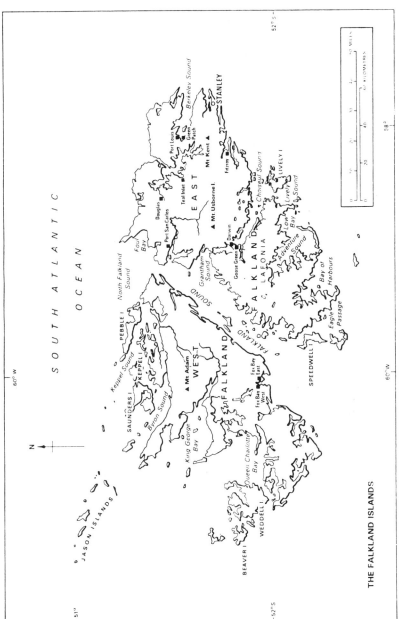

FIGURE 1.3. British official map of the Falkland Islands.

Source: British Information Services, *Survey of Current Affairs* 12, no. 6 (June 1982), p. 181.

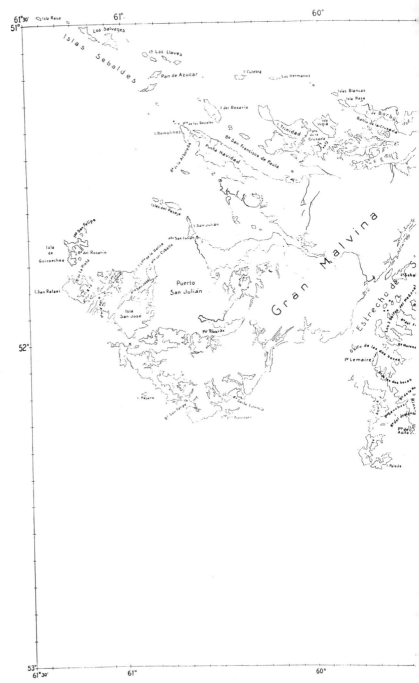

FIGURE 1.4. Map of the Malvinas printed in a typical Argentine textbook on the islands.

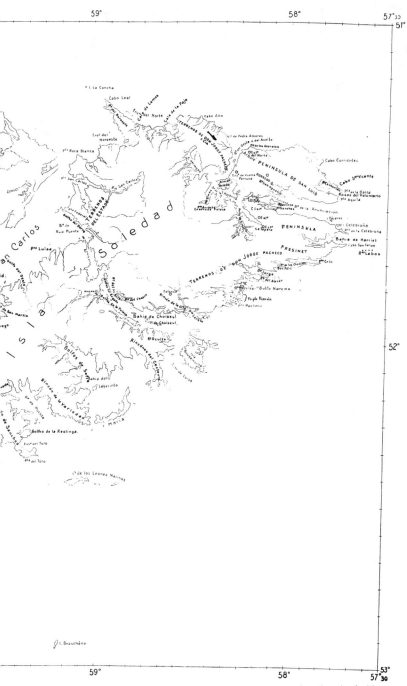

Source: Antonio Gomez Langenheim, *Elementos para la Historia de Nuestras Islas Malvinas*, vol. 2. (Buenos Aires: El Ateneo, 1939). Reprinted by permission.

FIGURE 1.5. Rockhopper penguins in tussock grass on Kidney Island. Photo by O. S. Pettingill.

called the diddle dee grows to a height of six to twelve inches. In the poorly drained areas the vegetation is replaced by brown rushes. In the higher hills and on the "stone runs," or streams, red dwarf sorrel, pink and orange ferns, lichens, and green and golden mosses cover with delicate colors the harshness of the rocky soil.

But *the* plant of the islands is a beautiful grass, the tussock (*Poa flabellata*), which forms clumps reaching up to nine feet in height. It used to cover the coastal regions of the large islands with a green belt 400 to 600 yards wide, and still does in the small islands. This was the vegetation that made early navigators like Bougainville, looking at the islands from the sea, believe at first that they were covered by medium-high forests. The dry blades, says Bougainville's chronicler, provided the French sailors with beds and with thatch for their houses on the islands.

The blades of the tussock, three feet or more in length, spread and droop on a pedestal formed from the decaying leaves on an outcropping of peat or other bases. Clumps of tussock grow very close together and interlace, forming passages or tunnels where thousands of birds nest, protected from the inclement weather. Birds and tussock achieve a perfectly balanced association, for the tussock cannot grow without the fertilizer provided by the birds. Seals and sea lions used to rest under its cover also. But sealers hunting these animals for meat and pelts started the destruction of the tussock, and the later introduction of sheep on the larger islands destroyed almost all of it.

The tussock is an extraordinarily rich winter feed. Cattle introduced by Bougainville thrived on it, attracted to it from a long distance by its smell, and even tried to eat the tussock roofs of the settlers' homes. Cattle and horses eat it in the winter and let it replenish itself during the summer, but sheep eat the buds, preventing its growth. It was the tussock that made possible the tremendous growth of the sheep industry during the nineteenth century, but since then this grass has almost disappeared from the main islands because of overgrazing. The number of sheep the islands could support has decreased from around 800,000 at the beginning of the century to 650,000 in 1977.

Starting with Bougainville, who brought 10,000 trees of different sizes from the Strait of Magellan, many efforts have been made to introduce trees into the islands, with meager results. Roses and lupines grow well, as do some vegetables, like potatoes and turnips. Almost every house in Stanley has a small garden, and many have greenhouses, which may also be found in some of the outlying rural establishments.

Wildlife

For centuries, perhaps thousands of years, the islands have been a wildlife paradise, until in the last century men discovered that seal pelts, whale oil, and penguin oil were profitable and began to kill sea animals and birds by the millions, almost exterminating them. Now, under protection, the seals and the king penguins, the most beautiful of penguins, are slowly returning. From late September to early March, the coastal areas of the islands become alive with the shrieking and squawking of millions of the birds emerging from the sea or dropping from the skies, coming back to their nesting colonies, to which they return faithfully year after year. The interior grasslands are not empty, either. Swarms of upland and ruddy-headed geese nest, feed, and rest there on their migrations.

Five of the fourteen existing species of penguins nest in the islands, and they are the most extraordinary group of visiting birds. They are the rockhoppers, the gentoos, the macaroni, the Magellanic, and a few king penguins returning at last. Some of their colonies number 100,000 pairs or more. The rockhoppers, emerging from the sea, climb up the rocky slopes with surprising agility. Together with some king cormorants and black-browed albatrosses, they nest on top of tall cliffs open to the full roughness of the weather. The gentoo penguins select sheltered beaches to land and proceed in single file to their crowded colonies a short distance from the sea. Several species of ducks, plovers, oyster catchers, gulls, skuas, and geese can be seen everywhere on their nests, while the magnificent black and white king cormorants and black-browed albatrosses glide toward their nesting places. And the flightless steamer duck is everywhere.

Nobody yet knows the importance of the islands as nesting places. Ian J. Strange, a naturalist who has lived in the Falklands for twenty years, tells of an experience he had not long ago when he landed for the first time on an apparently deserted island. He heard a roar coming from over the brow of a hill and thought it was coming from the sea on the opposite side of the island. When he reached the top of the hill and looked through the tussock grass, he saw a mass of black-browed albatrosses and rockhoppers so packed he could not have walked through them without stepping on birds and eggs. With careful surveys and aerial photographs, he calculated that the colony had some two million albatrosses and even more penguins (Strange 1982: p. 6).

Economy

This survey of the economic life of the islands is based in the main on the report of the Shackleton mission of 1976. The economy of the islands depends almost exclusively on the production of high-quality wool from sheep of mixed Corriedale and Romney Marsh stock with a high proportion of merino strains. In recent years, through strict selection, a "clean face" sheep has been produced without wool to obstruct its vision, and the average production of wool for each animal has increased from three to four kilograms (from 6.6 to 8.8 pounds) (Crosby, 1981: p. 26).

The sheep thrive on the rather poor native white grass, the tussock grass having almost disappeared from East and West Falklands. Some progress has been made in improving the pasture. It was noticed a few years ago that a weed called Yorkshire Fog (*Holcus lanatus*) thrived in acid soil, resisted overgrazing, and was well liked by the sheep. The new type of pasture was cultivated with much success in Roy Cove, the most progressive of the farms, which the government of the islands has recently purchased for subdividing.

The grazing land, approximately two-thirds of the total area of the islands, is divided into thirty-six "farms" (really ranches) ranging from 1,000 to 350,000 acres. Of these, four are owner-occupied, nine belong to sole traders and partnerships with headquarters in Stanley, and the remaining twenty-three are in the hands of fourteen companies, most of them with headquarters in England. Of these companies by far the largest is the Falkland Islands Company.

The islanders who work as managers or wool shearers on the sheep farms earn from $6,000 to $8,000 a year, plus housing, meat, milk, and fuel. They take their work seriously because there is no unemployment compensation. They have a rather comfortable life, but when the time comes for retirement they lose most of the benefits, including housing, and are forced to move to Stanley and adjust to new surroundings, which is not always easy. They may also then encounter financial difficulties.

The young, for their part, resent their apparently comfortable but dependent situation, as well as the lack of future improvement in their lives: The possibility of a sheepherder becoming a farm manager is remote indeed; the chance of being elected to one of the two councils and having a voice in politics is nonexistent; and the opportunity of buying or leasing land to farm independently is practically out of the question because little land and few loans are available. Outside the farms a source of livelihood for many islanders is the cutting of peat, the year-round fuel for heating and cooking. There are few crafts, no small enterprises, and no offshore fishing.

The islands, although a crown colony, belong practically to a group of private companies. The profits of the wool industry have been flowing to England, with virtually none used for reinvestment in the islands. From 1950 to 1974, from 10 to 12 million pounds were distributed among the shareholders of the companies owning most of the land and sheep. From this inflow of capital the British government collected about 4 million pounds in corporation and dividend taxes, while its administrative expenses during the same period amounted to 1.7 million pounds (Johnson 1977: p. 226).

Possible economic resources in the future include oil (of which no evidence has been found to date), alginates from the extensive belt of kelp surrounding the islands, and krill, a small shrimp-like sea animal that is high in protein and exists in huge quantities. It is estimated that with the rapid destruction of the blue whale, which fed on the krill, the annual harvest of krill could reach between 75 and 100 million tons a year, whereas the total world fish catch today is only about 70 million. None of these economic possibilities is being exploited (Shackleton 1977: p. 10).

As Lord Shackleton, former president of the Royal Geographical Society and chairman of the Economic Survey of the Falkland Islands, wrote in 1976:

> Far from the Falkland Islanders living off the British, the British have been doing very nicely out of the Falkland Islanders over many years. Far more has come back to Britain in the way of profits than has gone out in the way of new investment. More importantly, we concluded that the Chancellor of the Exchequer has, over the years, taken twice as much out in tax as has gone in in the form of aid to help develop the Falkland Islands. This is a crucial aspect of our findings (Shackleton 1977: p. 5).

The Falkland Islands Company

The economy of the islands is dominated by the Falkland Islands Company, a miniature replica of the East India Company and the British South Africa Company of the seventeenth and eighteenth centuries, with some of the characteristics of its mighty ancestors. It has a firm grip on the land, the economy, and the people on the islands. The company had its origins in the wheeling and dealing of a shady businessman in Montevideo named Samuel Fisher Lafone. In order to settle the islands (which until then had been only a naval way-station), the British government sold him a large tract of land in the islands in the 1840s at a cheap price. The project failed because of Lafone's incompetence. Heavily in debt, he launched a corporation in London named the Royal Falkland Land, Cattle, Seal and Whale Fishery Company. He sold shares in the company and successfully paid off his debts (The *Sunday Times* of London Insight Team 1982: p. 42).

In 1852 Queen Victoria granted the company a royal charter similar to the charter of the East India Company. The company's purpose was to exploit the wealth in cattle roaming wild over the islands, descendants of the cattle left by Bougainville and the succeeding Spanish and Argentine settlements before Britain took the islands in 1833. But soon the remoteness of the islands and the circumscription of their wealth to peat and cattle disillusioned the shareholders. Then sheep came to the rescue. There were only about 1,000 sheep in the islands in 1851. By 1880 there were 435,700. With the sheep came settlers, whom the British government intended to treat well by allotting them 160 acres each. But before long it raised the allotments to 6,000 acres, and through agents, third parties, and managers the company was able to acquire most of the best available land. Small landholders, instead of being independent farmers, soon became employees of the company. In spite of complaints the company continued to acquire land (The *Sunday Times* of London Insight Team 1982: p. 42).

Today the company owns eight farms, with 46 percent of the land (about 1.3 million acres) and about half the sheep. It also owns or controls almost everything that is vital to the economy of the islands—wholesale and retail business, banking, and shipping—and it employs a third of the work force of the islands. It runs the charter vessel that four times a year transports the wool clip to Britain and returns with necessary imported goods—that is, almost everything. In 1978 Ian Jack visited the islands for *The Sunday Times Colour Magazine*, for which he wrote the following:

> The men of the Camp—the country outside the town of Stanley—live in tied company houses on company land. They shop in the company store for goods delivered by company ship, and have bills deducted from company wages. Many of them use the company as a bank, the wool they shear from the company sheep goes to Tilbury, again by company ship, where it is unloaded at the company wharf, stored in the company warehouse and sold on the company wool exchange in Bradford. By means of directorships and shareholders, and by owning the only means of transport and marketing, the Falkland Islands Company extends its influence over the islands' few other landlords. For better or worse, the Falklands are company islands (The *Sunday Times* of London Insight Team 1982: p. 43).

Recent years, however, have not been so reassuring for the company. The negotiations between Britain and Argentina to resolve the ownership of the islands, which started in 1965 at the request of the United Nations, raised a serious question about Britain's rights to the islands as well as about Britain's true relations with the islanders. In 1976 the report of the commission headed by Lord Shackleton recommended drastic changes. No doubt these events were influential in making the company receptive to take-over bids when they came.

One such offer was from Héctor F. D. Capozzolo, an Argentine entrepreneur who had organized an Anglo-Franco-Argentine company for the purpose of acquiring the Falkland Islands Company. The negotiations ended successfully in February 1977, with an agreement to purchase the company for $7,500,000. Unfortunately for Capozzolo, an Argentine newspaper published news of the agreement before the contract could be signed, stirring up a storm of protest in England. The British government vetoed the transaction.

In spite of this setback, it seems that Capozzolo remained in touch with the president of the company, who was still interested in selling. But in March 1982, the Falkland Islands Company was merged with the Coalite Group, a private British fuel and transport conglomerate, with the provision that no part of the new corporation could be bought separately from the complete holdings (120,000,000 pounds). Apparently, that ended the attempt of an Argentine firm to buy the islands. If it had succeeded, it might have averted future trouble. And it would have saved the lives of a thousand young men.

Society

The Falklands have had European settlers since 1764, when Bougainville established his settlement there for the French. However, he soon returned it to the Spanish crown, which had protested that the Malvinas were Spanish. Spanish governors and garrisons remained on the islands until 1811, when with Spain occupied by Napoleon and Argentina rejecting Napoleon's rule, the Spanish governor of Montevideo (present Uruguay) withdrew the garrison. When Argentina obtained its independence, it claimed the islands as Argentine territory and soon sent settlers there. The first Argentine governor of the islands, Luis Vernet, brought some Europeans, some Argentine gauchos, and several Indians to the islands to help work the cattle that had multiplied from cattle left there by former settlers, both French and Spanish. These were the first permanent settlers, forerunners of the later population.

After the occupation of the islands by Britain in 1833, people from the British Isles were brought over, so that today the majority of the islands' inhabitants are descendants of these people. However, the population is more cosmopolitan than Britain likes to point out in its claims to the islands. The places of birth of heads of families in 1972 were as follows: Falklands, 431; Great Britain, 127; Argentina, 2; Australia, 1; Canada, 1; Chile, 9; Denmark, 1; Germany, 1; Ireland, 3; Tanzania, 1; United States, 3; and Uruguay, 1 (Crosby 1981: p. 74). Because of the extensive amounts of kelp that surround the islands, the inhabitants are frequently called "kelpers."

Juan Carlos Moreno, an Argentine who spent a long time in the Malvinas, has given us one of the few descriptions (and perhaps the best) of what the islander or kelper is like. He describes him as an artless man, neither mean nor refined, of medium education, and with manners different from those of the British. To the kelper the Englishman is a foreigner sent by the crown or by a company, well-educated, elegant perhaps, who comes to the islands to take an important job that the kelper cannot fill and may not fill no matter how competent he may be. The Englishman is respected and obeyed but not loved. The kelper dresses unpretentiously. His features are plain, unexpressive, almost gloomy, covering a kind heart. He is shy, of few words, but never mean or disdainful. He is generous and hospitable. The women are of Nordic appearance, modest and bashful, fresh-looking, reserved. The children are respectful, cheerful, talkative, and very friendly (Moreno 1938: pp. 50–53).

Members of the Shackleton mission to the islands in 1975 found the people loyal and splendid and as hospitable as could be found anywhere. One member went so far as to say that their ingenuity and toughness in coping with the immense physical problems of the island was a lesson in itself (Shackleton 1977: p. 5). In spite of the excellent human qualities of the kelpers, praised by English and Argentine writers alike, as a group they suffer from a serious lack of social cohesion. In the Falklands the normal difficulties of all societies are aggravated by the small population, the difficulty of communication and transportation among the outlying settlements and between them and the capital, the colonial status of the islands, the overwhelming dominance of the Falkland Islands Company and the related economic structure, and the fragmented and stratified society.

Some problems are caused by the age and sex structures of these communities. In West Falkland in 1975 there was only one unmarried woman over nineteen. Ten women had left the year before to become engaged to or marry members of the Royal Marines. The difficulty of finding a mate is one of the important reasons why young men leave the islands. A farm laborer told a reporter that he would not mind living under Argentine rulers if they sent the islands two plane-loads of women. (One wonders what the effect will be of having over 3,000 marines on the islands after the war with Argentina.) Moreover, there are no older people in the settlements able to provide the guidance, advice, and leadership so badly needed by the young people. On retirement, workers must leave the settlements and go to Stanley, because housing is tied to the job.

Isolation and lack of entertainment make life in the islands monotonous. In the winter the trails between settlements are often impassable for Landrovers and horses alike. The only way to reach all the settlements from Stanley is by boat: The mail boat makes the rounds about once a month and the supply boat every three months. In recent years an air service has been established, with two single-engine Beaver float planes on an on-call taxi basis, which has alleviated the situation somewhat, especially in emergency cases. Since 1972, as part of an Anglo-Argentine communications agreement, a temporary airstrip, built and run by Líneas Aéreas del Estado (LADE), a branch of the Argentine air force, has been in operation in Stanley, permitting flights from and to Argentina, with preferential rates for the islanders. In 1976 Britain finished the permanent landing strip, thereby permitting two flights a week by bigger planes between Stanley and Comodoro Rivadavia in southern Argentina and thus lessening the isolation of the islanders.

The main source of amusement is the radio-transmitter service that links all the settlements with each other and with Stanley. Via the transmitter the islanders can hear all conversations, a good source of gossip, on which the small population thrives. If they connect the transmitter service to the family radio, all the family can share in the fun. But not all the people in the settlements have access to the service. Also possible are an infrequent silent movie or a game of whist, the card game of the islands and the forerunner of bridge. Lack of recreation is particularly hard on single males and on the women, whose activities are limited to house chores. And an annual sports show (even if they look forward to it and prepare for it for months in advance) does not really fill the islanders' needs.

The islanders' lack of recreational initiative is linked to their standard of education, which is low, although no child between five and fifteen is out of school. A day school in Stanley, a boarding school near Goose Green, and thirty itinerant teachers (thirteen fully certified and seventeen with secondary education) are in charge of educating over 500 children. The itinerant teachers visit a settlement for fourteen days every two months. The effort to educate every child deserves praise, but the kelpers' ten years of schooling have failed to give them a sense of identity or group cohesion, to help them grow roots in their own land.

There is a general awareness of class differences among the islanders. Approximately a fifth of the population consists of expatriates (expats, as they are known in the islands). They are Britons who have come over on short-term contracts as public servants, specialists of various types, and professionals. Among themselves they constitute a homogeneous group, but in all respects they are foreigners to the islanders. They live in Stanley with their families, organize their own activities, and associate little with the natives. In the "camps," or rural settlements, there are also farm workers brought from Britain on short-term contracts to supplement the native work force eroded by emigration. Although generally well paid, both kelpers and Britons resent the dependence on managers that is forced on them by the isolation of the farms.

Since the visit of the Shackleton mission of 1975, some notable changes have taken place. Two of the large rural establishments have been subdivided and parcels of land given to several young islanders. Cohesion and teamwork have emerged among the workers, who have successfully organized a union by taking advantage of the scarcity of laborers. The union has 550 members, who, although already well paid, obtained in January 1980 higher wages, a forty-hour week, and extra pay for overtime. Thanks to these benefits some laborers earn more than the farm managers (Crosby 1981: pp. 75–77).

Yet, in spite of recent economic improvements, discontent persists among the kelpers. They speak of social injustice and preferential treatment of Britons. The education the kelpers receive on the islands permits them to occupy positions available to them but not public offices which are generally held by the British. An Anglo-Argentine professional who visited the islands has observed that the economic improvements obtained by the kelpers will permit them to emigrate more easily (Crosby 1981: pp. 69–70). Ironically, then, the very same economic and working improvements may hasten the depopulation of the islands.

A British businessman, well acquainted with the islands, has said, "Most visitors who come here develop a patronizing attitude. They find the people slow and inarticulate and think that they are, on the whole, a bit stupid. They are inarticulate, but they aren't stupid. They are actually quite shrewd. Given a chance, they could make a go of it" (*Buenos Aires Herald*, November 9, 1982: p. 9).

2
Who Discovered the Islands?

Early Discoverers and Explorers

Upon the return of Columbus from his first expedition, his sponsors Ferdinand and Isabella, the monarchs of Spain, and the crown of Portugal, interested in West Africa and a route around Africa to India, requested the Vatican to designate the areas each could control in the seas and lands being discovered. The pope, as head and arbiter of all European Christendom at this time, issued a papal bull in 1493 providing that the world not already governed by Christian princes be divided by an imaginary line running from pole to pole one hundred leagues west of the Cape Verde Islands. Spain was to get all land discovered west of the line and Portugal, Spain's most active rival at the time, all land east of the line. In 1494, by the Treaty of Tordesillas, the monarchs of Spain and Portugal changed the line to 370 leagues (approximately 1000 miles) west of the Cape Verde Islands, an action that later permitted Portugal to claim a part of Brazil. The Falkland Islands (Las Islas Malvinas) remained in the area under Spanish control.

Probably the first European explorer to see the Falklands was Amerigo Vespucci, who on his second expedition to the New World sailed along the eastern coast of South America, including present Brazil, Uruguay, and Argentina. His description of the islands he saw and the latitude mentioned in his account of the voyage coincide with those of the Falklands. Louis Antoine de Bougainville, a Frenchman who much later placed the first settlement on the Falklands, wrote in 1771 that Vespucci had sighted the islands, and as Julius Goebel, Jr., the distinguished scholar of the early explorations of that region, remarks, "One would seem to violate no canon of common sense in accepting this conclusion" (Goebel 1927: p. 4).

More is known about the circumnavigation of the globe by Ferdinand Magellan and his lieutenant, Sebastián del Cano. Magellan left Seville in August 1519 and arrived on the coast of present Argentina in January 1520. He established a base in the bay of San Julian (his chronicler said it was at 49° 30' south latitude) and explored the area. Esteban Gómez, one of his captains, deserted the expedition in the *San Antonio*, and found several islands at 51° south latitude. Members of the crew called them *Islas de Sansón* (Samson) *y de los Patos* (ducks). These were probably the Jason Islands, but the earlier names remained until the end of the sixteenth century, when for many years they were called the Sebaldes, for Sebald de Weert, a Dutch explorer who discovered them later. The islands of Sansón and Patos (Sebaldes or Jason) lie northwest of West Falkland Island and are a part of the Falkland group.

The first known map showing the Falklands is that drawn by the Portuguese cartographer, Pedro Reinel in 1522–1523. It was found in the Mosque of the Aghalar in Istanbul and is called the map of Top Kapu Sarayi. It was hailed as an important discovery at the International Congress of Geography in Amsterdam in 1938. After Esteban Gómez returned to Spain in 1521, Reinel was asked to come to Seville to draw the map in accordance with instructions from Gómez and his companion on board the *San Antonio,* Andrés de San Martín, the astronomer of the expedition, who had studied the ocean and adjoining lands while in the Patagonia area. Some geographers believe that Reinel's map is based on another given by the same Reinel to Magellan in 1519. The meeting in Seville began in 1521, it appears, and Reinel did the map in 1522–1523. Later, in Badajoz, Spain, Esteban Gómez and Diego Rivero (a noted cartographer of the period), both of Spain, and Lope Homem of Portugal approved the map. The map shows the islands at 53° 30', placing them in the region of the Falkland Archipelago.

Several other maps in the same period showed the Sansón and Patos islands. These are the Weimar-Spanish map of 1527, the world map of Diego Rivero of 1529 in the Vatican Library, and the Agnese Atlas (1536–1545) in the municipal museum and library of Venice. But the most important knowledge comes from an unknown crew whose log provided the information needed to settle the question of where the islands of Sansón and Patos were located.

After the Magellan expedition four others were sent out by Spain to the Strait of Magellan, the most important in respect to the Falklands being that of Francisco de Camargo, who left Seville in August 1539 to settle the strait area. He arrived at the entrance to the strait with difficulty because of violent weather. His flagship was wrecked, but the crew and Camargo were saved and went on to Peru in a second ship.

The third ship, whose name and captain are unknown but of whose log a fragment remains, was driven back to Cape Virgins, where soon another violent storm broke the anchor cable. It barely escaped shipwreck but was able to put out to sea. On February 4, 1540, its crew sighted islands whose latitude and description make it quite certain that they were the Falklands. The ship's crew remained in the area several months, finding much game, including fowl, foxes, and sea lions. There must have been many foxes, for on November 24 they left a place they called the Puerto de las Zorras (Port of the Foxes). Because of the weather, however, they could not leave the islands for home until December (Goebel 1927: pp. 17–28).

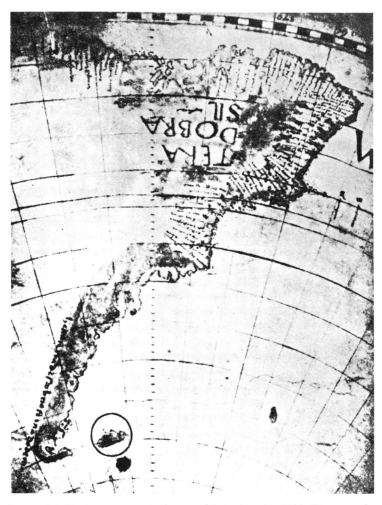

FIGURE 2.1. Portuguese nautical map of Reinel, 1522–1523. Discovered by Destombes in the Library of Istanbul and first made known at the Congreso Internacional de Geografía in Amsterdam in 1938. In a circle is the archipelago of the Malvinas. Inverted words (Tera do Brasil) mean "Land of Brazil."

Source: José Arce, *Las Malvinas* (Madrid: Instituto de Cultura Hispánica, 1950), following p. 16.

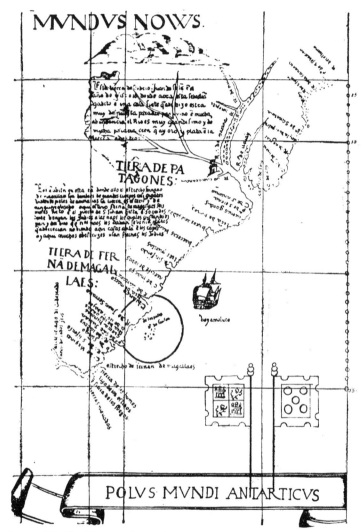

FIGURE 2.2. The Weimar-Spanish map of 1527 showing the Falklands (circled).

Source: La Nación (Buenos Aires), July 21, 1946.

FIGURE 2.3. Map from the Agnese Atlas (1536–1545) in the civic
library and museum of Venice. In the rectangle are shown the Malvinas
(islands of ducks and of San Son) to the northeast of the entrance
to the Strait of Magellan.

Source: José Arce, Las Malvinas (Madrid: Instituto de Cultura Hispánica, 1950),
following p. 18.

This expedition reported finding no people on the islands but did find good places to winter on the long journey to the Strait of Magellan. This is the first known mention of the most important reason to control the Falklands: to use them as a way station on the long route to the Pacific Ocean. It was important for Spain to control the eastern entrance to the Strait of Magellan, because the Pacific, like the Caribbean, was becoming a Spanish lake, and Spain would try to keep out all other Europeans. This was the underlying reason for the later conflicts over the islands among Spain, France, England, and, after its independence, the United States.

Another important consequence of the Camargo expedition was the *Islario General* (General Book of the Islands), the work of Alonso de Santa Cruz, the chief cartographer of Charles V of Spain. In it Santa Cruz, upon receiving the necessary information from the survivors of the expedition from both Peru and the Falklands, showed the islands as the *Islas de Sansón*, as did other mapmakers. Although not completely accurate, the map served to develop a chronological knowledge of the area. The name of Sansón for the islands continued until the seventeenth century, when cartographers began to delete that name from maps— probably because of the infrequency of visits to the region, for after the Camargo expedition no Spanish expedition arrived in that region for forty years.

The *Geography* of Ptolemy, officially published in 1561 by the senate of Venice and dedicated to Charles V of Spain, gives the same information as Santa Cruz's map. So does the map of Bartolomé Olives, made in 1562, named *Mundus Novus* (New World), and showing seven islands called the Sansón. Another map of Olives of 1580 also shows the islands. On two maps of Joan Martínez (1572 and 1580) the islands are designated as the Patos. Just before the turn of the century (1590) Sebastián López made a map of the region on which he called the islands Ilha Çam Çom (Portuguese for Sam Som).

Two years later John Davis, deserting his leader Thomas Cavendish, was in the region. Whether he saw the Falklands is not known, but he is still given credit today by British historians and politicians for having discovered the islands. He was certainly not the first man to see them, as the British claim. Many others saw them before him. Yet still today Davis's accounts are the basis for Britain's claims to the islands on the grounds of prior discovery.

Of all the British navigators in this region in the late sixteenth century, geographers owe most to Sir Francis Drake for his circumnavigation of the globe (1577–1580). He cleared up many false notions of the area of Tierra del Fuego and the Strait of Magellan. By sailing around Cape Horn he showed that the strait did not separate the South American mainland from a southern Antarctic continent. His discoveries south of 52° south latitude were put on a map by Richard Hakluyt in 1587. But Drake added little to solve the mystery of the Falklands.

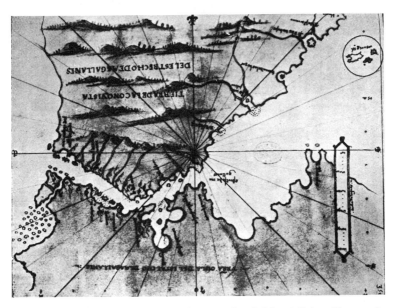

FIGURE 2.4. A 1541 map from the "Book of Islands" by Alonso de Santa Cruz, from the National Library of Madrid. In the circle are shown the Malvinas (islands San Son), to the northeast of the entrance to the Strait of Magellan.

Source: José Arce, *Las Malvinas* (Madrid: Instituto de Cultura Hispánica, 1950), following p. 20.

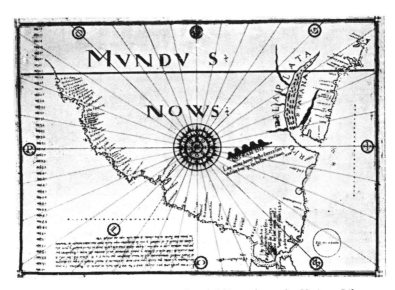

FIGURE 2.5. A 1562 map by Bartolomé Olives, from the Vatican Library. In the circle are shown the Malvina Islands.

Source: José Arce, *Las Malvinas* (Madrid: Instituto de Cultura Hispánica, 1950), following p. 22.

FIGURE 2.6. Map of Joan Martínez (1572) showing the Falklands and the entrance to the Strait of Magellan.

Source: José Arce, *Las Malvinas* (Madrid: Instituto de Cultura Hispánica, 1950), following p. 24.

25

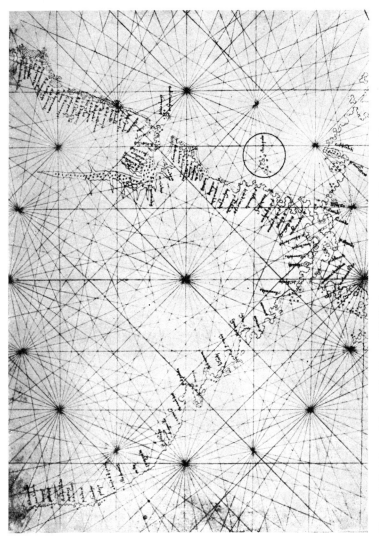

FIGURE 2.7. Map of Joan Martínez (1580) from the Angelica Library in Rome.

Source: José Arce, Las Malvinas (Madrid: Instituto de Cultura Hispánica, 1950), following p. 30.

British discoveries at the end of the sixteenth century, alleged and substantiated, form the basis for later claims to the Falklands. The claims of John Davis are especially tenuous. Davis was in command of the *Desire*, one of the ships of Thomas Cavendish's second expedition to the New World. He became separated from Cavendish off the coast of southern Argentina in May 1592, and decided to sail south to the Strait of Magellan to find him. On August 9, 1592, a severe storm battered his ship, driving him about fifty leagues northeast of the strait. There, according to his historian, John Jane, Davis took refuge "among certain Isles never before discovered" until the wind shifted and he could again set sail for the Strait, which he entered on August 19. Davis has been accused of having deserted Cavendish and making up the story of looking for him to justify his behavior (Goebel 1927: p. 35).

Soon after the Cavendish expedition visited the Patagonian coast, another Englishman arrived there. Richard Hawkins was commissioned by Queen Elizabeth to undertake discoveries in the East by way of the Strait of Magellan. He left England in June 1593, and arrived on the Patagonian coast early the next year. He discovered some land on February 2, 1594, which he named Hawkins's Maiden-land in honor of his Virgin Queen Bess. It was at 48° south latitude, and Hawkins had no idea where he was. Hawkins's discovery has been considered by English writers to be the Falklands, but his description does not fit the islands. He says that they saw many fires and people, with whom they could not get to speak. The land was temperate like England, with "great rivers" of fresh water that colored the sea water at their mouths. This description would seem to eliminate the Falklands.

Far too little scientific investigation has been made of the records left by Davis and Hawkins. Perhaps British writers have accepted their accounts out of deference to British rather than alien testimony. Davis's information is vague, and Hawkins's does not fit the description of the islands. Davis gives no latitudinal bearings, but says he sailed about fifty leagues northeast of the Strait of Magellan, which *might* have put him in the islands. Hawkins's mention of being in about 48° south latitude is of little help, as the Falklands lie between 51° and 53°. But his description of the islands (including people, fires, and huge rivers) is completely inaccurate. Hawkins's account has been reevaluated by a Commander Chambers, who after extensive study of the Hawkins account came to the conclusion that he had sighted land near Cape Tres Puntas on the mainland of Patagonia and thought it was unexplored land, and that when he later realized his error, he kept quiet (Chambers 1901). Moreover, Hawkins and his crew were captured by the Spaniards, and although the crew was freed and returned to England, Hawkins was a prisoner in Spain for many years. His *Observations* were written twenty-five years after the events occurred, probably without the aid of his ship's papers and influenced by information he gathered in Spain, a possibility that may explain many of the statements in his account of the expedition.

John Jane's account of Davis's explorations appeared in 1600, and Hawkins's *Observations* about eighteen years later. Considering the vagueness of detail and the improbability of many of the events he recounts, Jane may have appropriated some verbal reports of Hawkins's accounts, especially since Davis was suspected of having defected from Cavendish's command. Or perhaps Hawkins appropriated material from Jane's account of Davis's exploits, as an Argentine historian has suggested, because it can work just as well the other way around. As Dr. Goebel has so ably stated, after a thorough and scholarly examination of both accounts:

> Whatever view of these discoveries we take, there seems little excuse for accepting without challenge the statement that the Falklands were discovered by either Hawkins or Davis on the basis of data by no means more detailed or convincing than the accounts of the Spaniards we have already examined. Certainly the English cartographers of the period took no immediate notice of the claims of either Hawkins or Davis, for we find no record of them in the contemporary maps. The great map published in the 1600 edition of Hakluyt and attributed to Wright and Molyneux, depicts the Sansón group close to the Patagonian coast and calls it by that name. Undoubtedly the map makers were satisfied that whatever Davis saw, it must have been the same land that the Spanish claimed decades before to have discovered (Goebel 1927: pp. 42–43).

By the end of the sixteenth century, the English, French, and Dutch were actively challenging Spanish claims to exclusive rights to the New World. Spain, as the most powerful nation in Europe, predictably took measures to counteract what it considered acts of aggression against its rightful ownership of the New World, including the area of the straits in the South Atlantic. English voyages to the Strait of Magellan had aroused Spanish authorities to action. The area had to be colonized and consolidated. Pedro Sarmiento de Gamboa, one of the more outstanding and indomitable Spanish explorers, had made extensive surveys of the strait in 1579–1580. In 1581, because of his accounts, a large expedition was sent to the region with Sarmiento de Gamboa as governor. The endeavor was doomed to a heartrending failure, and Sarmiento de Gamboa was ultimately captured by the British. During this period, however, Sarmiento de Gamboa made two trips to the strait and three attempts to reach the colony he had left in that area, and never saw the Falklands. Soon the extension of Spanish power was checked by the defeat of Spain's Great Armada sent out to bring England to its knees, and also by the rise of Holland as a seafaring power. The great feats of Drake and Cavendish were repeated by the great Dutch sailors, Mahu, Cordes, Weert, and Spilberg, in the rush to obtain overseas possessions.

Later Discoverers and Explorers

Among the few known explorers to enter the South Atlantic and the Strait of Magellan at the end of the sixteenth century was the Dutchman Jacob Mahu. In command of five ships, he left Rotterdam in June 1598. In April 1599, he was halfway through the Strait of Magellan when he encountered storms so devastating that when he finally emerged in the Pacific, he decided to split the expedition. As a result, under the command of Sebald de Weert, the *Geloof* turned back to return to Holland. De Weert was able to return through the strait. On January 16, 1600, he left the strait and sailed eastward. On the twenty-fourth he sighted three small islands not on any map. He named them the "Sebaldes" after his given name. They were probably the present Jason Islands northwest of West Falkland Island, although the number of leagues traveled and latitude given by de Weert are not completely accurate. Dutch cartographers gradually replaced the Sansón group of the Spaniards with the Sebald Islands.

Another Dutch expedition, which sailed from Holland in 1614 under Le Mair and Schouten, reported sighting the Sebaldes. As a result de Weert's account was accepted. Moreover, a map in the first general English atlas, John Speed's *A Prospect of the Most Famous Parts of the World* (1626), showed only the Sebald Islands, indicating that de Weert's discovery was given credence and not those of Davis and Hawkins.

To make the early history of the Falklands even more confusing, Ambrose Cowley claimed in 1684 that he had discovered an island in latitude 47° 41', according to him covered with woods and with a harbor capable of holding 500 ships. He promptly named it Pepys Island in honor of the secretary of the Admiralty at the time (Goebel 1927: pp. 133–134). Another member of the same expedition, a semibucca-neering venture out of Chesapeake Bay, was William Dampier, a far more observing person, it seems, than Cowley. Dampier collected botanical and zoological specimens, contributing to contemporary science. Dampier made no mention of Pepys Island but did mention sighting the Sebaldes, stating that water might be obtained there before sailing south instead of going through the Strait of Magellan, thus making it easier to reach Cape Horn.

The visit of this expedition to the Sebaldes attracted no great attention, but the idea of a huge harbor on the so-called island of Pepys did. The British Admiralty even began a plan to establish a naval base on the island, but was deterred from it by treaties made with Spain in 1667 and 1670. These "antibuccaneering" treaties permitted Britain to retain the colonies it had in America but forbade its entrance into other areas held by Spain in the new world. Pepys Island was a myth, but a myth well known and sought after for over a hundred years before it was dropped from navigational charts.

There was no rush to the Sebaldes, for they had been described as windy places, inhabited by penguins, ducks, and sea lions, and not as lands of beauty and wealth, of adventure and romance. They did not even have people on them. Many decades were to pass before men finally walked on their shores.

Not long after Dampier's sighting of the Sebaldes, during the War of the English Succession when Spain and England were allied against France, England gave a privateer's commission against the French to Captain John Strong of the *Welfare*, who sailed from Downs in October 1689. Off the Patagonian coast westerly winds were so strong that he could not put in at Puerto Deseado as he had wished. Pushed by winds and currents, on January 27, 1690, he sighted the Falklands from the north and entered the sound between East and West Falkland, naming it Falkland Sound in honor of Anthony, Viscount Falkland (1659–1694), at the time Commissioner of the Admiralty and later First Lord of the Admiralty. Dr. Goebel comments on Strong's visit as follows:

> The visit of Strong was the first landing of Englishmen on the Falklands. It was of no conceivable legal consequence, for it involved neither a formal taking possession of the islands, nor an occupation. Inasmuch as the voyage was undertaken with the intention of violating the treaty between England and Spain and the Spanish rules of trade, and was so treated by the Spaniards, it can scarcely be said that as against Spain any acts of Captain Strong had the effect either of establishing or perfecting any claims of the English to the Islands. (Goebel 1927: p. 137)

3
The Falklands Come of Age

European Colonial Rivalry
in the Early Eighteenth Century

The eighteenth century was ushered in with the War of the Spanish Succession (1701–1713), the first of many wars in that century that were to have important consequences for the Falkland Islands. For years European rulers had been scheming to get control of the Spanish Empire when the feeble, heirless, yet long-lived Charles II of Spain died in 1700. During his thirty-five years on the throne intrigues and conspiracies had thrived in the European courts to see who would inherit the Spanish crown and thus the vast Spanish Empire.

The winner, as might have been expected, was the powerful Louis XIV of France, who quickly placed his grandson, the Duke of Anjou, on the Spanish throne as Philip V, the first Bourbon monarch of Spain. The result was the War of the Spanish Succession, for England, with visions of a union of the Bourbon families of France and Spain, would certainly not let the vast and rich Spanish Empire fall into the clutches of France without a struggle. Up to this war Spain had been quite successful in warding off the assaults of other countries that had tried, through smuggling and outright buccaneering, to obtain a share of the wealth of the New World.

Spain had been surprisingly successful, considering the vastness of its possessions—from the coast of Oregon to Cape Horn, and the whole Caribbean, as well as the Philippines. It is true that the French, Dutch, and English had obtained footholds in the Caribbean by 1700, and by treaty Spain had accepted British control of the North American colonies as far south as present Charleston, South Carolina, in 1670. But these were areas in which Spain was not interested.

Spain demanded that ships of other countries stay out of *its* South Atlantic seas and out of *its* Pacific Ocean, but little heed was paid to this demand. As we have noted, the Falklands were important as a stopover and watering place for ships on the long voyage around Cape Horn to the Pacific. This route was becoming more traveled by 1700 and less protected, for the Spanish monarchy had fallen into a sad state after thirty-five years of misrule and chaos under the demented Charles II.

The French had been especially busy in the South Atlantic before the death of Charles. The Compagnie des Indes Orientales had been granted a charter by the French government in 1664 to trade in the Pacific and in the region of the Strait of Magellan. But in 1698, because the company had not made use of the latter part of the agreement, another company, the Compagnie de la Mer du Sud, was given a charter to trade from Cape San Antonio on the Patagonian coast to the southern tip of South America. These charters had been granted without the blessing of Spain.

The center of French maritime activity had for many years been the port of St. Malo, on the northwest coast of France, where privateers had been fitted out and through which much contraband trade had been handled. During the War of the English Succession, when France and Spain were on opposite sides, Louis XIV even had dreams of conquering the Río de la Plata area in order to open Buenos Aires for the St. Malo trade. It is from St. Malo that the Spanish name for the Falklands springs. When the French arrived at the Falklands, they called them Les Iles Malouines. When the Spaniards took them over from the French, they called them Las Islas Malvinas, the name by which all Argentines call them today.

The Compagnie de la Mer du Sud sent its first expedition to South America under the command of Beauchesne Gouin. It left St. Malo in December 1698, passed through the Strait of Magellan, and sailed as far north as the Galapagos Islands in the Pacific. On his return Gouin sailed around Cape Horn and headed north, finding an "unknown island" at latitude 52° 50', about sixty leagues from Tierra del Fuego. He named it Ile Beauchesne and said it was a day's journey from the Sebald Islands. Guillaume Delisle's map of 1708 showed it as a single island, but later maps depicted it as two islands.

Spanish protests against these French expeditions were unheeded until France and Spain made an alliance after the ascent of Philip V to the Spanish throne. When France and Spain became allies against England in the War of the Spanish Succession in 1701, the Compagnie de la Mer du Sud was disbanded. After 1701, French sailors had the run of the South Atlantic. French expeditions ranged the sea, and some of them reached the Falklands. Two vessels of the Compagnie des Indes visited the southern shores of the Falklands in 1706 and reported that they had good ports of call. The same area was visited in 1711 by Jean Doublet de Honfleur. Also from St. Malo, a man named Porée explored the northern coast of the islands and named it Côte de l'Assomption (July 1708). At least one English ship also reached the Falklands during the War of the Spanish Succession. Captain Woodes Rodgers sailed from Bristol in September 1708, sighted the islands in December, but was unable to land because of strong winds.

The end of the war with a British victory terminated French endeavors in the southern seas. When Spanish officials in the New World colonies received news of the end of the war, they immediately ordered all French subjects out of their jurisdictions. The victors, the British, were now determined to get a monopoly of the trade with the New World, to the exclusion of all former enemies (the French) and allies (the Dutch). To Europeans it appeared as if the war had been fought solely over trade concessions in the New World, and not over the succession to the Spanish throne.

The Peace of Utrecht, signed in 1713, consisted of three treaties: the *asiento* treaty signed March 26, 1713, the treaty of peace signed July 13, 1713, and the treaty of commerce signed December 9, 1713. Under the *asiento*, or contract to traffic in slaves, the British were allowed to bring to the Spanish colonies in the New World 4,800 slaves a year for thirty years and one ship of 500 tons burden a year with British goods to be sold at the fairs of Jalapa (present Mexico) and Puerto Bello (present Panama). The Spanish crown was to share in the profits of this trade and the slave trade.

The British crown soon transferred the commercial privileges in the treaty to the South Sea Company, which promptly resorted to all sorts of practices the treaty had not provided for. Spanish officials were bribed. Smuggling became rampant. And the annual permission ship of 500 tons burden would dock in the port, unload, and at night reload from tenders bringing more goods from ships hidden in the daytime. Technically, the treaty was not broken, because it provided for one ship of 500 tons *burden* and not 500 tons of goods, as the Spaniards probably thought it meant. Because of these flagrant frauds the South Sea Company made huge profits, and other English subjects tried to imitate its practices. As a result the Spanish crown strengthened its naval protection around the Spanish Indies and even permitted a limited degree of privateering. The termination of the *asiento* agreement in 1750 ended the commercial ventures of the South Sea Company in the new world, but not the contraband trade to which the company's methods had given greater momentum.

The *asiento* treaty had a provision more closely related to the Falklands question. It provided that Britain was to be permitted the use of certain parcels of land in the Rio de la Plata region (present Argentina) for the housing and feeding of slaves to be sold under the treaty. However, the restrictions placed on the manner in which the station was to be erected and operated were so severe, and the process was to be supervised so carefully by Spanish officials, that the British government abandoned any plans to take advantage of the concession.

What if the British government had placed a station in this area? It might have become a permanent foothold in the South Atlantic area, and later an anchorage for ships sailing to the Pacific and to Australia. A strong military post in that area, which a weak Spain might not have been able to prevent, would have been of great advantage in any effort to take over the Falklands and retain them against Spanish attempts to recover them. This is not too farfetched, for Britain did try to conquer Buenos Aires in 1806 and 1807, in the English Invasions, famous in Argentine history. In both attempts Britain was defeated by a native, colonial army, unaided by Spain. If Britain had had a strong post in the area, it might have taken over the viceroyalty of Río de la Plata and fulfilled its plans in the English Invasions. After all, by the same Treaty of Utrecht, Britain received Gibraltar (captured during the war), which it has not relinquished to this day.

Britain had entered the war to prevent a union of Spain and France, but it had also during the war seen a chance to acquire territory (like Gibraltar and the island of Minorca) and special advantages in trade with the Spanish colonies in the New World. It had also wanted to return to the status quo of the treaties of 1667 and 1670, and the exclusion of France from the Spanish West Indies.

By the treaty of commerce in the Peace of Utrecht, England could trade in Spain and the Spanish colonies only insofar as previous treaties permitted. England demanded additonal benefits in the West Indian trade on the basis that they were necessary for English access to Jamaica and Barbados, which Britain already held. But Philip V refused all additional requests and remained adamant about it. Philip did accept a British demand that no other nations (such as the French) could obtain Spanish land in America. Indeed, the treaty went on to say that Great Britain would assist Spain in restoring its possessions in the West Indies as they had been held by Spain in the 1660s.

In short, Spain, England, and France all wanted to maintain the old colonial system: Spain to preserve her empire; England to prevent France from getting any advantages; and France to prevent Britain from doing the same thing. Britain, for example, strongly protested a Spanish concession to six St. Malo ships to sail to the Pacific, and offered to pay Philip V the 360,000 crowns he had received for the concession as well as to help him refit his navy to guard against outside aggression against Spanish commerce. Philip declined the last offer but cancelled the concession. But the sailors of St. Malo continued to engage in commerce in the Pacific, and the French crown, to forestall English objections, issued a decree forbidding that commerce on penalty of death. At the same time France joined with Spain to sweep from the seas vessels preying upon Spanish commerce. These measures were aimed at smugglers of all nations equally.

As far as the Falklands are concerned, the legal result of the Peace of Utrecht is the most important. By article eight of the treaty of peace of July 13, 1713, England agreed that, except for the slave trade and the 500-ton permission ship, the seas around Spanish domains were closed to outsiders and there was no relaxation of the legal system of exclusion. It is true that Lord Lexington, the British ambassador to

Madrid, who had negotiated and accepted the Peace of Utrecht, suggested in England to a private council of ministers that the treaties were a mere cloak for the future destruction of the Spanish legal order. But at least for the time being contraband trade was outlawed and Spain could legally destroy it. Indeed, the legal system restored by the Peace of Utrecht became binding on the powers of Europe for the next century.

The Plot Thickens: Attempts to Destroy Spain's Colonial Monopoly

As might be expected, after the war neither England nor Spain felt that the provisions of the Peace of Utrecht were observed by the other side. English officials complained of their treatment by Spanish officials in the colonies, and Spanish officials complained of liberties taken by officials of the South Sea Company in trading with the Spanish Indies. To the chagrin of the British, accustomed to the inefficient and lackadaisical administration of Charles II, the far more efficient Spanish administration under the new Bourbon monarch was bringing a political, economic, and military renaissance to Spain. No longer could the English smuggle at will. Their government had accepted Spanish exclusiveness in the New World as it had existed before the war, and now they were discovering that Spain meant to live up to the provisions of the treaty and maintain its monopoly in the New World.

Soon after peace was made London merchants began complaining about their treatment by Spanish officials in Spain, and to these complaints was added a long list of grievances of South Sea Company officials describing difficulties they were encountering in trading with the Spanish Indies under the *asiento* agreement. Because many influential English politicians were interested in the success of the company, King George I asked Parliament for relief for the company and protection of English trade both in Europe and overseas.

Actually, hostilities had already erupted, and in the battle of Cape Pasaro the British had defeated the Spanish fleet. Spain retaliated by issuing letters of marque and reprisal, and war was declared in November 1718. The Spanish government seized all the properties of the South Sea Company in America and suspended all trade with England. This was a serious blow to British commerce. Philip V tried to go further by demanding the restitution of Gibraltar and Minorca, so important to England's protection of its Mediterranean trade routes, but England refused to budge. A treaty was signed in Madrid in June 1721, in effect guaranteeing the Peace of Utrecht. The Spanish crown agreed to restore the *asiento* and pay an indemnity for all English property confiscated in Spain and the Spanish Indies. This was a great victory for Britain: The public law established by the treaties of Utrecht had been reaffirmed and the status quo reestablished. By the same token it was a victory for Spain, because the Spanish crown also won by the reestablishment of the provisions of Utrecht.

The short war had also proved that the bad faith underlying submission to the principles of Utrecht would not go unchallenged by the government of Spain. Not only the treaties but also the system they had been designed to mask were to be exposed to continued attack. Such attacks would be more difficult, however, because after the War of the Spanish Succession, Spain had been making a determined effort to reorganize and revitalize the economic and fiscal system of the country. This effort included strengthening the navy and coast guard, revitalizing colonial trade, and reforming the colonial administrative system. The English, if the ministers of the Bourbon kings of Spain had their way, would not have an easy time if they decided to thwart any Spanish restrictions against outside trade in the New World. The stage was set for continued conflict, which was ultimately to lead to England's loss of its original thirteen colonies (the United States) and later to Spain's loss of its own New World colonies except for some islands in the Caribbean.

Trouble was not long in coming. The English felt themselves set upon because the smuggling carried on by the *asiento* ships and the annual trading ship was no longer freely permitted by the Spanish navy. It is true that even legal *asiento* ships were halted on the high seas, searched, and taken as prizes, at times with cruel treatment of English crews. But most ships boarded in that manner were set on smuggling, as were many vessels from the English-American colonies that carried on a lively trade with the Spanish colonies under no pretext of any right.

The last straw for the British was the permission to trade granted by Spain to the newly organized Ostend Company, a Dutch trading company. The Netherlands, formerly a Spanish possession, had been given by Spain to Austria by the Peace of Utrecht, and were now returned certain trading privileges they had held under Spanish rule in the form of special privileges granted to the Ostend Company. This development infuriated English merchants, because it would mean strong competition for the South Sea and other British companies.

Robert Walpole, in charge of the British government, did not want war, but he had to show the strength of England. He sent a fleet to blockade the Spanish coast and another to the West Indies to capture the Spanish treasure fleet. Spain replied by seizing a South Sea Company ship, suspending the *asiento*, and laying siege to Gibraltar. It was a short war with few casualties. A peace was signed in March 1728, calling for a return to the status quo and the convening of a congress to discuss contraband, a proposal England naturally strongly opposed. The congress ended in November 1729, with a treaty calling for a "defensive" alliance among England, France, and Spain, a return to the status quo concerning commercial agreements, and a mutual payment of reparations for damages done to each other's trade. There was even a reciprocal agreement among the three countries to avoid future violence! Thus the *asiento* was restored and payment for confiscated property made. Walpole's aspiration to placate Spain without detriment to England's commercial advantages won the day. Occasional seizures of ships (about thirty-one in twelve years along the vast coasts of the Americas) were no real threat to the ever-growing British trade, but Spain's enmity was.

But as the Spanish saying goes, *no pueden con el genio* (they just can't help themselves). Neither the Spaniards nor the British could change their ways. Spain was determined to preserve its possessions in the New World for the Spaniards. England was just as determined to increase its commercial opportunities in the New World. Acts of violence by both English and Spanish captains continued, sometimes accompanied by extremely cruel treatment of the victims. Ships were boarded and frequently seized, and sailors were chained and thrown in the brig. In one instance, an English skipper caught in the act of smuggling had his ear cut off by the Spanish captain, who boasted that he would do the same to the English king if he were there. Captain Jenkins, the English skipper, pickled his ear for eight years, and just at the right time, in 1739, when Parliament was debating British relations with Spain, he showed it to the assemblage as proof of Spanish cruelty to English seamen. It had the desired effect. The War of Jenkins's Ear began in 1739, to be merged in 1740 into a wider conflict, the War of the Austrian Succession (1740–1748), which ended with the Treaty of Aix-la-Chapelle.

The issues over which the war had been fought were almost immediately forgotten for the far more important European questions occupying the various European chancelleries. The English, as usual, demanded free navigation of the Spanish Indies, but Spain insisted that free navigation applied only to European waters and the Spanish Indies were still closed to foreigners except insofar as Spain had permitted them to enter there. The treaty established the *status quo ante bellum*, with conquests made in Europe and the Spanish Indies restored to previous owners.

The public law of the Peace of Utrecht had again been accepted by both parties, although reluctantly. Britain especially wanted a more precise definition of British seamen's rights because of what had happened during the war. During the war British strategy had been to strangle Spain's South American trade by concerted operations on both the east and west coasts and to control the Caribbean and the Pacific by taking the isthmus of Panama. Captain Vernon attacked Puerto Bello, and Admiral George Anson set sail for the Pacific in six ships of which he lost three off the tip of South America. Further trouble made Anson forget about Panama and dedicate himself to taking prizes in the Pacific, including the annual Manila-to-Acapulco ship with a treasure of 1,500,000 dollars.

Upon his return to England Anson wrote a report in blunt language. To go to the Pacific around South America, English sailors would have to make some changes. Stopping off in Brazil and getting supplies there was out of the question, because the friendship of the Portuguese could not be relied on in any plan to interrupt Spanish trade from bases in Brazil. The Spaniards, however, were creatures of custom and always took the same route home from the New World. But when apprised of an enemy they would stop all trade. Anson suggested, therefore, that a base for concealing British ships should be established on Pepys Island (the mythical island no one had been able to find since Cowley's glowing description of it) or on the Falklands. Anson also denounced the frivolous manner in which English buccaneers reported on places that did not exist! Yet he accepted Cowley's report of the harbor big enough for 500 ships on Pepys Island. He suggested that an expedition be sent to the Falklands to survey them and added that "if, on examination one or both of these places should appear proper for the purpose intended, it is scarcely to be conceived of what prodigious import a convenient station might prove situated so far to the southward, and so near to Cape Horn" (Goebel 1927: p. 196). He also suggested that the area around Tierra del Fuego be surveyed for the same purpose.

The Spanish court at the time seemed to be more favorably disposed to England than it had been for many years, and the British crown suggested to Spain that as George II was determined to stand firmly by the Treaty of Aix-la-Chapelle, the Spanish crown might see fit to permit the British to explore fully Pepys Island and the Falkland Islands as well as the South Seas. To this disingenuous proposition, the Spanish government replied that it was sorry to see England, soon after the reestablishment of friendly relations between the two countries, propose a new project that would break this friendship or perhaps, even worse, bring graver disputes than the one that had caused the last war. The projected expedition of Anson, the Spanish minister contended, was a new attempt to create jealousies and suspicions. Wherever the two countries held possessions in the same areas, and commerce was forbidden in those areas, unpleasant incidents occurred, the very thing the Spanish government was trying to prevent.

The Spanish minister went on to say that he knew of Anson's plans, having read the printed account of his voyage. Why would the English want to visit the Falklands to obtain information about them that was already available? The Spaniards had long since discovered and inhabited them, calling them the Islas de Leones because of the many sea lions found there. If the British had no intention of establishing a settlement there, why did they want to go there? Perhaps taking advantage of the opportunity, the Spanish minister continued that the English had no possessions in the South Atlantic. If they were to be allowed to establish some at the mouth of the Strait of Magellan, they would be ready to enter the Pacific. Then the next step would be to occupy another island as a base to refit their naval forces for the long journey to China— naval forces that could be used to attack Spanish coasts, as Lord Anson had done!

After another attempt to convince Spanish officials that their interpretation of British proposals was distorted and their fears were unfounded, the British government decided to abandon for the time being any project that might give offense to the Spanish crown. But it insisted that anyone could send out expeditions to discover unknown and unsettled parts of the world. It must be noted that this was the first diplomatic exchange over the Falkland Islands. In it, the right to settle was not discussed. The British contended that their expedition would be a purely scientific one. This claim seems to indicate that they knew that they had no right to settle in that area under the treaties and were trying to secure the right under the guise of sending in a scientific expedition. The Spanish government took the stand that the British, having no possessions in that area, had no business there.

The question of the projected expedition by England having been resolved, the two countries turned to the knotty problem of commercial relations. By a new treaty of October 1750, Britain gave up its rights to the *asiento* and the annual vessel of 500 tons burden and was paid 100,000 pounds as compensation. Claims for damages were remitted by both sides, and Britain was satisfied with better commercial privileges within Spain itself, from which it gained greater profits than from the *asiento*.

In the years following the War of the Austrian Succession the British seemed anxious to secure Spanish friendship. They embarked on a far more statesmanlike colonial policy than they had demonstrated in the past, at least not openly antagonizing the Spanish court. As a result friction between the two countries was held to a minimum. When the Seven Years War between France and England broke out in 1756, Spain remained neutral for several years in spite of the efforts of France to involve it in the struggle.

Ferdinand VI of Spain wanted peace to continue Spain's economic and cultural rehabilitation. But with his death in 1759, his half-brother Charles III ascended the throne and a new era began in Spanish history. A man of great ability and strength, Charles combined during his long rule (1759–1788) a sincere desire to promote the well-being of his subjects with a strong hand on the government. He was a close friend of the French, but he did not want them to tell him what to do. So France used guile to get him into the war on its side. In August 1761, the machinations of the French foreign minister, the Duc de Choiseul, got Charles III into the Family Compact with his cousin, Louis XV, the king of France. The treaty provided that any enemy of either crown was the enemy of the other. Spain entered the war just as it was ending, and promptly lost Havana and Manila to British fleets.

As the war was drawing to a close with defeat for France and Spain, France ceded the Louisiana Territory to Spain. On the day that the treaty of cession was completed, France and Spain concluded with England the Treaty of Paris ending the war. It was February 10, 1763, a black day in the annals of the Family Compact. France relinquished Canada and all the land it possessed east of the Mississippi River to England. Spain ceded Florida to England in exchange for Havana (Cuba), captured by the British during the last months of the war. Spain also agreed to accept the decisions of English prize courts and to give up claims to the Newfoundland fisheries.

The Treaty of Paris also renewed and confirmed previous treaties in regard to public law, thus leaving undisturbed the fundamental basis of the existing colonial system. As strange as it may seem, Spain could still close its colonial settlements to outsiders. Spain still had exclusive use of its possessions, and its idea of the closed sea was undisturbed. Spain, indeed, had strict rules about the evacuation of territories occupied by Englishmen during the war, and so did France. By the treaty, ships arriving to remove British subjects had to arrive in ballast, have passports, and have Spanish officers on board—all measures to prevent illegal trading.

Now, however, it would be much more difficult to contain British encroachment on Spanish possessions. Spain faced England along the Mississippi and in Florida. Although the Gulf of Mexico was supposedly closed to foreigners, by Spanish law accepted by international agreement, how could Spain keep out every ship? The lands of the two powers had never been in such close proximity. The conflicts that had occurred in the West Indies were now threatening in other parts of America. One of these places was going to be the Falkland Islands.

France Settles the Islands But Returns Them to Spain

The Seven Years' War had brought England great stretches of territory, with prospects of fabulous wealth from any commercial ventures it might undertake. France had lost almost all its huge empire in the New World, retaining only a few islands. Spain had lost Florida to England, but had gained from France the Louisiana Territory west of the Mississippi. The question now was, Would England, at least for the time being, be satisfied with its gains, or would it try to expand its empire even more? The whole process of assimilation of new territories was not carefully planned but rather spontaneous and natural, and was closely related to political processes in Europe. The quest for additional possessions came from a desire to strengthen and protect lands already occupied, and also to obtain outposts for further expansion. Britain was driven to expansionist policies in part because of political alignments on the Continent (the Family Compact, for example, was still in effect) and in part because as victor in the last struggle it was openly disliked by all sides, a situation that augured future conflict.

England stood alone. Spain repulsed a British attempt at closer understanding and better relations. No paths anywhere led to an alliance. France and Spain immediately after the war were busy reorganizing their internal and external affairs, an ominous foreboding. Britain's only hope was that the economic exhaustion of its two enemies would provide a breathing spell in which to get ready for any emergency.

Choiseul was too shrewd to think of renewing war with England immediately. Outwardly he carried out all the terms of the treaty and urged Spain to do likewise, while in the meantime he dedicated himself to restoring the French Empire as best he could by establishing new settlements in unoccupied areas. In this he had to act alone, because Louis XV and the people around him refused to support his ideas. But as long as he did not bring France into direct confrontation with other powers, he was allowed freedom of action to sustain the dignity of France. Choiseul's plans included creating an Antillean empire by taking over a chain of islands in the West Indies and establishing a settlement in Guiana. He proposed to revitalize the remnants of French settlements in India and to establish outposts in Madagascar. Further plans embraced a possible base in the Spanish-owned Philippines, but Spain soon checked those dreams. That would be carrying the Family Compact too far. Moreover, it was absolutely necessary to maintain the closest friendship between the two allies, avoiding disputes over lands both crowns coveted.

Yet something had to be done to blot out the disgrace of losing Canada. The French Empire had to be restored and the good name of the Bourbons upheld. One result of this line of thought was the first settlement of the Falkland Islands. A young officer, Louis Antoine de Bougainville, whose name is better known for an island in the South Pacific and a beautiful tropical flower that bears it, had been with Montcalm at Quebec during the Seven Years' War, and was known as a distinguished military man. He suggested to the French crown that he and some relatives, all of St. Malo, be permitted to go at their own expense to Les Iles Malouines, as the sailors of St. Malo called the Falklands. The government consented, and Bougainville set sail from St. Malo in September 1763, in two ships with the necessary supplies and several Acadian families from Canada. It was definitely a colonizing expedition. He touched at Montevideo (in present-day Uruguay), a Spanish colony, and finally reached West Falkland in January 1764.

Finding no good bay in which to anchor, Bougainville sailed to East Falkland, where he founded the first known settlement on the Falklands on March 17, 1764. He called it Fort St. Louis. It was located on present Berkeley Sound. On April 5, he took possession of the land in the name of Louis XV, and a few days later he sailed back to France. He was back in the colony in January 1765, but soon crossed over to the region of the Strait of Magellan to get wood for houses and small trees to be planted in the islands. In April 1765, he again returned to France, and this time he sent out more supplies and additional colonists, bringing the total to 150, in those days considered enough for a well-established colony.

In the meantime Spain had followed Bougainville's activities with anxiety. Soon after he had stopped over in Montevideo, Spanish officials there had informed the Spanish government of Bougainville's expedition. The Marqués de Grimaldi, Spain's capable foreign minister, asked the Spanish ambassador in Paris, the Conde de Fuentes, to find out the purpose of the expedition. He was to tell the French crown that this was not the route to India and that the Family Compact did not authorize this action. Choiseul, the artful intriguer, answered that the expedition had gone to the South Atlantic to find an island that would facilitate the trip around the Horn, that the commander knew that he had no right to enter Spanish colonies or trade with them, and that he had entered Montevideo harbor only because his ships needed repairs.

Grimaldi and Charles III had already been planning on settling the Falklands as a protection to Spanish fleets using the Straits and Cape Horn. Grimaldi told Fuentes to inform the French government that a French settlement in the Falklands would be prejudicial to the interests of Spain, because the British might believe they had the right to take similar action. Fuentes was to ask officially for the abandonment of the settlement and to inform Choiseul that Spain could not understand why the French government had not informed Spain officially of this action, of which it had heard indirectly from foreign journals and from Spanish officials in Montevideo. Spain also asked for a conference to discuss the abandonment of the settlement by the French and Spain's taking it over.

Spain based its claim to the islands on the principle of territorial proximity: their nearness to the mainland under Spanish control (present Argentina). Perhaps because the Spanish government was not completely certain of the validity of this claim, or perhaps because it did not want to put any strain on the Family Compact, it suggested that Spain pay France for the expenses incurred in establishing the settlement. At first Choiseul did not want to give in, but he eventually did. Bougainville, who had just returned from his second trip to the islands, was sent to Madrid in April 1766 to come to terms with the Spanish government. Bougainville agreed to return the islands to Spain, and Spain areed to reimburse Bougainville for expenses incurred in establishing an illegal settlement on the islands. It must be noted that the official document said that the settlement was illegal. France therefore accepted Spain's claim to the Falklands. Bougainville received a liberal sum from Grimaldi, and France accepted the agreement.

On his trip to restore the Malvinas to the Spanish crown, Bougainville arrived in Montevideo in January 1767, and sailed across the Río de la Plata to Buenos Aires to arrange for the cession of the islands with the Spanish officials there. The combined Spanish and French fleet then sailed for the Falklands together, arriving at Fort St. Louis on March 25, 1767. On April 1, Bougainville delivered the settlement to the Spaniards. In accordance with the French king's wishes, the inhabitants could remain and become Spanish subjects or return to France. A few families remained, but most of them returned. The Spanish governor of the new colony was Felipe Ruiz Puente. He was under the governor of

Buenos Aires, Francisco de Paula Bucareli y Ursúa, a strong-willed person, as will be seen later.

Britain Attempts to Settle the Islands

The British government, in the meantime, was showing a renewed interest in the Falklands, probably because of Admiral Anson's interest in them and because of the possibility of great benefits to be derived from preying on Spanish commerce from bases in the islands. An expedition was organized in 1764 to sail to the area and report on these possibilities. On June 21, 1764, Commodore John Byron (grandfather of the poet) sailed from Downs on H.M.S. *Dolphin* with the frigate *Tamar*. He was to call at some islands located near the Strait of Magellan named Falklands and Pepys and make better surveys of them than had yet been made. In doing this he was to seek a place or places where a settlement or settlements could be made. Byron was chosen because he supposedly knew the area, having earlier performed the incredible feat of crossing Patagonia, about which he wrote a narrative published in 1768. The real object of the expedition was not disclosed to the crew until the ships reached the coast of Brazil. Until then they had been supposedly bound for the East Indies. It seems that the Byron expedition had actually been ordered to carry out Anson's plans of many years before.

Byron, using a chart of Anson's voyage, reached Puerto Deseado on the Patagonian coast after some difficulty. He searched the seas for several days for Pepys Island, and not finding it (because it didn't exist), he set sail for the islands of Sebald de Weert, which had been seen by enough people so that he could be certain they *did* exist. Storms, however, made him change his course. He entered the Strait of Magellan, going as far as Port Famine in search of wood and water. On January 5, 1765, Byron left Port Famine to seek the Falklands. He sighted West Falkland on January 11. He began making extensive surveys of the coast of this island, using as a base a place on present Byron Sound, which he called Port Egmont in honor of the First Lord of the Admiralty. Without giving the date of this action, he wrote that he had taken possession of that harbor and all neighboring islands in the name of King George III. He called them Falkland's Islands.

Leaving Port Egmont, Byron continued coasting along the northern shores of the islands, even past present Berkeley Sound, at the end of which the French colony was snugly concealed. Byron knew nothing of the French presence in the Falklands, because he had left England before any public announcement of the French occupation had been made. He did not explore the sound itself and seems to have gone no farther than the present Cape Pembroke, assuming that a point he saw at 52° 3' was the southernmost point of East Falkland. He sailed back to Puerto Deseado, where he met a provision ship with which he sent back news of his discoveries. Ironically, Byron later sighted the *Aigle*, in which Bougainville explored the Strait of Magellan for wood.

Byron's news reached England on June 21, 1765. One of the statements in his dispatch noted that he had seen no people in the islands and no signs of any people either then existing or having ever set foot on the islands. The British government immediately made plans to settle the islands. Henry Conway, secretary of state for the Southern Department, told the lords of the Admiralty on July 20, 1765, that the king desired that an expedition be sent to the Falklands as soon as possible. It was to consist of a frigate, a sloop, and a storeship with a military complement of twenty-five marines. The commanders were enjoined by all means possible to complete the settlement begun the year before at Port Egmont. Conway considered the planting of a vegetable garden by the surgeon of the *Tamar* as proof of a settlement—no people had been left at Port Egmont. Does this mean that it was difficult for the British government to find bases to bolster its claim to the islands? In addition, a ship was to be constantly in the islands for the protection of the settlers, and other vessels were to make additional surveys and also search for Pepys Island. It seems England was going to go all out to find that mercurial island of thick woods, fresh water, and a bay big enough for 500 ships.

Although he definitely knew by now about the French settlement in the Falklands, Conway nevertheless gave instructions that

If any lawless Persons should happen to be found seated on any Part of the Islands, they are to be compelled either to quit the said Island, or to take the oath, acknowledge & submit themselves to his Majesty's government as subjects of the Crown of Great Britain.

And if, contrary to Expectation, the subjects of any Foreign Power in Amity with Great Britain, should under any real and pretended authority, have taken upon them to make any settlement of any kind or nature whatsoever upon any part or parts either of the said Falkland's or Pepys' Islands, the commanders of His Majestys ships aforesaid are to visit such settlement, and to remonstrate against their proceedings, acquainting them that the said Islands having been first discovered by the subjects of the Crown of England, sent out by the government thereof for that purpose, and of right belonging to His Majesty, and His Majesty having given orders for the settlement thereof, the subjects of no other power can have any title to establish themselves, therein without the Kings permission; acquainting them further, that they are directed to warn them off the said islands & to transport themselves with their effects within a time limited, not exceeding six months from the day of the notice so to be given. (Goebel 1927: pp. 234–235).

In spite of this admonition, Conway also warned the admiralty that if a settlement of another power were found and it took no notice of a warning, the commanders should start no acts of violence or hostility except in self-defense. However, this prohibition did not apply to Port

Egmont, which must be held at any cost. In case a foreign colony were found, the settlers were to be warned off. If they did not obey, the British commanders should land and establish a joint settlement with the foreign colonists without hostility, and leave the question of future rights to the area to the British crown and the sovereign of the other settlers.

A very interesting explanation of the projected expedition was sent by First Lord of the Admiralty Lord Egmont to the duke of Grafton, the secretary of state for the Northern Department, in which he presented what he considered proofs of Britain's title to the Falklands, but told the duke not to let anyone see them except persons of the most complete discretion because they were of the most secret nature. The question is, Why should proofs of Britain's title be kept secret? Egmont added that the Falklands were without doubt the key to the whole Pacific Ocean, commanding the ports and trade of Chile, Peru, Panama, and Acapulco, "in one word all the Spanish territory upon that sea." And he insisted that possession of the islands would "render all our expeditions to those parts most lucrative to ourselves, most fatal to Spain and no longer formidable tedious, or uncertain in a future war . . ." (Goebel 1927: p. 236). What more need be said about Lord Egmont's intentions and hopes? His note is nothing less than a remarkable expression of British imperialism in the eighteenth century. The English settlement in the Falklands was well named: Port Egmont.

Regarding the claims of Spain and France to the islands, Egmont declared that no papal bulls and no treaties (as far as he could remember) gave Spain title to an island lying eighty or a hundred leagues east of the coast of South America in the Atlantic Ocean, and that France's attempted colonization there seemed to substantiate his argument. Egmont's logic confirms that Spain's fears, expressed to France at the time of Bougainville's expedition to the Falklands, were well founded. Egmont contended that Britain had made two discoveries of the islands before anyone else, no doubt referring to the expeditions of Davis and Hawkins, who as has been seen, were not the first discoverers and may never have been at the islands. Egmont assured the duke of Grafton that Byron had seen no French settlement on the islands, but that it was widely known that France was planning to send an expedition there. He therefore urged immediate action, for if the French really intended to settle the islands, and the British did nothing, the French would have a year's start on them. Then it might not be within Britain's power to expel them without open hostilities that would mean an immediate rupture with both France and Spain. This could be avoided by immediate action.

The expedition was prepared in extreme secrecy. It was placed under the command of Captain John McBride, commander of H.M.S. *Jason*. He was ordered to sail to the Falklands with the *Jason*, the sloop *Carcass*, and the storeship *Experiment*, there to erect a blockhouse mounted with guns from the ships and manned by twenty-five marines. Toward any alien he found on the islands he was to act as Conway had requested. The expedition landed in the Falklands on January 8, 1766, almost two years after the French had arrived there and fourteen months before the Spaniards arrived to take possession of their colony from the French. McBride sailed around the islands, but when he was unable to make accurate surveys in a large vessel, he took to using small boats. His examination of the islands was done hastily, and he reported no trace of a French settlement. He had to stop his surveys when winter set in, and started them again in September 1766. He finally found the French settlement, warned the French to leave, and returned to Port Egmont, whence he sailed for England in January 1767.

Under the existing public law, reinforced by the treaties of Utrecht and Aix-la-Chapelle, McBride's actions were highly irregular. Fort St. Louis was a French colonial port that McBride entered after having been warned not to, thus committing an act of aggression. He left when the French officer in charge of the settlement showed him Bougainville's commission, which may have intimidated McBride. Soon thereafter the French turned the colony over to the Spaniards, making the incident important only in relation to other events.

Evidently, the three powers came to grips with the Falklands question in a vacillating, almost faint-hearted way. Probably this indecisiveness was due to the fact that no one of them knew what the others were doing to establish a colony in the South Atlantic. Also, there was still a great deal of uncertainty, especially in England, as to whether the Malouines and the Falklands were the same. The surveys of the famous French cartographer Amédée François Frézier, upon whom the French relied, and of Byron, upon whom the English relied, were incomplete. Were the English and French settlements even in the same group? Neither Byron nor McBride (in their first reports) had mentioned a French colony. The ones who knew more about the islands were the Spaniards. At least they claimed exact knowledge about the region and had no doubt about the conflict of sovereignty. In the islands McBride had not been informed of the French colony until March 1766, and Britain had not been informed of the cession to Spain of Bougainville's colony until May 1766. Until then no official notice of a French colony close to the British station at Port Egmont had been received.

Hence a problem arose soon after news of the return of the Malouines to Spain was received in England: What was the Admiralty to do about revictualling Port Egmont? What effect would it have on Britain's relations with France and Spain? The question of sending supplies to Port Egmont was discussed in the British cabinet. In these discussions the full deceit and conspiracy of the Admiralty was revealed. The French chargé d'affaires in London procured an account of what happened in the meeting by giving a clerk in the Admiralty seventy-five pounds. If this account is to be believed, the British Admiralty knew about the French settlement in the Falklands and about French claims of sovereignty over them, and therefore could not justify the establishment of a colony there. Perhaps this is why Britain claimed title by discovery, a basis which had never been considered valid.

When Choisuel heard of the revictualling expedition even before it sailed, he sent a note to the French embassy in London in which he declared that it seemed as if the British were planning to show who was ruler of the seas. He reiterated that the Spanish government rested its claims on the Peace of Utrecht.

In August 1766, Egmont forcefully explained to a meeting of the cabinet what in his opinion had prompted the previous ministry to determine to establish a settlement on the islands, and strongly supported sending the fleet to protect it. The Duke of Grafton, however, denied that the motives alleged by Edmont were those of the previous ministry, and demonstrated how the sending of the fleet could cause grave difficulties. Others in the cabinet supported Grafton's suggestion and proposed a delay of one week during which they would prepare to take a vote. Egmont strongly opposed delay, insisting that Lord Chatham (William Pitt) had approved the scheme in his last term in office. But Chatham said nothing and the meeting adjourned. Egmont thereupon handed in his resignation. The Admiralty had lost its case, and for the time being the Falklands were to be free of British ships.

The spy-clerk in the Admiralty advised the French embassy of another interesting tidbit. The British government would be willing to negotiate with Spain and France a mutual agreement that all parties should refrain from occupying the islands. Prince Masserano, the Spanish ambassador in London, advised his government not to wait or negotiate but to destroy the English settlement before the fleet could reach it. If at this time Spain had followed Masserano's advice and explained why it had destroyed the settlement, it could have saved itself many headaches later.

Soon thereafter Chatham had a change of heart (or had he waited until Egmont had resigned to break his silence?); he now supported the continuance of Port Egmont on the grounds that Franco-Spanish opposition would be slight, that the fleet was ready, and that England needed a station in the Falklands in time of war. The cabinet decided to send the fleet unless within a week Spain and France should object.

Choiseul wanted no war at this time and advised Masserano to adopt a moderate tone with England. He hoped to prevent a hasty act by the Spanish ambassador while he tried to cool off the Spanish court. However, to the British ambassador in Paris he asserted that Spain had good claims to the islands and had received them from France in consequence of the Treaty of Utrecht, by which only Spaniards could settle in that part of the world. Choiseul reminded the British ambassador that Spain had objected to the British expedition to the South Sea (the Anson project) and had succeeded in stopping it in 1749. He also said that he was not alarmed, and that he would make the same suggestions to the Spanish government that he had made to Britain.

But Choiseul had difficulty in convincing Charles III not to rush into a dangerous situation. Charles wanted to attack the British immediately because it would become more difficult to do so later on. His ministers advised him, however, that the worst step would be a war, because France and Spain were not prepared for a conflict. Instead, the Spanish crown should preserve its right to the islands through protest and representations while making preparations to place the two allies on a basis of naval equality with Britain. This was Choiseul's idea, and a report on the state of Spain's readiness for a naval war bore him out. Charles finally gave in. Choiseul had won the day, and his general design for the Family Compact, whereby France was to control Spanish foreign policy, seemed to be working like clockwork.

In the meantime, Prince Masserano had asked Lord Shelburne, the new secretary of state, about British designs. Lord Shelburne lied by disclaiming any knowledge of the matter and said that England would observe the treaties. Then he added that the Treaty of Utrecht did not apply in this case because it regulated only the acts of individuals and not those of the states themselves, a specious argument, to say the least, as governments, not individuals, had made the treaty. Shelburne refused to admit the existence of an English colony on the Falklands and said that it was ridiculous to forbid England the navigation not only of the Atlantic but of the South Seas as well. Anyway, according to him, things had gone too far and Britain could not turn back. Without consideration of the possible consequences the ministry would proceed with its plans. In a huff, Shelburne said that the English would continue to navigate in those waters and asked what the limits of the Spanish possessions were. It was Spain's task to prove her rights to the islands; England had many navigators to testify to British rights.

Commenting on Shelburne's original complaint, that Spain had not protested the first British expedition (Spain had, but Shelburne had not been told about it), Masserano replied by asking why, if the Falklands and the Malvinas were the same, England had never protested Bougainville's occupation. Perhaps exasperated, Masserano conceded that trying to reason with Shelburne was futile, because he was obviously ready to go to war before giving up Port Egmont.

Choiseul's reaction to this turn of events was to make a strong attempt to persuade Spain to avoid war at all costs, at least for eighteen months. He suggested to Charles that Spain accept a delay in action. In the meantime Spain should send out a fleet to see if there were an English colony on the Malouines, and if it found one to destroy it immediately. It was easier, he said, to discuss a destroyed colony than one that was to be destroyed—a frivolous and strange suggestion from someone trying to avoid war. Choiseul proposed that the Spanish crown should send out singly various Spanish ships to different places and then assemble them at a given place in order to destroy all settlements made contrary to the treaties. By the time news of this action reached Europe, Spain and France would be ready to fight.

Meanwhile, the Comte de Guerchy, the French ambassador to London, would return to England and there join with Masserano in speaking plainly with George III, pointing out that Spain and France were bound by treaty to enter into war if either were attacked, and that both Louis XV and Charles III were inclined to peace and were doing everything they could to avoid war. For this reason, when Spain had protested Bougainville's settlement, France had not taken advantage of Charles's great affection for his royal cousin and had handed over the settlement. Louis XV would make any sacrifice for peace, but it was necessary that England do likewise. All the sacrifices should not be made by Spain and France. In short, France wanted peace but would not buy it, according to Choiseul.

Choiseul's idea of temporizing was not adopted at once, but later developments led to its execution, with Spanish emendations. Grimaldi sent Masserano instructions to the effect that he was to tell George III that Spain had heard about Byron's and other expeditions to the region of the Strait of Magellan, for the purpose of establishing settlements there, and that if these reports were true, they meant that Britain was aiming to strike a mortal blow to the Spanish crown and its rights.

Spain's rights, he said, were based on the Treaty of Utrecht, "the political foundations of Europe," under which Spain had recognized the British ruling house and the British had recognized the Spanish ruling house. For this reason as well as others the two crowns should respect and not oppose the terms of the pact. By article eight of the treaty Spain had been given exclusive possession of the American continents and adjacent islands, and it could not legally alienate any part of these possessions. It was *England* that had exacted these provisions, and it had been *England* that in the past had given proof of the need to recognize these provisions. England in 1740 had resisted attempts by Russia to get a foothold in the Pacific by openly declaring that Spain was the mistress of the Pacific. Abandonment of the Anson project of 1749 and the French surrender of the Bougainville colony to Spain were further proof of the validity of the Spanish claim.

Masserano was to tell George III that Charles III most solemnly protested the projected settlement in the Malvinas or in any other place in the vicinity of the Horn, and that he would counter any such settlement at any cost in spite of the great hurt he would feel under so cruel a necessity. The dispatch ended in a flowery appeal to George III's sense of justice and a devout hope for the preservation of peace.

Fortunately for Spain, when Britain learned that Bougainville had ceded the settlement of Fort Louis to Spain, the situation changed. The British had been assuming that the Spanish government was basing its demand for Port Egmont on the violation of the principles of the closed sea as established in the American Treaty of 1670 and the Treaty of Utrecht. Now that the Spaniards were in possession under the agreement of cession, by which they succeeded to the rights of an occupant anterior to the British, the Spanish position was greatly strengthened. Moreover, Masserano considered the question of the Malvinas a point of honor for Spain; it would be better to go to war than to give in. Charles III agreed.

But Choiseul did not. He was afraid of war with England. With him the Family Compact was not a question of honor. In September 1766, the Spanish court had accepted the idea that war could not be declared for eight months, but by November 1766, it felt that it would be ready in 1768. But Choiseul insisted that France would not be ready until the end of 1769. Later he changed it to 1770, insisting that the two courts would be more ready to fight in 1770 than in 1769 and more ready in 1769 than in 1768.

But other problems made Charles III delay confrontation. In 1767, as part of a widespread and drastic ecclesiastical reform, he banished the Jesuits from all Spanish territories, a measure that produced a hue and cry in the populace because in most places the Jesuits were much loved and considered a genuinely Spanish religious order. The measure was viewed as the beginning of a reduction in the temporal and spiritual power of the church. To such measures there was much opposition in that devoutly Catholic country. It is little wonder that for two years Charles was too busy at home to worry about some islands in the South Atlantic. This preoccupation probably made it easier for Spain to accept Choiseul's refusal to be drawn into immediate war, a decision that amounted to his refusal to live up to the Family Compact. Other minor problems helped to calm down Charles III. In October 1767, for example, some British warships entered Havana harbor illegally, an incident that was soon forgotten but caused Spain some fearful moments.

However, Spain did not forget Port Egmont, to the Spanish government a blot on the scutcheon that had to be removed. Spain was aided by the doctrine of possession, which in the seventeenth and eighteenth centuries became the basis for all territorial claims. The doctrine *uti possidetis* ("as you possess" or "according to as you now possess") was the foundation stone of the American Treaty of 1670 and the Treaty of Utrecht, but even before these treaties no state had successfully maintained the so-called doctrine of discovery, that is, finding and thereafter claiming an area without settling it. Britain or Spain, under the doctrine of possession, would have to occupy a territory like the Falklands to claim sovereignty over it. But Spain also had the American Treaty of 1670 and the Treaty of Utrecht to back it up.

Lord Egmont, however, insisted that mere discovery gave England rights to the islands. He asserted, erroneously, that the English (Davis's and Hawkins's expeditions) had discovered them first and that Byron's expedition had been made to cinch this claim based on discovery. By

1768, then, Britain claimed right by discovery and by occupation, persistently maintaining that the Treaty of Utrecht did not exclude Britons from settling in the South Atlantic. Spain claimed right by occupation, as the sole power authorized to colonize that area under the Treaty of Utrecht. The French had not only settled there before the British but had also ceded the islands to Spain. Having received clear title to the islands from France, Spain was in law to be treated as the prior occupant. If the legality of the treaty is accepted, the British claim is destroyed.

There is little doubt that the British were on the Falklands without any right, and that establishing a settlement there was an act of aggression. By this act England repudiated a treaty of over fifty years and denied the legality of a prior settlement by another state. By 1768, the Spaniards felt that a grave injury had been done them. Realizing that they could no longer depend on the French to support them under the Family Compact, they decided to eject the English themselves.

Spain Ejects the British from the Islands

On February 25, 1768, the Spanish crown ordered the governor and military commander of Buenos Aires, Francisco de Paula Bucareli y Ursúa, to expel any English settlers in the Malvinas by force if they did not obey warnings to leave peacefully. He needed no further instructions, but he was ordered to be careful and not expose himself to a superior force. If he faced a superior force he was to resort to protests, declaring that he would take no action until he had informed his king and additional orders had been received.

Bucareli was a man of energy and action, but he was also careful. His fleet had to be well provisioned, and that took time. He was probably also delayed by the bad weather and the lack of exact information about the location of the English settlement. It is not known whether he received further orders that might have delayed him. In any case, it was not until December 1769 that Bucareli sent out the frigates *Santa Catalina* and *Santa Rosa* and the xebec *Andaluz*. Bucareli sent along two Englishmen who claimed to know the location of the English settlement, but this precaution proved unnecessary, because when the Spaniards arrived at Puerto de la Soledad, as the new Spanish and former French settlement was now named, they heard that the English settlement had been found. In fact, a clash between the two opposing groups had almost occurred.

The month before, in November 1769, Felipe Ruiz Puente, the Spanish governor of the Malvinas, had sent out a schooner to survey the islands. The pilot, Angel Santos, encountered Captain Hunt of the English colony, who was on a similar expedition. Hunt warned off the Spanish schooner, but it reappeared a few days later where Hunt was anchored, with letters and presents from Ruiz Puente. In the letters the Spanish governor expressed surprise that Hunt had been so disrespectful of the Spanish king as to have the Spanish ship put about. He said that he supposed Hunt's being on those coasts was purely accidental, but that he should leave with the first formal warning of the Spanish officer. If he did not do so, he would be in violation of treaties and in breach of faith.

Hunt replied that the islands belonged to His Britannic Majesty and that the subjects of no other power whatsoever could inhabit them. He warned the Spaniards to leave and gave them six months to get out. He also told the Spanish lieutenant who brought the message that he would be fired on if he continued his survey of the islands, and forbade him to enter the harbor of Port Egmont. The Spanish lieutenant protested in writing against this treatment and forbade Hunt to enter the harbor of La Soledad. The Spanish governor again demanded that Hunt withdraw from the islands, as his stay was a breach of treaty. Hunt again refused and repeated his previous ultimatum.

When the squadron sent by Bucareli arrived at La Soledad and was informed of what had happened, Fernando de Rubalclava, commander of the *Santa Catalina,* set sail together with the *Andaluz* for Port Egmont, where he arrived on February 20, 1770. Rubalclava sent a note to Hunt advising him that the British settlement in the area was in violation of treaties allowing no intrusion into the dominions of Spain. He protested strongly against the presence of the English, but said he would take no action until he had received orders from his king. Unless he had noted a superior force at Port Egmont, this inaction was contrary to the orders issued to and presumably passed on by Bucareli. Hunt replied that the islands belonged to Britain by right of discovery and warned the Spaniards to get out. But Rubalclava stayed eight days before he left. Meantime the *Santa Rosa* had been sent back to Buenos Aires to report the first meeting with the British, and soon thereafter the *Andaluz* left with news of Rubalclava's encounter with Hunt. Hunt sailed for England in March 1770.

Bucareli immediately organized a new expedition consisting of four frigates and a xebec, with 1,400 troops, a fifth of whom were seasoned veterans. It was under the command of Juan Ignacio de Madariaga, whose orders were to reduce the British settlement should it offer resistance. On June 4, 1770, he anchored in the bay of Port Egmont and sent notes to the two English captains there, demanding the withdrawal of the English from Spanish territory and offering to help them leave. The English refused, and the Spaniards attacked the settlement, which surrendered very quickly. By the terms of capitulation the frigate *Favourite,* the sole protection of the British colony, was to remain in port for twenty days after Madariaga had dispatched a frigate to take news of the surrender to Spain. To make sure that the *Favourite* did not sail sooner, its rudder was removed.

Spain had gone it alone. It did not need the aid of Choiseul and the Family Compact. Spain should have remembered this in 1790, during the Nootka Sound controversy, when France again abandoned its partner.

The incident at Port Egmont left both sides feeling that their honor had been insulted and their pride hurt. But neither side had wanted war.

Diplomatic Crisis over Port Egmont

Lord North had just become prime minister, in February 1770, with Lord Weymouth as secretary of state for the Southern Department. It was a weak combination considered incapable of pursuing a vigorous foreign policy. It was certainly not like the William Pitt government so feared by Choiseul, who had warned the Spanish crown four years before about the dangers of war with England so long as Pitt was in command.

Now the British government was not only weak; it was also facing troubles with its American colonies. But Francés, Choiseul's chargé d'affaires in London, warned his chief that although the English ministry was vacillating and not disposed to go to war over the Falklands, it would have to be watched, because pride and a sense of honor would not let it abandon the colony completely, especially as long as William Pitt captained the opposition and would seize any pretext to embarrass the government. Pitt was constantly harassing the government, accusing it of having done nothing for three years about the Falklands question and of doing nothing now in response to the acts of Spain, which he called a declaration of war.

In Francés's view, the British people in general believed that Britain had no right to the islands, but that the colony established there could not be abandoned without dishonor. But he insisted that war would be very risky for North's ministry. It is not known whether Choiseul at that moment considered going to war, but in July 1770, he instructed Francés to present to the British government a demand for reparation for an incident that had taken place in India and that Choiseul considered an insult to the French flag.

Perhaps Choiseul was looking for a war to save his neck; he was out of favor with Madame Du Barry and other people close to Louis XV. Spain had assured him in 1766 that it would be ready to go to war in eighteen months, and more than eighteen months had passed since this assurance. Certainly Choiseul seemed justified in believing that he could go to some lengths to back his ally in a war with Britain. So now the shoe was on the other foot; Choiseul was ready for action, but Spain had become cautious. Realizing that England's reaction to the events at Port Egmont was deeply rooted in a sense of national honor, Charles III was disposed to heal the wound inflicted on England's pride by restoring Port Egmont exactly as it had been when the Spaniards expelled the British, provided they would return it soon and in that manner accept the sovereignty of Spain over the islands. This would avoid war, which Spain did not want at the moment because the Jesuit question was still a matter of lively discussion with the Vatican and the country was not yet adequately prepared for war.

Charles III's minister, the Marqués de Grimaldi, informed Choiseul that what the Spanish ships had done was in agreement with what he had previously told the French court: that when Spain had learned vaguely that the British had established a settlement in the vicinity of Port Egmont, it decided that a reconnaissance should be made, and if the settlement were on the Pacific side of Cape Horn it should be destroyed immediately, but if it were on the Malvinas the Spanish forces should merely protest. This is actually what had been done at first. Grimaldi added that Bucareli's patriotic action had been too violent and had been disavowed. Grimaldi and the Spanish court were not willing to go to war over a Franco-English conflict in India or over a proposed treaty Choiseul was thinking of making with Turkey, an action that would certainly mean war with England.

There was a long period of negotiation before the nations came to terms. As was natural, each court was looking out for its own country's interests. The Spaniards did not trust the English or the French, the French did not trust the English or the Spaniards, and the English did not trust the Spaniards or the French—all for good reason.

War Is Averted: A King's Honor Is Rescued

Between England and Spain the main conflict was a question of honor. Charles III, always solicitous of his honor, could not understand why the English crown would not give way on a matter he felt involved the honor of the Spanish crown. Each side felt itself insulted, and for that reason, during the negotiations emphasis was placed on the immediate events rather than on the matter of right, the real question. Moreover, for the Spaniards, unconditional acceptance of British demands meant the risk of prejudicing a discussion of the fundamental problem: the ownership of the Malvinas.

The British minister to the Spanish court, James Harris, insisted that George III was anxious to make all possible concessions to the Spanish court that were compatible with his honor, and that the demands made by the British crown were the only ones that could be made consistent with honor. Grimaldi told Harris that Charles III, anxious to keep the peace, was willing to give every reasonable satisfaction to the king of England if he felt himself insulted. This satisfaction would be given in the manner the British crown desired. However, Charles III also thought that since he had gone out of his way to preserve the honor of George III, George III should reciprocate.

This kind of haggling went on for months after the Spanish troops had ejected the English garrison at Port Egmont on June 10, 1770. England threatened war if the settlement were not returned. Spain did not budge except to suggest that it might return Port Egmont for a while provided the settlement were restored in due time to Spain by England. This suggestion eventually settled the issue.

Prince Masserano, the very able Spanish ambassador in London, received from the British government a secret, verbal agreement that if Port Egmont were returned to England, it would in time be restored to Spain. But the public, written agreement also contained a clause stating that possession of Port Egmont by the British for a short while could not and ought not to affect in any way the Spanish right to the Malvinas. This is the crux of later misunderstandings, but the clause was never misunderstood by Spain or, later, by Spain's heir, Argentina. The mutual agreement was signed January 22, 1771. Masserano's declaration was as follows:

His Britannick Majesty having complained of the violence which was committed on the 10th of June, 1770, at the island commonly called the Great Malouine, and by the English Falkland's Island, in obliging by force, the commander and subjects of his Britannick Majesty to evacuate the port by them called Egmont; a step offensive to the honour of his crown; the Prince de Maserano, Ambassador Extraordinary of his Catholick Majesty, has received orders to declare, and declares, that his Catholick Majesty, considering the desire with which he is animated for peace, and for the maintenance of good harmony with his Britannick Majesty, and the reflecting that this event might interrupt it, has seen with displeasure this expedition tending to disturb it; and in the persuasion in which he is of the reciprocity of sentiments of his Britannick Majesty, and of its being far from his intention to authorise anything that might disturb the good understanding between the two Courts, his Catholick Majesty does disavow the said violent enterprise,—and, in consequence, the Prince of Maserano, declares that his Catholick Majesty engages to give immediate orders, that things shall be restored in the Great Malouine at the port called Egmont, precisely to the state in which they were before the 10th of June, 1770: For which purpose, his Catholick Majesty will give orders to one of his Officers, to deliver up to the Officer authorized by his Britannick Majesty the port and fort called Egmont, with all the artillery, stores, and effects of his Britannick Majesty and his subjects which were at that place the day above named, agreeable to the inventory which had been made of them.

The Prince de Maserano declares, at the same time, in the name of the King, his master, that the engagement of his said Catholick Majesty, to restore to his Britannick Majesty the possession of the port and fort called Egmont, cannot nor ought in any wise to affect the question of the prior right of sovereignty of the Malouine Islands, otherwise called Falkland's Islands. In witness whereof, I, the underwritten Ambassador Extraordinary have signed the present declaration with my usual signature, and caused it to be sealed with our arms. (Goebel, 1927: pp. 358–359)

The British declaration was signed by William, Earl of Rochford, Lord North's secretary of the Southern Department, recently appointed to succeed Thomas Wentworth, with whom Masserano had had no success in negotiating. Wentworth, in fact, had wanted war. The British acceptance of Masserano's declaration stated:

His Catholick Majesty having authorized the Prince de Maserano, his Ambassador Extraordinary, to offer, in his Majesty's name, to the King of Great Britain, a satisfaction for the injury done to this Britannick Majesty by dispossessing him of the port and fort of Egmont; and the said Ambassador having this day signed a declaration, which he has just delivered to me, expressing therein, that his Catholick Majesty, being desirous to restore the good harmony and friendship which before subsisted between the two Crowns, does disavow the expedition against Port Egmont, in which force has been used against his Britannick Majesty's possessions, commander, and subjects; and does also engage, that all things shall be immediately restored to the precise situation in which they stood before the 10th of June, 1770; and that his Catholick Majesty shall give orders, in consequence, to one of his Officers to deliver up to the Officer authorized by his Britannick Majesty, the port and fort of Port Egmont, as also all his Britannick Majesty's artillery, stores, and effects, as well as those of his subjects, according to the inventory which had been made of them. And the said Ambassador having moreover engaged, in his Catholick Majesty's name, that what is contained in the said declaration shall be carried into effect by his said Catholick Majesty, and that duplicates of this Catholic Majesty's order to his Officers shall be delivered into the hands of one of his Britannick Majesty's Principal Secretaries of State within six weeks; his said Britannick Majesty in order to shew the same friendly disposition on his part, has authorised me to declare, that he will look upon the said declaration of the Prince of Maserano, together with the full performance of the said agreement on the part of His Catholick Majesty, as a satisfaction for the injury done to the Crown of Great Britain. In witness whereof, I, the under-written, one of his Brittanick Majesty's Principal Secretaries of State, have signed these presents with my usual signature, and caused them to be sealed with our arms. (Goebel 1927: pp. 359–360)

This agreement was to play a significant role in the future history of the islands. Goebel has shown that at the time of the exchange of notes, Lord North and his secretary for the Southern Department, the Earl of Rochford, gave their solemn word that the fort and port of Egmont would be returned to Spain in the not too distant future. This was a secret agreement (a gentlemen's agreement). Immediately after the pact was signed, a rumor circulated in London that a secret article preserved Spain's sovereignty over the islands. The agreement did not say that exactly—it merely provided for the return of the islands to Spain after England had occupied Port Egmont for a while, without doubt to preserve King George's honor in the public eye.

Many years later, when during the British seizure of the islands in 1833 the Argentine minister to England, Manuel Moreno, protested to Lord Palmerston and mentioned the gentlemen's agreement, Palmerston told him that there never had been such an agreement, because there were no papers in the archives to prove it. But it was made verbally, and Palmerston, as a diplomat and foreign minister of England, knew very well that no records are kept of "secret" agreements. Moreover, even contemporary works mentioned the agreement.

The day after signing the declaration, Masserano attended a party at the royal palace, where George III greeted him effusively as the father of Britain's well-being and told him that he would learn to trust the good faith of the British crown. To this Masserano replied that his king relied on that good faith and for that reason had commanded him to do what he had just done, and that his master would be very glad to hear that he could rely upon the good faith of His Britannic Majesty in the enforcement of the treaty. These exchanges verify the ratification by King George of the verbal promise of North and Rochford.

What legal basis did Spain's declaration and its acceptance by Britain have? It was a mere statement of satisfaction. It disavowed Bucareli's violent action of 1770 (actually an insult to an energetic and loyal servant of the Spanish crown) and temporarily restored the colony, a mere restitution of possession not affecting any right.

During the negotiations, which lasted several months, the British demand had been whittled down to a mere satisfaction for the injury done to the British crown by Bucareli's attack. This demand was based (and here perhaps Masserano's skill is best shown) on an attack on a royal force and not on any violation of territorial sovereignty. Another illustration of this distinction might be the Tampico incident of 1914, when a Mexican president's troops fired on American sailors. The United States considered the act an affront to the United States, as represented by its troops.

Masserano's skill as a diplomat is also shown in the failure of the British to make a reservation of right. Does this mean that the British government felt that it had no sovereign rights to the Falklands, or at least that it wasn't certain about them? It is possible that both Masserano and the French minister in London, Francés, who supported Masserano's negotiations, not only tried to prevent a British reservation, which would weaken Spain's claim, but also realized that the previously made assurance that the British would evacuate the islands made it unnecessary for the British to reserve the right to the islands. Later the British ministry insisted that no assurance had been given, either officially or confidentially, but the fact is that it was given and that it was the basis for Spain's acceptance of the agreement. The British promise to evacuate amounted to a waiver of all question of right. That is how Masserano, and Spain, understood it. Later the British government realized its mistake and demanded a reciprocal abandonment of the islands by the two countries, but it was too late. Spain would not hear of it. However, the British admission of Spain's right to the islands would become legal only when the British actually abandoned the islands. As a result, Spain was going to pass some anxious months wondering whether the British would really abandon them and thus make legal the intent of the agreement.

Finally, it is important to note that during the long negotiations, North and his colleagues tried to assure the Spanish and French envoys that England no longer wanted the islands, had no further use for them, and would never go to war over them. Indeed, the last of these protests was made by Rochford at the moment of exchange of the two documents of agreement. Whether Masserano believed these protestations is questionable, in view of his low opinion of the English government. Is it possible that by the time the agreement was confirmed, the British officials had repeated them so often that they had come to believe them themselves? In any case, these protests of British lack of interest in the Falklands may be used as further proof, if any were needed, that a "secret" gentlemen's agreement did exist, and that the British government was sincere in its promise to leave the resettled Port Egmont in a short time.

Although agreement had been reached and everything seemed to be going smoothly, Masserano had a few days of fright. During the defense of the agreement in Parliament, North stated that Britain ought always to have a base of operations in the South Seas and the right to navigate them. Whether North knew it or not, this statement was a full repudiation of Spain's claims under the Treaty of Utrecht, and it certainly went against North's verbal agreement. A few days later Masserano received dispatches from Grimaldi with copies of the orders sent by his government to the governor of the Malvinas, the governor of Montevideo, and the commandant of Buenos Aires to return the British property at Port Egmont. Upon reporting this action to Rochford, he also told him that Charles III was very satisfied that peace had been established through the efforts of George III, in whom he had great faith, and who, Charles III hoped, would now finish what had been planned to end the matter in an amiable fashion.

To this Rochford replied that the point of honor had been saved, the chief consideration, and the rest had been accomplished. Again, honor was the most important consideration in the whole controversy, it seems, and the occupation of the islands was a minor matter. Rochford was surprised that the Spanish king had suggested no procedure for returning Port Egmont, an omission that astonished Masserano, who quickly said that his master relied on the good faith of the British monarch and his statements after the declaration was signed and wished to see how the promises of the British ministry regarding the evacuation of the *Gran Malvina* would be carried out. This riposte seemed to catch Rochford by surprise, but he quickly recovered himself enough to declare that the British were planning to send two small frigates and a supply ship with food for the few people being sent, fewer than Spain had there.

Masserano had again obtained what he wanted, but, perhaps to be sure, he repaired to the royal palace and repeated Charles III's message, reminding George III of the conversation of January 23. George III assured Masserano that he remembered his promises and would carry them out in good faith. His greatest desire was to avert war, he said. Masserano had again had the secret gentlemen's agreement confirmed by the highest law of the land, the king himself: Port Egmont was to be in British hands only temporarily and then be returned to Spain.

Masserano had good reason to fear British intrigue. Rochford dilly-dallied with the thorny question of how the port was to be returned, not accepting the Spanish suggestion that the British go to Port Soledad, the Spanish capital of the islands, to receive possession of Port Egmont, and suggesting instead a complicated method of returning the port that Spain could not possibly accept. Rochford also brought in the two French envoys, Francés and de Guines, and discussed the matter with them before broaching it to Masserano. The latter was astounded, especially since Rochford had declared Charles III's orders to the Spanish governor, Ruiz Puente, to be satisfactory.

The explanation of the seemingly unusual attitude of the British government was that a public announcement of the conference had made the stocks of the East India Company and other companies drop several points. Was Rochford, in bad financial straits, trying to influence the market? He was a stockholder in the East India Company and might have been trying to save his money. Masserano did not mince words in reminding Rochford that he, Rochford, had approved the orders to Ruiz Puente, and now was raising difficulties. Especially shocking was Rochford's suggestion that perhaps a year hence Port Egmont could be abandoned. Masserano did not explode at this remark, but, as the good diplomat he was, calmly suggested arbitration as the best course, knowing that the British aversion to arbitration would bring Rochford around. Rochford then said that if Spain did not want the English on the island, it could always eject them. Even this frivolous statement did not faze Masserano, who merely said that that was exactly what he was trying to avoid—a war.

The whole Falklands question was again causing political turmoil in England. Pitt, Earl of Chatham, and his colleagues were attacking the government in Parliament for having given up on the Falklands, and were demanding to know whether there had been any secret agreements. In all this Masserano was convinced that the North ministry was acting in bad faith, as indeed it was, thanks to the troubles it was having with the parliamentary opposition. "Hawks" like Pitt made life miserable for the ministry. North also felt that Spain was diplomatically isolated thanks to a change in the French ministry, and therefore he could hold off on the question of a date for the evacuation. Masserano frankly told several British ministers that England was acting in bad faith.

After several more days of acrimonious discussion, Masserano, firmly convinced that the English were trying to squirm out of their agreement in order to gain an advantage over their opponents in Parliament, was somewhat relieved to receive instructions stating that the reason for having the British go to Port Soledad to receive back the command of

Port Egmont was that there was no one living on the Gran Malvina (West Falkland); that Spain had no intention of increasing its armaments (a strong British fear), for it sincerely wanted to avoid a break; and that, with reference to the evacuation of Port Egmont, Spain would see whether Britain sincerely desired to show by its own acts that its word could be relied upon.

Both sides said they wanted peace and both talked about disarmament. But neither wanted to take the lead in advancing either goal. Masserano unfortunately caught Rochford in several evasions and downright lies during the discussion, yet he held his temper as a good diplomat, although several times he hinted at the bad faith of the British in the whole affair. Rochford finally expressed pleasure at not having to hurry about evacuation, since the ministry wished to avoid any appearance of a secret promise, *a fact which it always intended to deny*. This was an open confession of Rochford's deceit.

In a personal meeting with George III, Masserano was told by the king that Spain could rely on his good faith. In the light of this assurance, Grimaldi told Masserano to take it easy, suggesting that Spain should not press the British but ask them in conversation how they would carry out their promise and convince Spain of their good faith. This Masserano had done often in discussions with Rochford; he did not need to be reminded about it. Spain had decided to commit herself to a policy of watchful waiting.

What Spain did not want was Britain's use of Port Egmont as a base for more widespread operations in the South Atlantic and the Pacific. The British had said they would keep only a small force at Port Egmont, and that fact, together with a larger force of Spanish troops at Port Soledad, would surely prevent the use of Port Egmont as a means of violating the Treaty of Utrecht. Now all Spain had to do was wait. There was no further need for discussions of the meaning of the treaties and agreements, because the abandonment of Port Egmont would signify that Britain agreed to forsake the whole idea of a right to free navigation and settlement in that area.

Port Egmont was finally returned to the British crown on September 15, 1771. A British squadron under Captain Stott had arrived two days earlier, and found there a small Spanish force under Lieutenant Francisco de Orduña. Stott delivered the orders of the Spanish king, and after arranging for the delivery of the stores and the restoring of possession, the British troops landed and formally took possession. After the English flag was raised and a salute fired, the Spaniards departed. Later Stott reported that the entire procedure had been effected with the greatest appearance of good faith.

The question now was, When would the British government evacuate Port Egmont as it had promised? The Foreign Office had assured Masserano that Britain would reduce the force there to a minimum, and it now approached the admiralty on the matter. The Admiralty suggested a reduction of the force, as a smaller force would keep up a temporary *mark* of possession anyway, and the garrison was not large enough to defend the port. As a public justification for the abandonment of Port Egmont Rochford used the excuse of economy. Nothing was said about a prior promise to Spain. Caution had to be continued even if Parliament was now more tractable. There was nothing in the records that would show what really had been done.

But Spain was not concerned about the reasons—all it wanted was for the British to leave the Falklands and fulfill the promise of January 1771. The Spanish government informed its governor on the Falklands that as the English had promised to abandon the islands, he was to make sure that they did, and that he should report any future attempts at colonization.

On May 20, 1774, the English abandoned Port Egmont, leaving a lead plate fastened on the blockhouse with the following inscription: "Be it known to all nations that the Falkland Islands, with this fort, the storehouses, wharfs, bays, and creeks thereunto belonging are the sole right and property of His Most Sacred Majesty George the Third, King of Great Britain, France, and Ireland, Defender of Faith, etc. In witness whereof this plate is set up, and his Britannic Majesty's colors left flying as a mark of possession by S. W. Clayton, commanding officer at Falkland Islands, A.D. 1774."

Did Clayton's action give the British government a legal right to the Falklands? It did not, as Goebel, Caillet-Bois, Hidalgo Nieto, and other eminent diplomatic historians have pointed out. In spite of Clayton's leaden plate, England had declared its intention to surrender the islands in a few years. Therefore possession could not have been constructively retained. When Spain received notice of Britain's intention to leave Port Egmont, the Spanish government sent orders to the Spanish governor at Soledad to see to it that the abandonment was complete. Spain was careful that Britain should have no claim to a title by prescription, that is, through continued use or possession over a long period of time. Moreover, even if Britain had retained any semblance of a legal title to the Malvinas, it would have lost that title by signing the Nootka Sound Convention in 1790, by which, as will be seen later, Britain agreed that no English vessel could land at the Falklands Islands because they were already occupied by Spain, thus recognizing Spain's sovereignty over the islands. The Nootka Sound Convention very importantly destroyed any claim to the Falklands that the English might have kept alive.

Dr. Samuel Johnson, the most noted English scholar of the eighteenth century, in 1771 put his thoughts about Britain's claim to the Falklands on paper at the request of the government. In his *Thoughts on the Late Transactions Respecting Falkland's Islands* Johnson recognized Spain's legal title to the islands in spite of the transitory return of the islands to Britain, stating that the decision to restore Port Egmont temporarily to England should not and could not in any sense affect the prior sovereignty held by Spain. Lord Rochford accepted this conclusion for the government over the loud protests of the opposition in Parliament, led by Pitt and Edmund Burke. Incidentally, Johnson's *Thoughts* is one of the best written of his many works and ends with a brilliant condemnation of war. Today Argentines use it to condemn Britain's usurpation of the islands, pointing out that this usurpation was declared illegal by one of England's greatest sons, so great that he lies buried in Westminster Abbey.

But Charles III was not going to be caught napping. As Spain's contribution to the series of eighteenth-century European enlightened despots he was very energetic and anxious to modernize Spain and make it powerful. To check further British-Portuguese encroachment from Brazil, in 1776 he created the viceroyalty of Río de la Plata (or viceroyalty of Buenos Aires, so named after its capital), which included present-day Argentina, Uruguay, Paraguay, and Bolivia. The Malvinas were placed under the jurisdiction of this new viceroyalty. One of Charles's first subsequent acts was to order in 1777 the complete destruction of Port Egmont to prevent its use by itinerant foreign vessels, and thus to avoid new complications. This order had been carried out by February 8, 1781 (the date of the royal approval of the measures taken).

There is little doubt that the Spanish government did everything possible to secure its sovereignty over the islands during these years. It appointed governors to rule them right down to the outbreak of the independence movement in Buenos Aires in 1810. In this period there appear to have been seventeen governors, several serving more than one short term. The governors, usually naval officers, frequently explored the islands for interlopers, leaving other officers as governors, and these in turn would do the same.

In this period many foreign ships, mostly English and American, were reported hunting for whales and seals. When possible they were chased away, and at times their land posts were demolished and the sailors arrested. However, during this entire period no attempt was made by Britain to reestablish a settlement on the Falklands. Indeed, it did just the opposite. In 1790, England signed the Nootka Sound Convention, whereby it gave up any rights to settle in the Spanish-claimed areas on the mainland and the islands of the South Atlantic.

The events leading to the signing of the convention were similar to the earlier conflict of Britain and Spain over the Falklands. In 1789, Spain had established a settlement on Nootka Sound, an inlet on the western shore of Vancouver Island, an area that had been claimed by Spain since the 1540s. When the British arrived later in the same year, 1789, the Spanish commander seized them and their vessels and sent them to Mexico to be tried. When the news reached Europe of these events, the same reaction took place that had occurred about twenty years before: the same preparations and threats of war, the same endless exchanges of view, and the same obstinate refusals to give in to the other side. However, there was a difference: Charles III was no longer king of Spain. The king was the weak Charles IV, and when he appealed to France to come to his aid under the terms of the Family Compact, he was refused. The French Revolution had made Louis XVI helpless and in fact had spelled the end of the Family Compact.

This was a new challenge to Spain's exclusive rights to the Pacific and the lands thereof. England, according to the Spanish government, was again encroaching on Spanish territory contrary to existing treaties. England countered that Spain had broken international law in its treatment of British sailors while committing a violent hostile act, and in addition denied vigorously that Spain held exclusive sovereignty in the Pacific. In October 1790, Britain gave Spain a ten-day ultimatum: Accede to Britain's demands in regard to occupation of the lands and navigation of waters Spain considered its exclusive properties, or there would be war. Spain had to submit, surrendering the northern Pacific coast exclusiveness to save the vast, richer areas of Central and South America. The Nootka Sound Convention was signed on October 25, 1790.

By this agreement each side returned property taken from the other on the northwest coast of North America since April 1789. Thus Spain returned to England the latter's holdings on Nootka Sound. But Britain agreed that its subjects would not fish within ten maritime leagues of any part of the coast already occupied by Spain. It also agreed not to permit fishing and navigation by its subjects to be a pretext for illicit trade with the Spanish colonies, although on the northwest coast of North America subjects of both powers would have free access to the area and be permitted to trade. It would appear that these provisions of the convention once and for all destroyed Spain's monopoly of the Pacific and Atlantic oceans in those areas where the Spanish Empire continued, and that Spain had thus made earth-shaking concessions. But Spain's concessions were not as broad as they might at first appear. Britain could *colonize* only the northwest coast of North America. It could not establish settlements in other parts of the Spanish dominions. There British subjects could navigate only for the purpose of fishing. Both parties agreed not to establish new colonies in the South Pacific and South Atlantic; areas already settled (which would include the Falklands) would remain in *statu quo* unless a third party tried to settle them.

By the Nootka Sound Convention the British government admitted that Spain's occupation of the Falkland Islands was legal and agreed not to establish colonies to the south of the regions already occupied by Spain. British subjects could land on the islands in the vicinity of Tierra del Fuego and farther south, but only temporarily. Britain by the convention renounced *possession* of the Falklands, and only by possession could Britain claim right to them.

Spain now made a decided effort to keep all fishermen from its coasts, a very difficult task. Spanish ports on the mainland of South America were closed to foreign fishermen, and without these ports, it was exceedingly hazardous to fish in the South Atlantic. The Falklands now assumed an increasing economic importance, and Spain became ever more vigilant to keep foreigners out of them. This extra vigilance extended to the areas surrounding the islands. Britain did not contest these acts, and indeed through the Nootka Sound agreement accepted them. It appeared as if Spain had finally obtained complete sovereignty over the islands. England would have to wait until that sovereignty was transferred to Argentina after that country obtained its independence from Spain. Then it would try again, and this time be successful in taking the islands by force.

4
British Might Makes Right

Argentina Inherits the Islands from Spain

Spain obtained British recognition of its sovereignty over the Malvinas by the Nootka Sound agreement only two decades before its colonies in the New World began their movement for independence from Spanish rule. Already the year before the agreement was signed the French Revolution had begun bringing tumult to France and Europe. The revolutionary government in France had refused to live up to the Family Compact, and Spain had had to face England alone, in spite of which Spain came out of the Nootka controversy with most of its territories intact. But the French Revolution and the subsequent Napoleonic Wars affected Spain disastrously. Spain's alliance with Napoleon in 1795 opened Spain to attacks by Britain. The naval defeat of France and Spain at Trafalgar in 1805 meant British supremacy on the seas, while Napoleon tried to keep his supremacy on land and prevent the British from landing on the Continent.

Britain now tried again to obtain a base in the South Atlantic. An English force under Lord Beresford attacked Buenos Aires in 1806, only to be ignominiously defeated by a quickly organized army of colonials under Santiago de Liniers. England sent a larger force to retake Buenos Aires in 1807. It too was promptly defeated and the English sent home. These two English Invasions and the consequent Reconquest, as the Argentines call them, hold a hallowed niche in Argentine history books. The Argentines had had to fend for themselves, for they could expect no help from Spain under the venal, bankrupt, and helpless Charles IV and with Britain ruling the seas. They elected Liniers viceroy, as the Spanish-appointed viceroy had fled before the first invasion. This is the only case in which Spanish colonists elected their own viceroy. Liniers, although he had fought the British army, promptly asked some of the British traders who had come with it to stay. He also established free trade. This was the beginning of English economic relations with Argentina which in later years were to become so dominant.

There is little doubt that the Reconquest had a great effect on Argentine history. A nondescript army of Argentines quickly assembled and badly trained had twice defeated the armies of the most powerful empire in the world. Moreover, the introduction of free trade opened people's eyes. But it was Napoleon who was to give them the best reasons for independence. To prevent England from getting a foothold on the Continent, Napoleon would have to close off Spain and Portugal. Napoleon marched into Spain in 1808, arrested Charles IV, who had just abdicated, and his son and heir Ferdinand VII, and put his own brother, Joseph Bonaparte, on the Spanish throne. But the upper-class colonists in the capitals of the Spanish possessions in the New World had no use for Napoleon and in 1810 called open town meetings to discuss the crisis. In Buenos Aires in May 1810, an open town council meeting declared that it did not accept Napoleon's brother as the new king of Spain, and would govern the colony until Ferdinand could return.

From that point it was easy to move on to complete independence after Ferdinand (even worse than his father) was restored to the Spanish throne in 1814 and promptly persecuted all who had dared rule in his name during his absence. On July 9, 1816, Argentina formally declared its independence from Spain as the United Provinces of Río de la Plata. With few resources, the new government immediately began organizing a large army to free Chile and later Peru from Spanish rule, in order to prevent a Spanish attack from that viceroyalty against Argentina's flank. In the meantime, the colonists on the Malvinas had been evacuated by the governor of Montevideo by a decree of January 8, 1811. After independence the United Provinces, struggling to survive, for a while paid no attention to the Malvinas. But neither did any other nation. Whalers and sealers still visited the islands as they had before, and found them useful as havens from storms and sources of water and wild game.

The United Provinces were finally able in 1820 to send a ship to the Malvinas to secure the territory as part of Argentina. It was the *Heroína*, captained by David Jewitt, an American in the service of the United Provinces. On November 6, 1820, he took formal possession of the Malvinas in the name of the United Provinces, reading a declaration to that effect in both Spanish and English, the latter authorized by an English consul. He did this at the foot of a flagstaff flying the flag of the United Provinces and with a twenty-one-gun salute. The event was described in newspapers in Spain, Argentine, Chile, and the United States. The U.S. notice was published in the *Salem Gazette* in June 1821, from a message sent to a friend in Salem by Jewitt, who stated that the ceremony was witnessed by several U.S. citizens and British subjects.

Jewitt found as many as fifty vessels of different nationalities in the islands. He notified the masters of these vessels of the new laws of the United Provinces forbidding hunting and fishing in the islands. It must be noted that although most of these vessels were U.S. or British, the British government made no protest of Jewitt's actions. James Weddell, the captain of one of these vessels, left a very interesting account of his voyage to the area, printed in London in 1825. Jewitt sent Weddell a letter announcing that he was commissioned by the government of the United Provinces to take possession of the islands in the name of that nation, to which the islands belonged by natural law. In a personal interview with Jewitt, Weddell noticed that he meant business and that he planned to bring people and supplies to the islands to establish a formal settlement. But threatened by scurvy and, worse still, mutiny, Jewitt asked to be relieved of his command.

Soon after Jewitt's visit to the Malvinas the government of Buenos Aires became more and more disturbed by reports of indiscriminate sealing and fishing in the southern seas. An expedition was sent to the Patagonian coast, and an attempt was made to control and tax fishers and sealers. It failed, probably because of the vastness of the region to be covered and the ease with which culprits could operate without being observed.

In 1823 Pablo Areguati was appointed governor of the islands, and at the same time a concession was granted to Jorge Pacheco and Luis Vernet giving them land on East Falkland Island and use of the fish and cattle in the islands. An expedition of three ships under the command of Robert Schofield was sent out, but his venture was abandoned in 1824. Vernet and Pacheco seemed not to be discouraged by the failure, quickly organizing a second expedition. Sailing in January 1826, Vernet took charge and established a settlement on the Malvinas.

Luis Vernet seems to have been an unusual person. Of French Protestant extraction, his ancestors having left France for Germany in the days of religious persecution, Vernet was born in Hamburg in 1791. At fourteen he was sent by his father to the United States to learn the merchant trade with a firm in Philadelphia. This is probably why he is sometimes called a French-American or German-American in the service of Argentina. Vernet lived in the United States eight years, becoming well versed in business, especially trading and shipping. He made several voyages to Europe and South America. In 1817 he set sail for Buenos Aires, where he immediately joined a friend, Conrad Rücker, and began, through his business relations in Europe, a commercial venture on a large scale. Perhaps it was on too large a scale; after a few years all kinds of troubles caused the dissolution of the partnership.

Vernet and Pacheco had known each other since 1819 and had had business relations of sorts. Pacheco had been in the Spanish colonial army and had later fought in the revolution against Spain. When he left the armed forces, the government owed him money, which he had great difficulty in collecting. Vernet lent him money to take care of his family and to run his business, a meat-salting plant, which was on the rocks. The two men made an agreement whereby Vernet would help Pacheco financially until he obtained back pay from the government, and Pacheco agreed to pay Vernet half of whatever he received from that source.

Vernet asked for the exclusive right to fish in the Malvinas, knowing that the new state from its inception had taken a great interest in the preservation of fisheries. His request was granted in January 1828, through a second concession giving him the island of Staatenland and those off the big island of Soledad (East Falkland), with the exception of those belonging to Pacheco by a previous grant and a ten-square-mile strip on the Bay of San Carlos reserved for government use. The colony had to be established within three years and for twenty years was to be free of all taxes except those needed to maintain local authorities. For the same period fishing was to be free of duty in all the islands as well as off the Patagonian coast south of the Río Negro. The decree's purpose, so it stated, was to promote fishing and to establish a secure base for the government's privateering operations.

The new colony was a success, thanks to the methodical plans of Vernet. He brought in immigrants for the various types of work that needed to be done, he granted land on the basis of need and the use he wanted made of it, and he advertised his project in foreign papers. He even had his own agents in foreign countries. Later, when Vernet put a stop to indiscriminate sealing and fishing, and his colony was destroyed by Captain Duncan of the USS *Lexington*, bringing about a break with the United States, Vernet was called every kind of name. But that was because he was a thorn in the side of his vilifiers. Vernet seems to have been a man of strong character and of great energy, an organizer and a good businessman. He was far from the barbarian his detractors made him out to be. Voyagers in the islands were surprised to see a good piano and shelves of good books in his home. Captain Robert Fitzroy, commander of Charles Darwin's ship, the *Beagle*, in his *Narrative* (London, 1839), speaks of the kindness shown a brother officer by Vernet. There are other indications that U.S. officials who later denounced Vernet were lying and had specific reasons to vilify him.

Vernet's colony was such a success that the Buenos Aires government issued a decree on June 10, 1829, stating that as the government of the new republic had inherited all the rights formerly exercised by the mother country, Spain, in these areas, it was establishing the office of military and political governor to rule the Malvinas and all the islands adjacent to Cape Horn on the Atlantic. The governor was to reside at Port Soledad (on the island of Soledad or East Falkland), where a fort flying the flag of the republic was to be erected. He was to enforce the law of the republic in his jurisdiction and to protect the fishing and sealing industry. Vernet was appointed to the new position.

This decree made Vernet an official of the Buenos Aires government and no longer merely a merchant. He was the sole concessionaire of the fishing industry, but he was also to enforce the laws against indiscriminate fishing. Already in 1820, Jewitt had warned the government about this, especially the indiscriminate killing of whales, seals, and sea lions, all very numerous among the islands. Vernet even requested a

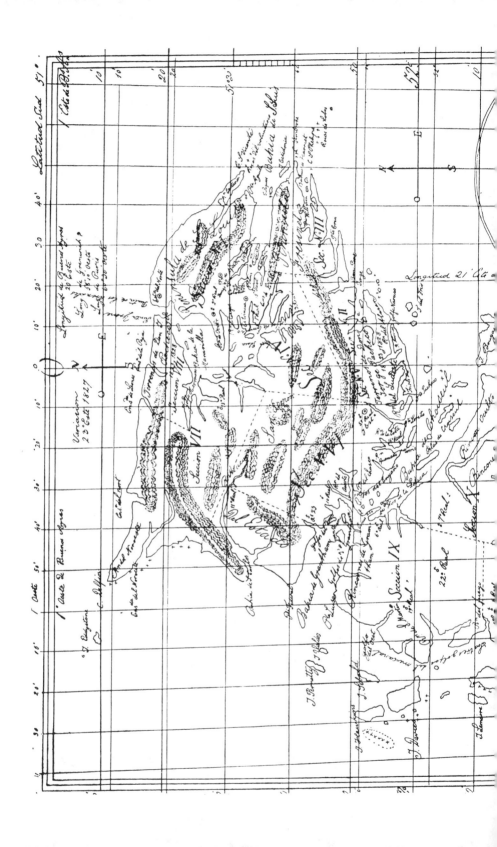

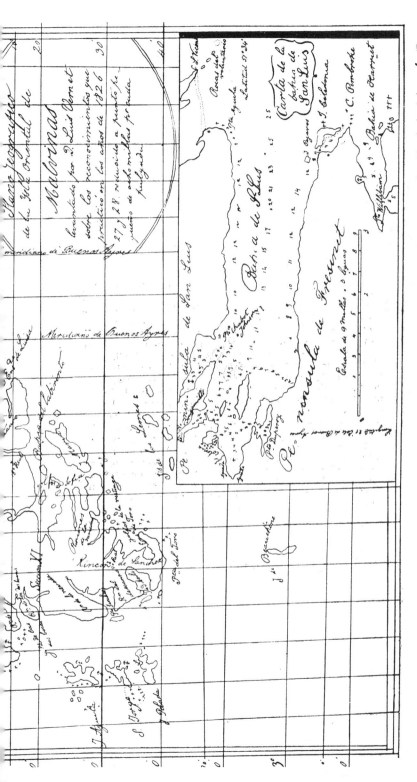

FIGURE 4.1. Map made by Luis Vernet of his explorations of the islands in 1826, 1827, and 1828. (Original in the Archivo General de las Indias, Buenos Aires.)

Souce: Antonio Montarcé Lastra, *Redención de la Soberanía* (Buenos Aires: Talleres Graficos Padilla y Contreras, 1946), following p. 56.

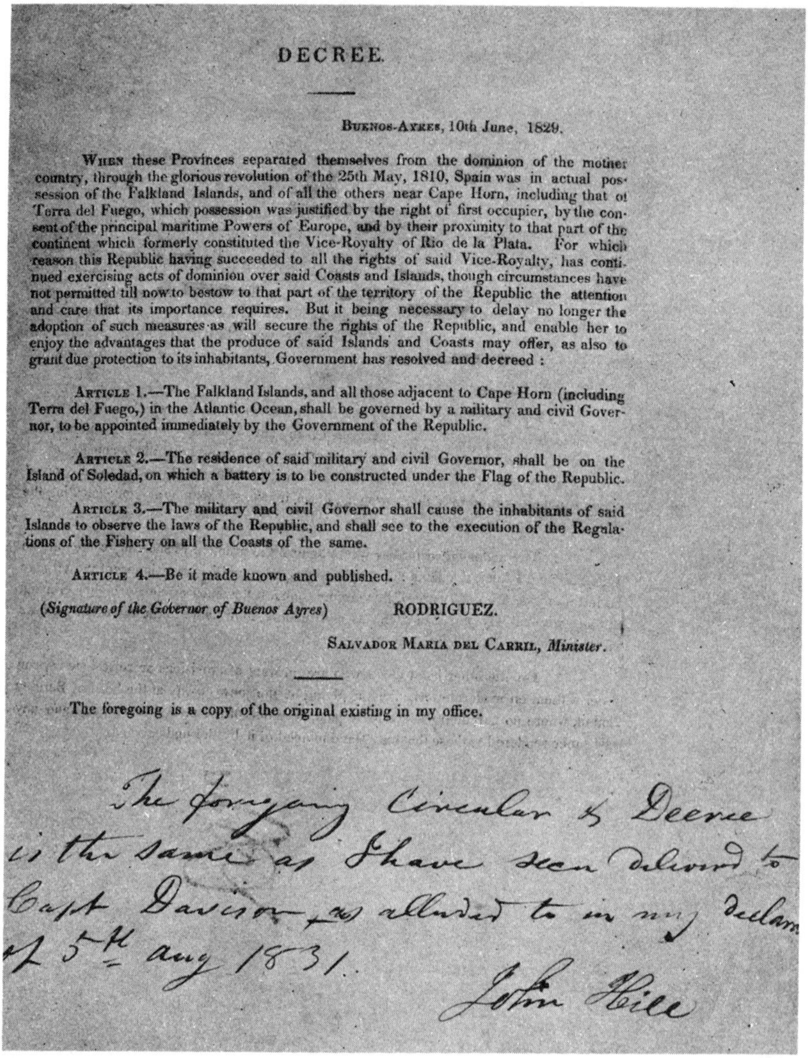

DECREE.

BUENOS-AYRES, 10th June, 1829.

WHEN these Provinces separated themselves from the dominion of the mother country, through the glorious revolution of the 25th May, 1810, Spain was in actual possession of the Falkland Islands, and of all the others near Cape Horn, including that of Terra del Fuego, which possession was justified by the right of first occupier, by the consent of the principal maritime Powers of Europe, and by their proximity to that part of the continent which formerly constituted the Vice-Royalty of Rio de la Plata. For which reason this Republic having succeeded to all the rights of said Vice-Royalty, has continued exercising acts of dominion over said Coasts and Islands, though circumstances have not permitted till now to bestow to that part of the territory of the Republic the attention and care that its importance requires. But it being necessary to delay no longer the adoption of such measures as will secure the rights of the Republic, and enable her to enjoy the advantages that the produce of said Islands and Coasts may offer, as also to grant due protection to its inhabitants, Government has resolved and decreed :

ARTICLE 1.—The Falkland Islands, and all those adjacent to Cape Horn (including Terra del Fuego,) in the Atlantic Ocean, shall be governed by a military and civil Governor, to be appointed immediately by the Government of the Republic.

ARTICLE 2.—The residence of said military and civil Governor, shall be on the Island of Soledad, on which a battery is to be constructed under the Flag of the Republic.

ARTICLE 3.—The military and civil Governor shall cause the inhabitants of said Islands to observe the laws of the Republic, and shall see to the execution of the Regulations of the Fishery on all the Coasts of the same.

ARTICLE 4.—Be it made known and published.

(Signature of the Governor of Buenos Ayres) RODRIGUEZ.

SALVADOR MARIA DEL CARRIL, *Minister*.

The foregoing is a copy of the original existing in my office.

The foregoing Circular & Decree is the same as I have seen delivered to Capt Davison, as alluded to in my declaration of 5th Aug 1831.

John Hill

FIGURE 4.2. Decree (1829) in English that Luis Vernet gave to all foreign fishers and sealers in the Falkland Islands advising them of government regulations concerning their occupations.

Source: Ricardo R. Caillet-Bois, *Una Tierra Argentina: Las Malvinas,* 2nd ed. (Buenos Aires: Ediciones Peuser, 1952), following p. 256.

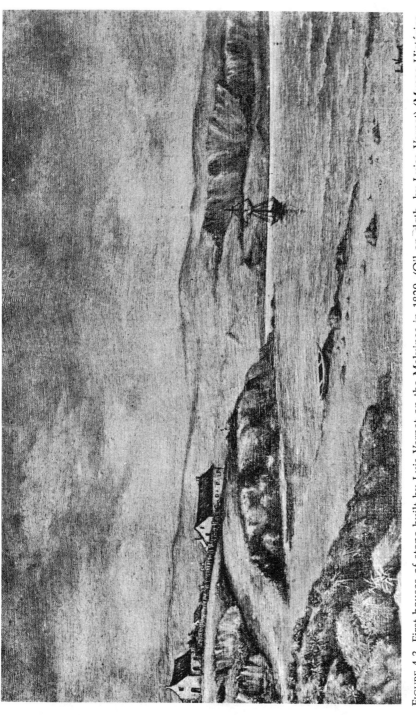

FIGURE 4.3. First houses of stone built by Luis Vernet on the Malvinas in 1829. (Oil on cloth, by Luisa Vernet) (Museo Histórico Nacional, Buenos Aires)

Source: Academia Nacional de la Historia, *Los Derechos Argentinos sobre Las Islas Malvinas* (Buenos Aires, 1964), following p. 62.

FIGURE 4.4. Seal used by Luis Vernet as political and military commander of the Malvinas and adjacent lands.

Source: Secretaría de Educación de la Nación, *Las Malvinas Son Argentinas* (Buenos Aires: Subsecretaría de Cultura, Publ. no. 1, July 1948), p. 41.

FIGURE 4.5. Money circulated by Luis Vernet in the Falklands.

Source: Ricardo R. Caillet-Bois, *Una Tierra Argentina: Las Islas Malvinas*, 2nd ed. (Buenos Aires: Ediciones Peuser, 1952), following p. 256.

war vessel to help him enforce the laws and stop the depredations of foreign sealers and whalers, which seemed to be getting worse. He did not get the warship, but on August 30, 1829, he issued a decree telling the captains of ships in the area to stop their operations under penalty of being sent to Buenos Aires for trial. His warnings were disregarded.

U.S.-Argentine Conflict over the Malvinas

The American schooner, the *Harriet*, after being duly warned, returned to seal and was seized with two other American vessels, the *Superior* and the *Breakwater*. Although it was later proved that the proceedings had taken place under due process of law and with no violence, at the time the American masters of the vessels claimed that they had been badly treated and their cargoes plundered. The *Breakwater* got away, but Vernet discussed with the masters of the other two vessels the procedure to be followed: *By contract*, the *Superior* was to go free and the *Harriet* was to proceed to Buenos Aires with all the necessary documents and with Vernet aboard, to stand trial for breaking the law. This contract was signed by Vernet and the captains of the *Harriet* and the *Superior*. Are these the actions of a pirate, the word used to describe Vernet later by U.S. diplomats in Buenos Aires?

The *Harriet* arrived in Buenos Aires on November 19, 1831. At the time there was no minister at the U.S. legation, and it was a calamitous misfortune that American interests were being handled by the consul, George W. Slacum, a person without diplomatic experience and devoid of tact. The master of the *Harriet* here saw his chance to equal scores with Vernet. He told Slacum that Vernet had treated him cruelly and stolen his goods. These colored views of what had happened in the Malvinas threw Slacum into a rage. He informed the Department of State of what supposedly had happened, and also the Argentine minister of foreign affairs, Tomás de Anchorena, an unruffled, cultured diplomat.

Slacum demanded to know from Anchorena whether the Buenos Aires government intended to support the actions of Vernet. Anchorena, after four days, replied that a message concerning the matter had been sent to the ministry of war and navy and would soon be sent to the chief executive. This reply infuriated Slacum, who told Anchorena that this meant support for Vernet's actions as well as his right to regulate the fisheries, a right the Buenos Aires government did not possess. Then he insisted that the decree of June 10, 1829, and all decrees before and after that date regulating fisheries were illegal, and that U.S. citizens could not be kept from the freest use of the fisheries. He asked that his note be considered a formal protest against Vernet's actions.

Anchorena replied that the matter was being considered in an inquiry under way, but that he could not consider Slacum's note as a formal protest because Slacum did not appear to have the authority to make a protest, being a mere consul, and because the United States had no rights to the fisheries in the first place and therefore no basis for protesting against their being closed. Then, seemingly adding insult to injury, he said that he presumed that Slacum was motivated only by the most upright considerations and that he hoped the matter could be settled in a friendly manner.

Unfortunately, during this tense situation there appreared in Buenos Aires the U.S.S. *Lexington* under the command of Silas Duncan, who, upon hearing of the events on the Falklands, decided to proceed to the islands to protect his compatriots. Slacum notified Anchorena of Duncan's decision. When Anchorena did not react as he had expected, he wrote him again, this time to inform him that Duncan's departure would be postponed until December 9, so that Anchorena could reply in regard to the suspension of Argentina's rights to capture U.S. vessels and Slacum's demand that the American's property be restored. He again maintained that he did have a right to protest. At the same time, Duncan jumped into the troubled waters and demanded that Vernet be surrendered for trial as a pirate and a thief or that he be tried and punished under the laws of Buenos Aires.

And here English officials entered the picture. It is very possible that Slacum's strange behavior was prompted by Woodbine Parish, the British consul general. In 1829, he had officially protested the Argentine occupation of the Falklands on the basis that they belonged to Great Britain, whose withdrawal from the islands had not invalidated English rights to them.

According to Parish, when the British left the islands in 1774, they had left marks of possession (the now-famous leaden plate), and other formalities had been observed indicating rights of ownership and intention to resume occupation—a blatant untruth. After a formal acknowledgement of receipt of his protest, Parish had heard no more about it. In 1831, he told Slacum that Britain had never given up her claim to the islands and that Argentina had no legal right to them. This seemed to strengthen Slacum in his dispute with Anchorena. He promptly informed Washington of Parish's assertion. In the meantime Duncan sailed for the Falklands before Slacum received Anchorena's reply to his ultimatum.

Anchorena's reply probably would not have stopped Duncan, and it infuriated Slacum even more. Anchorena asked Slacum not to interfere in questions not concerning him, and told him that if Duncan or any one else related to the U.S. government were to take any actions that sought to nullify Argentina's legal rights to the islands and the coasts bordering on Cape Horn, he would send a formal protest to Washington. Argentina would also take any measures to maintain its rights to that area and to see that they were respected.

Slacum, perhaps in a quandary now that he could not lean on Duncan, turned to the British minister Henry Fox and the British consul-general Parish for support. Parish showed Slacum the protest he had sent to the Argentine government in 1829 and told him that it had been filed merely to keep alive a latent claim of which the British would avail themselves when it was suitable. This put Slacum in a difficult position: He had gone too far in protesting against the Argentines' claims to the Malvinas, and yet he did not like the idea of the British taking over the islands. All he could think of doing was to report that things would look black for American commerce if the Argentines retained the Malvinas.

During the interim Captain Duncan had entered the harbor of Puerto Soledad on December 28, 1831, not under the U.S. flag but under the French flag! He invited Vernet's lieutenants, Matthew Brisbane and Henry Metcalf, on board the *Lexington*, and promptly arrested Brisbane and let Metcalf go free. Going ashore, he and his men arrested almost all the people there, pillaged the houses, stole sealskins and other articles out of warehouses, spiked the cannon and burned the gunpowder, and confiscated smaller arms. Then he sailed away, taking along Brisbane and six others in irons. Duncan did not enter any of these actions in his logbook. Also, he sailed to Montevideo and not to Buenos Aires. From Montevideo, now the capital of the new nation Uruguay, Duncan

75

3. *Ruines de l'Établissement Français aux Malouines.*

FIGURE 4.6. Ruins of the settlement founded by the French and Spanish in Puerto Soledad: "The remains of these buildings are still almost intact." (*Viaje pintoreso alrededor del mundo*, etc., by Dumont d'Urville, vol. 3, p. 294. Barcelona, 1841.)

Source: Ricardo R. Caillet-Bois, *Una Tierra Argentina: Las Islas Malvinas*, 2nd ed. (Buenos Aires: Ediciones Peuser, 1952), following p. 240.

advised Slacum of his actions and told him he would free the prisoners if the U.S. government supported his conduct. Slacum told him that it did.

The reaction of the Buenos Aires government to these proceedings can well be imagined. It issued a public proclamation to tell the people of what had occurred, and at the same time declared Slacum *persona non grata* because of his and Duncan's actions and because of Slacum's insulting language in his notes. It requested that Slacum appoint a substitute for his office. Slacum refused to do so, claiming that he had no such authority, and said he was surprised at the accusations against him. But the Argentine government refused to deal any further with him.

In the meantime President Andrew Jackson had heard of the capture of the *Harriet* and other sealers from news brought by the *Breakwater*. He did not accept Vernet's appointment as legal, claiming that Vernet's actions did not have the consent of the Buenos Aires government and that he had merely pretended to act under its consent. He added that because the United States had always traded freely in that area, he would send an armed vessel to those seas and a minister to Buenos Aires to investigate Argentina's claims to the islands. He asked Congress to provide for a military force adequate to protect American fishing and trading in the South Atlantic.

In one hasty action Jackson thus destroyed the U.S.-Argentine friendship and good will begun in 1824 by Caesar A. Rodney, the first U.S. minister in Buenos Aires. Jackson took the word of the people on the *Breakwater*. On top of this, as chargé d'affaires in Buenos Aires Jackson selected Francis Baylies, a person completely unfit to deal with the delicate problem of hunting and fishing in the Malvinas.

Although Vernet had copies of his official instructions of June 10, 1829, sent to the U.S. Department of State by his agent in Philadelphia, Secretary of State Livingston in his instructions to the American chargé d'affaires, Francis Baylies, called Vernet's actions piracy, on the grounds that the U.S. consul had not said anything about Vernet's instructions and anyway no government would permit acts of this type! President Jackson, Livingston said, had ordered a force sent to the area to protect U.S. citizens, because the decree of 1829 was an excuse to commit piratical acts.

In other words, Jackson called the Buenos Aires government a nest of pirates. Baylies was to demand a complete disavowal of Vernet's actions, the return of property seized by Vernet, and an indemnity for damages done, because the United States had been using the islands for over fifty years and had capital invested there. Baylies was to make a treaty with Buenos Aires (pirates?) dealing with sealing and fishing, demand the return of seized ships, and if Vernet's claims were disallowed, order the U.S. squadron to the Falklands to return Vernet to Buenos Aires for trial as a pirate.

The right to fish and seal in the Falklands or on the coast of Patagonia had never been granted by Spain to any country, and the Nootka Sound agreement had never extended general rights to all nations but had limited further rights to Great Britain alone. Indeed, Spain had used the agreement to emphasize her rights to the Falklands and the Patagonian coast. Certainly no legal right had ever been granted to the United States or conceded by Spain. For some reason, possibly lack of information on the subject or pressure from certain interests, Livingston falsified or at least misstated the facts.

Manuel V. de Maza, the Argentine foreign minister, informed Baylies that his charges were enough to present to the governor of the province (at this time there was no national government and the governor of the province of Buenos Aires was charged by all the provinces with conducting the foreign affairs of the nation), and that Vernet would be requested to explain his actions. The government, he said, would discharge its obligations with due respect for the rights of U.S. citizens, but Argentina was a sovereign state and as such would not surrender its rights as an independent nation. He added, and this must have galled Baylies, that the government would not bow before unreasonable and pretentious claims against Vernet's rights.

Baylies naturally did not like this cool reply and immediately informed Maza that Vernet's destructive actions had been admitted (by whom?) and therefore did not have to be explained, that only their extent had to be determined. He did not doubt Argentina's rights, but he wished to know definitely whether Argentina claimed the right to harass and interfere with U.S. fishing in the Falkland Islands. Maza kept Baylies waiting for a reply for two weeks; so Baylies wrote Maza a long letter containing the essence of Livingston's instructions to him and a lengthy dissertation on the history of the Falklands, quite inaccurate, trying to prove that Argentina had no rights to the islands. After another long wait for a reply, he sent another note demanding a reply. It came in two days, but it was addressed to the Secretary of State. Outwardly it appeared to discuss the unbelievable conduct of Slacum, but it also defended Argentina's posture in the whole matter. Argentina, Maza pointed out, was the heir of the viceroyalty of Río de la Plata and as such had complete jurisdiction over all the lands that had been a part of that viceroyalty. As a result, the case of the *Harriet* was a national, internal problem.

Soon another note arrived from Maza stating that the government had studied the documents in the case and now believed that Baylies had brought up the question of the fisheries in order to confuse the issue and avoid the real question, which was Duncan's outrageous and barbarous conduct in the islands and his commission of completely illegal acts. Even if Vernet's actions had been unjustified, they had not broken international law, for they had been committed by an Argentine official within the jurisdiction of Argentina. But there was no justification for Duncan's raid on the colony. Therefore, Maza added, Argentina demanded prompt satisfaction, including reparations and indemnity for losses resulting from Duncan's attack. As to the other points raised by Baylies, Maza refused to discuss them before this demand was met. Maza included in this note a detailed report by Vernet showing that Vernet had a remarkable comprehension of history and international law (Goebel 1927: p. 452).

Baylies returned this document to Maza immediately and asked for his passports. At the same time he sent a letter to Livingston explaining what he had done. When Maza asked Baylies why he had returned Vernet's report and demanded his passports, he said he did not want the United States to become involved in a case against Vernet that might be tried in Argentine courts. Maza indignantly denied trying to make the United States a litigant in an Argentine court. But Baylies insisted that he could do nothing further than demand his passports. Maza tried again, unsuccessfully, to make Baylies see that there were two questions: a question of fact and a question of right. The question of fact was Duncan's raid, and it had to be settled before the question of right was debated. Baylies adamantly demanded his passports, refusing further conferences. He left for the United States in September 1832.

Upon his arrival in the United States he told Livingston that the Argentines thought they could capture American fishing vessels at will, and therefore there was no use trying to discuss anything with them. It is peculiar that he said nothing about Argentina's claim to the Falklands. To Henry Fox, the British minister in Argentina, Baylies had said that the United States had no rights to the islands except for the right to fish, a right it would demand from the British as well as the Argentines. Baylies noted also that Fox had protested against Argentine occupation of the islands, and he assumed that Great Britain would soon take some action to get them back. Did Baylies's talks with Fox have any effect on that action? Certainly Baylies was indiscreet in his talks with Fox. Even his dislike for the Argentine government is no excuse for these indiscretions. The diplomatic dispute between Argentina and the United States assured Britain that the United States would not support Argentina if Britain decided to take over the Falkland Islands by force, as it did.

Britain Takes the Islands by Force

The British take-over of the islands took the form of a small military expedition of two war vessels, the *Clio* and the *Tyne*, which arrived in the Malvinas in December 1832, at Port Egmont. It was commanded by Captain John James Onslow. At Port Egmont he set to work to repair the ruined fort and put up a sign that the islands were a British possession. On January 2, 1833, Onslow put into Puerto Soledad, where the Argentine schooner *Sarandí* under José María Pinedo had just recently arrived with a new governor, Juan Esteban Mestivier. When Onslow

OBSERVATIONS

ON THE

Forcible Occupation

OF THE

MALVINAS, OR FALKLAND ISLANDS,

BY

THE BRITISH GOVERNMENT,

IN 1833.

LONDON :

PRINTED BY CHARLES WOOD AND SON,

POPPIN'S COURT, FLEET STREET

1833.

FIGURE 4.7. Title page of an 1833 British account of the forcible occupation of the Malvinas.

Source: El Hogar, October 10, 1947, p. 8.

demanded that Pinedo strike the Argentine flag, Pinedo refused and strongly protested Onslow's forcible occupation. Onslow struck the Argentine flag and sent it to Pinedo, who sailed for Buenos Aires on January 4, 1833. Since then Great Britain has been in possession of the islands.

Britain justified its seizure of the islands on the basis of its brief possession of them during the eighteenth century, a questionable basis when the so-called secret agreement is taken into account. Britain also contended that it had never accepted any rights of the Buenos Aires government to the islands and had protested both Vernet's and Mestivier's appointments as governors. However, it had not protested Jewitt's proclamation (not even the English translation of it) when he officially occupied the islands in 1820 for the Buenos Aires government. Other justifications included the abandonment of the islands by Spain in 1810–1811, at the time of the revolution for independence, and the abolition of Argentine control of the islands by the Americans' destruction of the Vernet colony. Both at best were weak or even specious arguments.

From the correspondence among British officials for several years before the British take-over, it is clear that one good reason was the need for a way station on the long voyage around the Horn. British merchants were clamoring for such a port because trade and commercial relations with the south sea islands and Australia were expanding rapidly. Parish mentioned a necessary layover in the Falklands for British ships. One merchant who had stopped over in Puerto Soledad when Vernet was still there, to take on food and water and products to be sold in Europe, had even said that Vernet had authorized him to say that Vernet was not opposed to a British take-over as long as the right to private property was guaranteed.

It is true that the *Lexington's* raid on Vernet's colony had temporarily removed the control of any visible authority over the colony. But was that a good reason for Britain to take it over? What about the people who remained on the island after Pinedo withdrew? These now began a kind of guerrilla action against the British. When Vernet came to the Malvinas he brought with him a brother and a brother-in-law, ten white people from Buenos Aires, ten English or American sailors, eighteen black men indentured for ten years, twelve black girls, seven single Germans, and four English families and six single Englishmen. By the time the English took over, a penal colony had been established at San Carlos, east of Puerto Soledad on East Falkland (Isla de la Soledad). The new governor, Mestivier, had taken it over just before the British arrived. As soon as he did, however, a mutiny broke out led by an army sergeant, and Mestivier was murdered. At the time of the arrival of the British force, Pinedo had just succeeded in reestablishing order.

Upon Pinedo's withdrawal at Onslow's demands, he appointed Juan Simón as governor. Simón was the leader of the "gauchos" who had remained on the islands after the raid on Vernet's colony. British historians claim that this appointment was illegal. Perhaps it was from the British viewpoint, but it followed a custom of centuries under the Spanish legal system. The gauchos, with Vernet's former storekeeper and Matthew Brisbane and William Lowe, two former ship masters, decided to band together to keep Vernet's plans alive. But on August 26, 1833, three gauchos and five convicts of the former penal colony at San Carlos murdered Brisbane, Simón, a German settler, and a Spanish settler, stole everything they could find, and fled into the interior to hide. The surviving settlers, including a woman and three children, hid on a small island, where, after much hardship, they were rescued in January 1834, when the H.M.S. *Challenger* with the new English governor, Lieutenant Henry Smith, arrived. Smith and six royal marines hunted down the murderers. One gaucho was killed by his companions, one turned state's evidence, and one, Antonio Rivero, was imprisoned in England for a while and then returned to Buenos Aires.

Vernet, in an attempt to salvage some of his investment at least, in 1835 asked the British government to return his property rights in the islands. Britain permitted him to get back any of his removable personal goods, but refused to recognize his land titles for fear that such recognition might imply tacit recognition of the Argentine government's rights to make such grants. Vernet's friend, Lieutenant William Langdon of the British navy, to whom Vernet had made a grant of land, also was refused recognition of the grant given him in the name of the government in Buenos Aires.

Argentina Protests in Vain

News of the British action in the Malvinas brought indignant protests from the government of Argentina. Maza immediately protested to the British chargé, Philip G. Gore, calling Onslow's operation an insult to the honor and dignity of Argentina and demanding official explanations. Gore, not having been informed of his government's invasion plans, had to think quickly. He pointed out to the Argentines that the British government had repeatedly broached the question and had never received an answer—at best a questionable justification. Gore and the British government knew full well Argentina's position on the question. Gore also said that Fox, before him, had protested the appointment of the late governor and had never received a reply.

To Manuel Moreno, the Argentine minister in London, was given the infelicitous task of protesting to a stiff-backed, pompous, self-righteous Lord Palmerston, the British foreign minister. On April 24, 1833, Moreno asked whether the British government had actually given orders to British military forces to drive the Argentine settlers out of the islands and occupy them. On April 27, 1833, Palmerston answered that that assumption was correct. Moreno waited several weeks before making a formal protest that drew its historical facts from Vernet's report on

82

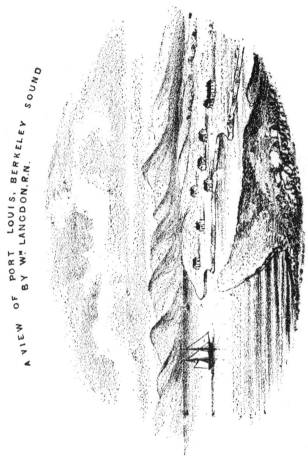

A VIEW OF PORT LOUIS, BERKELEY SOUND
BY Wᴹ LANGDON, R.N.

FIGURE 4.8. A view of Port Luis by William Langdon, 1841.

Source: Ricardo R. Caillet-Bois, *Una Tierra Argentina: Las Islas Malvinas*, 2nd ed. (Buenos Aires: Ediciones Peuser, 1952), following p. 256.

the islands. This seems to indicate that the report had had fairly widespread distribution. Moreno dwelt on the events of 1770–1771 and insisted that Britain's abandonment of the islands was in keeping with a secret promise to quit the islands soon after reoccupying Port Egmont, and was a legal abandonment (Goebel 1927: pp. 456–457).

Palmerston waited six months to reply. Greater disdain and contempt of one government for another could hardly be expressed. Palmerston reminded Moreno that Parish's protest against Vernet's appointment as governor of the Falklands in 1829 had been ignored by Buenos Aires, and suggested that Moreno should not expect the British government to accept continued illegal possession of the Falklands by Argentina. He based Britain's claim to ownership of the islands on the Anglo-Spanish discussion of 1770–1771 and the subsequent restoration of Port Egmont to Great Britain. He added that if the British government thereafter denied any right to the islands to Spain, it certainly would not permit any other country to exercise that right. Here Palmerston made a mistake that Moreno failed to catch. Britain *did* permit Spain to keep the islands for thirty-six years after it returned them to Spain in 1774. And after that Argentina, as the heir of Spain, had held them since 1811, another twenty-two years. Why had England not recovered the islands much sooner?

Palmerston insisted that there had never been a secret agreement because no document existed to that effect. He suggested to Moreno that when the facts were brought to his attention, Moreno would see that only His Britannic Majesty exercised sovereignty over the islands. Palmerston with his indignant self-righteousness had won the day, for he knew that Argentina, at the moment rent by internal strife, had no strength or resources to back up its claim.

In December 1834, Moreno tried without success to reopen the question. It was not until seven years later that he tried again, this time to salvage at least one big island for Argentina. He insisted that there was no proof that Spain had ever given to England or that England had ever held the Isla de la Soledad (East Falkland) and that for fifty years it had been in the undisputed possession of Spain. This seems to be true, for when Spain permitted England to return to the Falklands for a short period to save George III's honor, it was understood that England would reoccupy Port Egmont on West Falkland only. Spain still occupied East Falkland. Moreno's representation went unheeded; Britain, through Lord Aberdeen, rejected this attempt also. Moreno made one more attempt to get Aberdeen to listen to reason, giving him an impassioned note protesting British acts in the Malvinas. His contentions were in vain. For the British government the question was closed.

Later, however, some British government officials began to doubt Britain's claims to the islands. In 1910, for example, the British ambassador to Argentina asked the foreign secretary, Sir Edward Grey, what he should do about a new map of Argentina recently issued in that country on which the Falklands were designated as a part of Argentina. The advice sent him was to do nothing, the same procedure that had been used for seventy years. This seems not to have satisfied Sidney Spicer, head of the American department in the Foreign Office, who asked Gaston de Bernhardt, a researcher in the Foreign Office, to investigate the question of sovereignty over the islands. After Spicer read the result of Bernhardt's work, he commented that "it is difficult to avoid a conclusion that the Argentine government's attitude is not altogether unjustified and that our action has been somewhat high-handed" (The *Sunday Times* of London Insight Team 1982: pp. 39–40).

Bernhardt's findings showed that Palmerston's argument was completely false. The agreement of 1771 had omitted the question of sovereignty; Britain had no right to the island of East Falkland, not even claimed by England until 1829; and Palmerston had looked only at *official correspondence* (Bernhardt's italics) when looking for proof of the secret agreement, although there was plenty of it in other sources. In 1911 a Foreign Office official wrote that because England could not show a good claim for the Falklands, the office had decided not to discuss the subject with Argentina (The *Sunday Times* of London Insight Team 1982: p. 40).

After World War I Britain began to base its claim to the islands more and more on the principle of prescription, or the right to own land because of a long continued occupation of it, no matter how originally acquired. However, the Foreign Office, especially the American department, had doubts about openly advocating such a claim. Why? John Troutbeck, head of the American department, explained why in 1936. He wrote: "The difficulty of the position is that our seizure of the Falkland Islands in 1833 was so arbitrary a procedure as judged by the ideology of the present day. It is therefore not east to explain our possession without showing ourselves up as international bandits" (The *Sunday Times* of London Insight Team 1982: p. 40).

Rejection of Argentine Claims
Against the United States

Britain's adamant rejection of Argentina's demands also sounded the death knell for any claims Argentina had against the United States growing out of Duncan's foray on Vernet's colony. For the United States it was convenient to accept Britain's contention that it had occupied the islands in 1766–1770 and again in 1771–1774, and had left a lead plate of ownership on the islands when it pulled out in 1774. That would place Britain's claims in a period before the American Revolution and long before the Monroe Doctrine was announced in 1823 to keep European nations from colonizing in the New World. England had been in the islands before 1823, and so Argentina could not ask the United States to invoke the Monroe Doctrine against Britain. President Jackson's hands were clean. He did not have to accept any Argentine claims against Duncan.

Jackson's government did ask the Spanish government whether the Falklands had been a part of the Viceroyalty of Río de la Plata and whether a secret treaty existed by which Britain had given up all claims to the Falklands. To the first question, the answer was yes; to the second, the answer was inconclusive. The Spanish investigator had not found a copy of the secret agreement. If there was one it would no doubt have been in the archives of the secretariat of state, but it seems there was no effort made to search those archives. There are documents in the Spanish archives mentioning the secret agreement, but the investigator did not refer to them. Jackson's government should perhaps have investigated such an important matter further, but maybe it did not find an investigation necessary or convenient. And Jackson's government said nothing about Britain's abandonment of the islands for fifty-nine years, long enough for it to have lost all rights to them under international law, as another country had occupied them in the meantime.

Jackson's new secretary of state, John Forsyth, in sending a new consul to Buenos Aires, wrote the Argentine minister of foreign affairs on July 29, 1834, that he was sorry that Argentina had not sent a minister to the United States but that President Jackson was disposed to confer with Argentina in a conciliatory manner. According to the U.S. consul in Buenos Aires, the United States was delaying sending a minister because of the negotiations between Great Britain and Argentina. He also informed his government that he felt it unwise to send a minister under the existing conditions.

Buenos Aires, however, soon sent Carlos M. de Alvear as minister to Washington. Alvear immediately presented his country's claim for losses incurred in the Duncan raid on Vernet's settlement, but was advised by Secretary of State Daniel Webster on December 4, 1841, that the United States could give no answer to his request until the question of title to the islands had been settled.

Now British and American aims and intentions seemed to be working hand in glove. Just as Duncan's raid on Vernet's colony and the consequent diplomatic quarrel with the United States, ending in Baylies's asking for his passports, had given Britain an excuse for seizing the islands, so now Britain was giving the United States an excuse for avoiding discussion of the claims arising from the raid of the *Lexington*. The United States need not condemn Duncan's pillaging of Puerto Soledad. Neither need it protest Britain's occupation of the islands. It continued to maintain this rather quibbling position, maintaining that the Falkland claims could not be included in a discussion of outstanding claims between the two countries because the question of title to the islands had not been resolved.

But that position was not the only one that irritated the Argentines. Several times during the discussion of the claims, the U.S. government referred to Vernet's settlement and the arrest of U.S. sailors as illegal and piratical acts. For instance, in December 1885, Grover Cleveland, referring to a renewed Argentine request for the settlement of these claims, stated that Argentina was demanding indemnification for losses incurred when the commander of the *Lexington* destroyed a "piratical" settlement on the Falklands Islands in 1831, and because of the later occupation of the islands by Great Britain and the derelict state of the islands both before and after their occupation by Argentina, the United States considered the claims completely groundless.

How could Cleveland have been so poorly informed about the whole question of the Falklands? Either he was badly advised or he did not want to know the facts. Indeed, the new Argentine minister to the United States, the able scholar and diplomat Dr. Vicente G. Quesada, so informed the Department of State, but very diplomatically. Secretary of State Thomas F. Bayard replied on March 18, 1886, that the responsibility of the United States for Duncan's acts could not be separated from the question of the ownership of the Falklands, and that any decision on the former could be interpreted as an opinion on the latter. In other words, the United States could not discuss indemnification for damages from Duncan's foray without giving an opinion about the ownership of the Falklands. Moreover, Bayard said, the Monroe Doctrine did not apply in this case because it could not be applied retroactively, i.e., to any event that occurred before 1823, and Britain had held the islands before 1823, in fact before the United States was created. Did Bayard by this statement give an opinion after all? He had in fact accepted Britain's position that it had held the islands before the Monroe Doctrine and therefore the doctrine could not be applied (Goebel 1927: pp. 463–464).

Bayard then stated that even if it could be proved that Argentina possessed the islands at the time of Duncan's raid, there was plenty of proof to show that Duncan's acts could be defended, a shocking statement, to say the least, if Bayard was impartially advised. Quesada, in a long and masterful essay, tried in vain to show Bayard in what respects he was wrong. Argentine history books dwell on this unfortunate incident in United States–Argentine relations.

5
Britain Strengthens Its Hold
on the Islands

Rosas and the Islands

The British takeover of the Malvinas coincided with the rise to power of the Argentine dictator Juan Manuel de Rosas. Rosas had been elected governor of the province of Buenos Aires in 1829 for a three-year term. Upon leaving office in 1832, he took charge of the war against the Indians in the southern part of the province, making himself more popular with the powerful *estancieros* (ranchers) by adding more lands to their use. He himself acquired extensive areas of grassland for his cattle. In 1835 the provincial legislature reelected him governor, this time with complete dictatorial powers. Because attempts to establish a national government had failed, the provincial governments were satisfied to give Rosas the power to conduct foreign military affairs for the whole nation, now called the Argentine Confederation. Until his overthrow in 1852, Rosas was reelected to this supreme position every three years by his hand-picked legislature.

Rosas mentioned the need to recover the Malvinas in his annual messages to the legislature, but nothing came of them. Rosas was friendly to the British, whose support he needed against an aggressive French government trying to get a foothold in the Río de la Plata area, and it seems he was really not interested in retrieving some isolated, wind-swept islands in the farthermost reaches of the South Atlantic. "Cows and sheep not whales and seals were the preoccupation of his principal supporters, and the main objects of their affection and capital investments" (Ferns 1960: pp. 232–233).

Between 1838 and 1840 Argentina suffered the consequences of a French blockade that was bringing economic disaster to the country. As a result, during an exchange of notes between the British government and Rosas, he offered the islands to Britain in exchange for abrogation of Argentina's million-pound debt to the British-based Baring Brothers Bank. Lord Aberdeen, the British foreign minister, shrugged off this offer with the excuse that the loan had been made by a private bank, and the British government could not legally take it over. Probably the

87

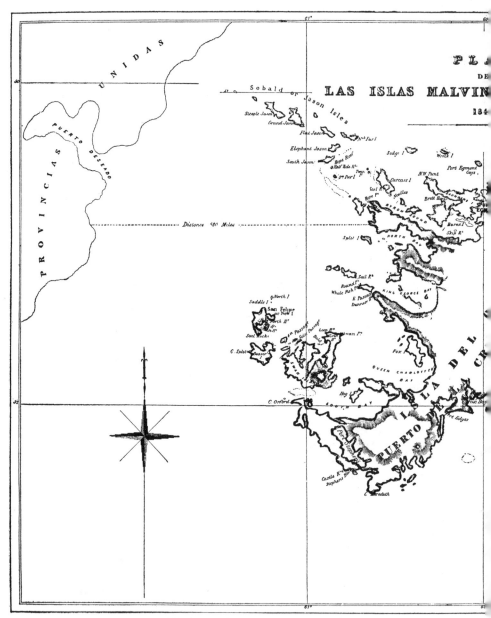

FIGURE 5.1. Map of the islands included in a message sent by Manuel Moreno, Argentine minister to Britain, to the British foreign minister, protesting British occupation of the islands in 1841.

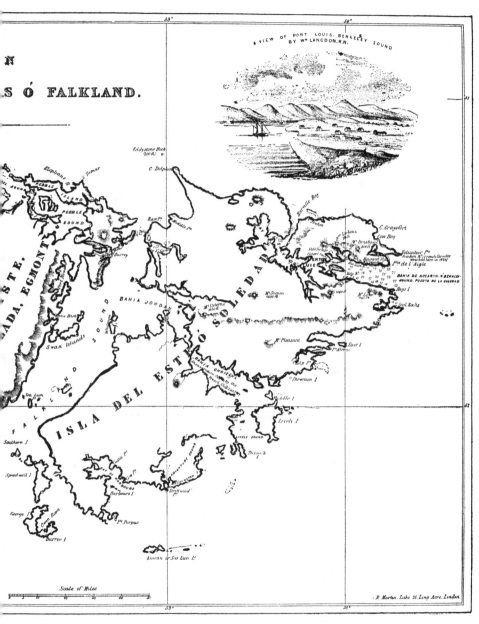

Source: Antonio Montarcé Lastra, *Redención de la Soberanía* (Buenos Aires: Talleres Graficos Padilla y Contreras, 1946), following p. 80.

real reason was that Aberdeen believed it would be ridiculous to buy something Britain already occupied. There seemed to be little danger of any Argentine attempt to get the islands back. Aberdeen was right.

Britain Establishes a Government in the Falklands

The first British officer to govern the Falklands was Her Majesty's Lieutenant, Henry Smith, who arrived at Port Luis, the former Spanish and Argentine capital of the Malvinas, in January 1834, and stayed four years. He was replaced for a short while by Lieutenant Robert Lowcay, who in turn was succeeded by Lieutenant W. Robinson. In mid-1839 Robinson delegated his functions to John Tyssen.

The islands did not prosper. In 1840, a count of the people at Port Luis showed only twenty-five adults and a few children living in the only known settlement on the islands. The town was dying of inanition when Queen Victoria in 1842 dispatched Captain Richard C. Moody to the islands, invested with the title of lieutenant-governor of the Falkland Islands, to reorganize the settlement and move it to a nearby bay named Port William, where the winds were not so strong. The place had been called Beau Port by the French and had been strongly recommended as a better port by Vice-Admiral Robert Fitzroy, who had been in that area in 1834 as the commander of H.M.S. *Beagle*, on which Charles Darwin had made his famous voyage. The suggestion raised a tempest in a teapot, but once the Antarctic explorer James C. Ross had recommended it, the evacuation of Port Luis was assured. At the last moment Governor Moody tried to save it by renaming it Port Anson, but Lord Stanley, the secretary of the colonies, stood firm, and Port Luis was gradually abandoned. The new capital initially took the name of Port William but was soon renamed Port Stanley.

On June 23, 1843, Queen Victoria issued a letter patent incorporating the islands into the dominions of the crown, an act that in theory would permit them to have their own legislative council and issue their own ordinances.

Sheep Take Over the Islands

The California gold rush of 1849 brought U.S. and other vessels to the islands for supplies and repairs on the long voyage around Cape Horn. But Americans were not always welcomed guests. For example, British officials charged the crews of the *Hudson* and the *Washington* with killing hogs on their stay in the islands. As in the case of Captain Duncan and the U.S.S. *Lexington*, the U.S.S. *Germantown* arrived in the islands to protect U.S. shipping, but this time against the British, not the Argentines. With the *Germantown's* thirty-two-pounder guns trained on the government house in Port Stanley, the British authorities decided to sentence the captains of the two U.S. vessels to a fine of only one pound for each of the twenty-two pigs slaughtered by the Americans.

The hogs were the property of the Falkland Islands Company, organized by a group of enterprising British merchants. In 1852 it received a royal charter from Queen Victoria to develop the colony. In the same year the company sent forty-six Cheviot sheep to the islands. By 1860 the company had 200 Cheviot and Southdown sheep and 6,000 mixed breeds on the islands, was sending over shepherds from the British Isles to tend them, and was buying up all the land it could. It ultimately owned 1.3 million acres, approximately half of all the land in the islands, in addition to all the warehouses, the ships in which it sent the wool to Britain and brought supplies to the islands, and the market in which the wool was sold—as well as the sheep.

Anglo-Argentine Relations Improve After 1852

The overthrow of Rosas in 1852 launched Argentina on an era of stable government and economic growth under the leadership of Presidents Justo José de Urquiza, Bartolomé Mitre, Domingo Faustino Sarmiento, and Nicolás Avellaneda, and of other statesmen whose aim was to steer Argentina on a secure democratic path under the new liberal constitution of 1853 and to develop the enormous agricultural potential of the country. Expansion and prosperity set in, with huge foreign investments (especially British) flowing into the country.

British investments in Argentina grew rapidly: from over 2,000,000 pounds in 1857 to 5,375,000 pounds in 1865. By 1874 they had reached 23,000,000 pounds (Ferns 1960: p. 492). British companies soon built most of the Argentine railways and ran them. Others furnished the finished goods sent to Argentina, while Argentina sent food and raw materials to Britain. Both Britain and Argentina profited from this hand-in-glove arrangement. Britain exported to Argentina textiles, coal, iron and steel, hardware, railway equipment, and tools and machinery, while Argentina sent Britain hides and skins, wool, tallow, cereals, flax, meat, and animals.

But the most important export of Britain to Argentina was capital to develop the country. By 1886, when 45,602,000 pounds had been invested there, Argentina had become the golden dream of British investors. In 1889, when the first rumblings of trouble began to appear, Argentina was receiving "between 40 and 50 percent of all British funds invested outside the United Kingdom" (Ferns 1960: p. 397). It seemed as if to all intents and purposes Argentina had become a part of the informal British empire.

Everything might have continued as before had it not been for the unsound fiscal policies of the Argentine government under Miguel Juárez Celman (1886–1890). The national and provincial governments borrowed extensively for railways, port improvements, farm machinery, meat-packing plants, and the like. The money came from bonds sold to British investors and payable in gold or sterling. But few people seemed to realize that investments in long-term projects like railways and port improvements would take a long time to produce the eagerly awaited dividends, and even longer in frontier areas such as Argentina. Railways, for example, did not overbuild in 1885–1890, as later utilization would show, but at the time building outpaced immediate use. Railway earnings lagged far behind railway capital investment by 1892, when the trend began to be reversed. Added to the troubles was corruption by public officials and private entrepreneurs.

When Argentina could no longer pay its debts in gold or sterling, it resorted to printing more and more money. This inconvertible paper money policy led to the overthrow of Juárez Celman in 1890. When in 1890 and 1891 Argentina defaulted on its bond payments and British investors no longer received dividends on their investments, the Baring Brothers bank (which had given Argentina its first loan in 1824) faced bankruptcy, with 21,000,000 pounds in liabilities. The Bank of England intervened and through a bankers' committee headed by Lord Rothschild obtained a liberal arrangement to pay Argentina's immediate debts with a loan, provided it cleaned house and employed stricter rules of doing business. The agreement failed to avoid the collapse of Argentine bonds but gave Argentina a breathing spell. Britain and Argentina now entered a golden age of Anglo-Argentine relations, lasting from the Boer War to World War II.

Before the 1890–1891 crisis, Argentina had imported much more from Britain than it had sold to Britain. This trade was now turned around, and from 1901 to 1914, Argentina sold much more to Britain than it bought in British goods. By 1913, the balance of trade in Argentina's favor had reached over 22,000,000 pounds (Ferns 1960: p. 485). But Argentina also had a favorable balance of trade with the world. Its surpluses paid the claims of investors abroad and paid for services it bought from foreign sellers. How did this come about? In the first place, Argentine products, especially cereals, increased by leaps and bounds, and Argentine produce was sold at high prices. Second, this happened at a time when food prices were favorable in relation to those of manufactured goods and services, such as sea freight. Third, the rise in production and sales led to advantageous investments. Between 1900 and 1910, British investments in Argentina jumped from 189,040,000 to 291,110,000 pounds (Ferns 1960: p. 493).

By the turn of the century some Argentines were looking with jaundiced eyes at the British economic supremacy in Argentina. Was Argentina becoming a British colony? Words like *colonialism* and *imperialism* were bandied about more frequently. And one writer noted that almost all Argentine industrial, commerical, agricultural, and mining companies bore the symbol *Limited*. He wondered if perhaps the distribution of Argentine wealth was "limited" also (Ferns 1960: p. 487). Gradually more and more Argentines came to believe that Argentina was too much under the thumb of British interests.

Yet, if imperialism implies political control, Argentina was certainly not under British control. If imperialism implies economic control the answer may be different. It is true that Argentine businesses sought out English investors and that the Argentine government permitted this policy. The question is, then, How much influence did British economic interests have on Argentine politics? This is a question difficult, almost impossible, to answer. Whether Britain influenced Argentine economic and political life too much or not, many Argentines by the 1930s believed that it did. And it would be only natural that the question of the Malvinas would arise to plague the good relations between the two countries. The Second World War helped to intensify the vexed question.

Why didn't the Argentine government make stronger and more frequent claims to the Malvinas during the last decades of the nineteenth century and the first three decades of the twentieth? Probably, at the time, people in government thought it was better not to rock the boat with tough demands that Britain return the Malvinas, because with Britain's help Argentina was experiencing an economic growth such as few countries have known. Since the 1860s British investments in Argentina had increased enormously. In general, therefore, until the 1940s Argentine governments, if not necessarily pro-British, did not challenge the over-whelming British supremacy in the economic life of the country.

At times, it is true, there were individuals and groups who brought up the question of ownership of the Malvinas. But protests and demonstrations were mild in comparison to what they became after World War II broke out and Argentines chose sides in that conflict. After the war the Perón regime did question Britain's economic position in Argentina more and more openly, until finally there began a lively campaign to terminate British dominance. With this came an ever-growing demand that Britain return the Falklands to Argentina.

6
The Pot Begins to Boil

Anglo-Argentine Relations Begin to Weaken

The turn of the century saw a gradual change in Anglo-Argentine relations as more and more Argentines began to question the role of Britain in Argentine life. Although those with economic and cultural ties to Britain continued to favor British influence, growing numbers of Argentines, especially among the working poor, were beginning to feel that Argentina's economic ties to Britain were at least one of the reasons why they toiled in ships, in factories, and on farms for so little pay.

Added to this was the rise of nationalism, with politicians, to get votes, extolling the virtues of "Argentinism." Some even declared that Argentina was made great by the hard work of Argentines and not by foreigners, conveniently forgetting the immense British and other foreign investments in Argentina and the European immigrants who came in by the thousands after 1870. Children and grandchildren of these immigrants were now among the most vociferous, jingoist, antiforeign elements in the population.

In 1916 the Unión Cívica Radical (the Radical Party) was successful in wrenching the presidency from the conservatives who had held it most of the time since 1890 and who were closely allied to British interests. The new president, elected on a populist platform supporting the masses, was Hipólito Yrigoyen, who, after the United States entered the First World War, almost single-handedly kept Argentina out of the war in spite of a widespread clamor that it should join the United States, England, and France in the conflict.

Because Argentine law forbids the immediate reelection of a president, another Radical, the more moderate Marcelo T. de Alvear, was elected president in 1922, but in 1928, Yrigoyen was reelected. Now an old man, Yrigoyen became more and more stubborn in desiring to rule personally, delegating little authority and making a mess of things. His anti-American and anti-English attitude, together with his personal aloofness and the ending of the social reforms begun in his first administration, as well as the general incompetency of the government under his personal direction, made it relatively easy for a military coup to overthrow him in 1930.

Thereafter for fifteen years civil governments consisting of conservative and reactionary people of several parties aligned under the label of La Concordancia were able to prevent any change in the status quo. The coming of the Second World War polarized political alignments even more. Yrigoyen's success in keeping Argentina out of the First World War and the economic prosperity enjoyed by Argentina in that war were used by pro-Axis elements to prevent Argentina from joining the Allies, with other Latin American nations, after the United States entered the war. By this time the Concordancia president was Ramón S. Castillo, who was determined to keep the Argentines neutral. But for some military leaders, even Castillo's regime was not reactionary enough.

Fearing that in the approaching elections the Concordancia might win with a strongly pro-English candidate, they overthrew the government in June 1943, with a revolution that soon brought Juan Domingo Perón to power. He was elected president in 1946 through dubious electoral procedures and a strong appeal to the masses. Aided by his beautiful, ambitious wife, María Eva Duarte de Perón ("Evita"), Perón was able by force and through patriotic appeals to various sectors of the populace to stay in power until 1955. Perón's rule saw the rise of a strong anti-British sentiment in Argentina. By skillfully accusing the upper-class commercial, industrial, and ranching groups of being in league with British economic interests in Argentina to exploit the working classes, he convinced many Argentines that it was time to overthrow British economic domination in Argentina.

The Postage-Stamp Controversy over the Falklands

Soon after Perón's election to the presidency, Britain issued stamps for the so-called Falkland Islands Dependencies showing maps of the South Atlantic with all the islands Britain claimed. Additional stamps of the Falklands has maps showing overprints of "South Orkney Dependency of Falkland Islands," "South Georgia Dependency of Falkland Islands," "South Shetlands Dependency of Falkland Islands," and "Graham Land Dependency of Falkland Islands." Perón's newspapers made hay of this flagrant attack on Argentina's sovereign rights over all these lands. But even liberal, anti-*peronista* papers could not let this glaring indiscretion slip by. Among the latter, *La Prensa*, in long accounts, pointed out that South Georgia, the South Orkney Islands, the South Shetlands, and Graham Land Peninsula, as well as some other Antarctic islands, were Argentine possessions, and that Argentina had maintained a meteorological station on the South Orkney Islands since February 22, 1904. In spite of this Britain, which had occupied none of the islands mentioned, decreed their annexation on July 21, 1908, through letters patent, giving the area the name "Falkland Island Whaling Sector." In this "sector," continued *La Prensa*, some eager-beaver British official had even included a section of the Patagonian mainland of Argentina,

FIGURE 6.1. British stamps of the Falklands (1946) that claimed sovereignty over additional territory.

Source: La Prensa (Buenos Aires), May 17 and June 7, 1946.

but this error was soon rectified. In 1909, Britain had declared these islands annexed to the British Empire, although it had never occupied them—a fact emphasized by the newspaper, perhaps because in seizing the Falklands, Britain had claimed that Argentina had not occupied them.

La Prensa also attacked another letter patent of March 24, 1917, through which Britain attempted to delineate the boundaries of the region. In 1923, Britain had made a public announcement of the annexation of the area and had included a part of the Antarctic continent. The so-called Falkland Whaling Sector was to comprise two zones, one south of 50° south latitude between 20° and 50° west longitude, and the other south of 58° south latitude between 50° and 80° west longitude. The islands shown on the much-discussed stamps were in the first zone.

In 1923, *La Prensa* continued, the Argentine postal service had protested to the Universal Postal Union against a stamp issued by Britain of the Falkland Islands Dependencies. The protest stated that Argentina's jurisdiction extended by right and in fact over all the seas and islands situated along its maritime coast, over a part of the island of Tierra del Fuego, over the archipelago of the Staaten, New Year, South Georgia, and South Orkney islands, and over the polar lands not yet delimited. This jurisdiction, it said, included the Falkland Islands (*La Prensa*, May 17, 1946).

In the meantime Argentina had established a rudimentary radio station at its meteorological station in the South Orkneys and had informed the Universal Postal Union of this action. Britain had protested to the Argentine government, declaring that the South Orkneys were under the jurisdiction of the governor of the Falkland Islands. Argentina, according to *La Prensa*, had replied with a counterprotest, but the matter remained pending because technical difficulties had kept the radio station from operating. When a new transmitter had gone into operation from the South Orkneys on March 30, 1927, Great Britain had protested again, decrying Argentina's repeated notes to the Universal Postal Union and presuming that these communications indicated that Argentina assumed sovereignty over all the islands, a claim the British government could not admit. Notes had continued between the two governments, with each claiming sovereignty over the islands. However, in its colonial reports published in 1928, the British government had admitted that the Argentine government had been permitted to maintain a radio station at the meteorological station on Laurie Island, one of the South Orkneys.

La Prensa ended its long commentary on the stamp dispute by recalling that at the end of 1939, in a special meeting in Panama of the foreign secretaries of the American nations, called to confront the growing danger from the actions of Axis powers, the question had arisen of the fate of European colonies in the Western Hemisphere, should they be attacked by these powers. The Argentine delegation had immediately declared that Argentina recognized no European colony or possession in the New World and moreover retained its legal title and rights to the Malvinas and other Argentine lands within the zone suggested by the conference to be defended against possible attack. The same position, *La Prensa* pointed out, was assumed by the Argentine delegation to the second special meeting of American foreign ministers in Havana in 1940. During discussion of what to do regarding foreign colonies in the Western Hemisphere, Argentina had again insisted that the question did not apply to the Malvinas, because they were Argentine territory, as were other regions in the south Atlantic area.

La Prensa's defense of Argentina's rights to the Malvinas is an excellent example of the unity among Argentines on the question of the islands. *La Prensa*, constant enemy of Perón, who later seized the paper and gave it to some henchmen to run as a *peronista* paper, used the dignity of the pen and honest reporting to defend Argentina's right to the Malvinas, whereas Perón used demagoguery, inciting mobs to a frenzy through rousing speeches against the English, but both insisted that "las Malvinas son argentinas."

Perón Attacks the British Economic Predominance over Argentina

In 1947 Britain suggested that the question of the Falklands be taken for study before the International Court of Justice, in appearance a turnabout, as Britain had shied away from arbitration after its own John Troutbeck, head of the American department of the Foreign Office, had in 1936 found that British possession of the islands could not be explained "without showing ourselves up as international bandits." Argentina quickly rejected the proposal on the grounds that the islands were Argentine, and therefore no question concerning them could be taken to an international court, but only to national court within Argentina.

On July 9, 1947, the anniversary of Argentina's declaration of political independence, Perón proclaimed Argentina's "Declaration of Economic Independence," vowing to free Argentines from the "reprehensible" economic hegemony of foreign interests and the native agrarian oligarchy connected with them. He acted quickly. By purchase and/or expropriation he took over important businesses. Included were the British-owned railways, the biggest investment in Argentina.

The task was fairly simple, although it later proved to be an economic disaster for Argentina. During the Second World War Britain had imported huge amounts of food supplies from Argentina, on which it postponed payment by freezing the debt due for the supplies until after the war. When the war was over Argentina had about $750,000,000 in frozen assets in England. Perón was willing to wipe out part of this debt in exchange for the British-owned railways. On March 1, 1948, he was able to announce to thousands of his cheering followers that the railways were no longer British, shouting at the end, in unison with his wife,

"Now they are ours!" The chant was soon taken over by their followers, who rushed to the railroad yards to paint on the cars, "Perón and Evita say that now they are ours!" Perón had paid $600,000,000 of the frozen assets for the railways, an amount he could well have used for other purposes. But he had to show that he was a nationalist and a patriot. His action was the best demonstration of his plan to bring economic independence to his country.

During the negotiations for the transfer of the railroads, the U.S. Department of State had warned Perón not to go ahead with his plans, pointing out that little had been done during the war years to maintain the railways and they were in the worst state possible. In not heeding this warning, Perón saddled the nation with a debt whose effects are still being felt today. Not only did he have to replace almost all the rails and rolling stock, but he would have to pay much more in wages to the many followers who were now hired as employees. Most stations during the British administration had been run by single families; now they had three or four times the number of employees, for political debts had to be paid. As some Argentines pointed out at the time, if Perón had had any sense at all he would have waited until the railways were in such bad shape that they could not function, and he would have been able to take them over through expropriation for failure to perform contractual services. He would have saved $600,000,000, with which he would have been able to replenish the worn-out stock. Instead, the huge debt incurred to keep the railways running was to plague Argentina for many years.

The purchase of the railways was the most spectacular step in Perón's march to economic independence from Britain, but it was not the only measure taken. By 1952, Perón had been able to reduce British investments in Argentina from $1,287,005,000 (estimate for 1940) to about $17,300,000 by buying and/or expropriating other industries and services, like electric and telephone companies and food-packing plants. Perón and his followers were happy to free Argentina from foreign economic domination, but future Argentine governments were going to be burdened with heavy debts.

The Falklands Question in the OAS:
The Rise of the Anticolonialism Theme

Perón's campaign to get back the Malvinas stressed that Argentina no longer accepted colonialism in the New World—not in British Honduras, nor in British Guiana, nor in the Malvinas. This theme was emphasized by his delegates at the inter-American conferences that took place after the Second World War: at Río de Janeiro (1947), Bogotá (1948), Washington (1951), and Caracas (1954).

At the Río conference, called to establish a hemisphere defense zone for protection against outside attack, Argentina succeeded in having the

Malvinas and a sector of the Antarctic included as territories under its sovereignty. The conference also accepted the principle that the American states would come to the aid of any conference members under outside attack. Argentina appealed to these treaties when in 1982 Britain sent a fleet to dislodge the Argentine armed force that had taken possession of the Falklands. But the United States pointed out that England had not attacked the islands, and so the matter did not come under the provisions of the Río agreements.

The Bogotá conference of 1948 called for an end to European colonies in the New World, on the grounds that they were contrary to American ideals and a threat to the defense of the Western Hemisphere. Again, the United States, unwilling to offend Great Britain, refused to approve the resolution, although it had been watered down from one the Argentines had supported. At the Washington conference of foreign ministers of the American states, called by the United States in 1951 to prepare for the defense of the American republics and support the action of the United Nations against communist aggression in Korea, Argentina refused to send troops anywhere in the world without prior consent of the Argentine people and congress. During the discussion of the status of the European colonies in the New World, Argentina again affirmed its rights to the Malvinas and other lands in the Antarctic. When the Tenth Inter-American Conference met in Caracas in 1954, Argentina once more expressed its strong opposition to colonialism in the New World. Although by now Perón was receiving increasing support from other Latin American countries for his stand, the United States still refused to support it, remaining loyal to its European allies.

After the overthrow of Perón in 1955, Argentina never wavered from this stand. Every government, and there have been many, has stood firm on this position. For instance, in the Act of Washington of December 1964 (during the First Extraordinary Inter-American Conference), the Argentine delegation made a special declaration that their country reserved to itself and kept intact the legitimate title and rights to the Islas Malvinas, South Georgia, and the South Sandwich Islands, none of which constituted colonies or possessions of any nation whatsoever but formed a part of Argentine territory and were included under Argentine dominion and sovereignty. According to the Argentine delegation, the Malvinas, Belize (British Honduras), and that part of British Guiana claimed by Venezuela could not be admitted into the Organization of American States if they succeeded in becoming independent nations, because they were not colonies but really parts of independent states. Thus the Organization of American States, by its own legal actions, recognized Argentine sovereignty over the Malvinas. The twenty nations making up the organization would, supposedly, back up Argentina's claim.

In April 1974, at the meeting of the General Assembly of the Organization of American States in Atlanta, Argentina, supported by

Guatemala and Venezuela, strongly opposed permitting Britain to be a permanent observer in meetings of the Organization of American States. The Argentine delegate accused Barbados, through its representative at the conference, of trying to speak for the United Kingdom, which had been denied an observer at the meeting. He pointed out that Argentina could not accept Britain's admission as a permanent observer until the question of the Malvinas was resolved. Britain's entrance into the organization as a permanent observer was overwhelmingly defeated, although the United States voted for it.

7

The Falklands/Malvinas Question in the United Nations

The Problem Reaches the United Nations

Argentina's contention that colonialism in the New World was un-acceptable (so frequently stressed in inter-American conferences) was approved by the United Nations on December 14, 1960, when the General Assembly passed Resolution 1514 by a vote of eighty-nine in favor, none against, and nine abstentions. The resolution called for an end to colonialism in the world. A committee of fourteen, later expanded to twenty-four, was formed to enforce the resolution. Countries were asked to list their colonies. Britain placed the Falkland Islands on its list of possessions.

Argentina, fearing that Resolution 1514 might be mistakenly inter-preted, quickly explained its position vis-à-vis the resolution: the Malvinas had always been a part of Argentina and were a colony of no country. It would never accept the thesis that they could be decolonized, because they had never been a colony (except illegally). Argentina began a campaign to remind the international community of the special case of the Malvinas as well as the adjacent islands and other South Atlantic areas, so as to prevent any pretext for applying to them the principle of self-determination. In this manner Argentina hoped, by constant repetition, to keep Argentina's position before the public eye.

The Argentine position was actually aided by a petition presented to the United Nations on September 8, 1964, the first time that the Malvinas as such were mentioned in that body officially. The petition, presented by the British delegate to the Committee of 24, had been sent by the inhabitants of the Falklands, and stated that they wanted to remain British. It can be imagined what the reaction of Argentina was to this petition. Its spokesman pointed out that the islands had a total population of about 2,000, of whom perhaps half were permanent residents, only enough to fill a large movie theater in Buenos Aires. Only twelve inhabitants owned land. Most of the rest of the population were employees of the Falkland Islands Company. Moreover, only four members on the legislative council of the island were elected. It would be completely impractical to make an independent state out of a territory so desolately unpopulated. Therefore, the only way to decolonize the islands would be for Great Britain to return them to the rightful owner, the Argentine Republic.

With the Falklands inscribed by Britain in the list of colonial territories (an action Argentina had refused to accept on the usual basis that they were Argentine territory), the Committee of 24 adopted on November 13, 1964, a resolution to the effect that the Falklands came under the designation of a colony that could become an independent country, but that as the United Kingdom and Argentina both claimed the islands, the two governments should begin negotiations, taking into account the objectives of the Charter of the United Nations, Resolution 1514, and the interests of the inhabitants of the islands.

Resolution 2065 Is Passed

In November 1965, the then extraordinary ambassador of the Argentine Republic to the United Nations and chief of the Argentine delegation to the plenary session of that body's committee on decolonization, Bonifacio del Carril, pointed out that Argentina had always been a strong supporter of autodetermination of peoples, but that in the case of the Malvinas there were no people to receive self-government. He characterized as pure sophistry the British delegate's affirmation that the people of the islands had a higher standard of living than those of Britain (and of course by inference than those of Argentina) and that therefore, if the islands were returned to Argentina, their people would lose a veritable earthly paradise. Del Carril declared that the islands had a population of 2,043 in 1901 and 2,172 in 1962, and that a U.N. report had indicated that the Malvinas had no possibility whatsoever of an increase in population. Del Carril went on to argue that the Malvinas had a harsh and inclement climate. The greater part of the people who lived there did so of necessity and not for pleasure. In fact infant mortality rates were low because there were few children; adult mortality rates were low because adults left the islands before dying. This did not mean that the British administration of the islands was not efficient and exemplary for the few people who lived there. But it did emphasize the point that in the Malvinas land was more important than people.

The speaker went on to say that he meant no offense to the inhabitants of the Malvinas. They fulfilled their mission as an advance guard of civilization in inhospitable, isolated regions. For that reason Argentina without reservations, theoretical or practical, accepted the principle that the destiny of those settlers could not be negotiated. But he was convinced that if Britain would truly accept negotiation of the problem, with the intention of reaching a solution that would conciliate all parties, as the Committee of 24 had recommended, some formula could be found that would recognize and guarantee the rights and aspirations of the people of the Malvinas. After all, thousands of people born in Great Britain or descendants of Britons were living in Argentina and had been for a century and a half, and the 2,000 islanders would probably be happy to live in Argentina too (*La Nacion*, November 11, 1965).

Bonifacio del Carril, a noted writer and historian, is the great-grandson of Salvador María del Carril, who as Argentine minister of grovernment drew up and signed the decree of June 10, 1829, whereby the Political and Military Command of the Malvinas was created and under which Vernet became the first Argentine governor of the islands. Del Carril's long discourse may have had some effect, for on December 15, 1965, the Twentieth General Assembly of the United Nations adopted Resolution 2065, which ratified the resolution of the Committee of 24 inviting Argentina and the United Kingdom to start discussions leading to a peaceful solution of the Falklands question.

Argentina was immensely encouraged by this action of the United Nations, but its hopes were soon shattered. Before long it appeared that England had no desire to negotiate, as according to its government the inhabitants of the islands desired to remain British subjects and their wishes had to be respected. Argentina, on the other hand, continued to insist that the sovereignty of the islands was the most important question, for the Malvinas had been Argentine since the independence of Argentina, had been occupied by Argentines, and had been wrested from Argentina by force in 1833.

Operation Cóndor

The seriousness of the situation is illustrated by an incident that occurred on September 28, 1966, and that could have developed into a dangerous confrontation between the two countries had not saner minds prevailed on both sides. On that day a group of young Argentine "nationalist" commandos hijacked an Aerolíneas Argentinas plane bound from Buenos Aires to Río Gallegos and ordered the pilot to fly the plane to the Malvinas. They were under the command of Dardo M. Cabo and María Cristina Verrier, an actress and the only woman in the group. They called the exploit Operation Cóndor. At the time Britain and Argentina were secretly negotiating the prospect of oil and gas exploration in the Malvinas area, and the hijacking hurt the negotiations.

As there was no airport in Stanley to accommodate the plane (a DC-4), the pilot dexterously made a dangerous landing on a soggy race track, where the plane promptly bogged down. The hijackers, heavily armed, left the plane, took hostage several curious persons who had come to see what was happening, and planted Argentine flags around the plane. The passengers were permitted to leave the plane, and were quickly given shelter in private homes through the intervention of the Catholic and Anglican priests in town. The hijackers kept the crew with them in the plane as hostages.

The Catholic priest, Rudolf Roel, noting the nervousness of the commandos, tried to quiet them down and conducted religious services for them inside the plane. They told him they had come to reclaim Argentine territory as good Argentine patriots, because the long-drawn-out diplomatic negoitations had gone nowhere. At the request of the priest they released the hostages, but they said they would not surrender to British authorities unless the Argentine government asked them to do so. Becoming weaker because of the cold and lack of food, the hijackers requested twenty-four hours to consider the conditions of surrender. They surrendered on the night of September 29, and were interned in a church and guarded by the local constabulary.

The incident set off a chain of reaction of anti-British demonstrations in Argentina. In Rosario a group of young nationalists attacked the British consulate, destroying furniture, and the Anglo-Argentine Cultural Institute, where they burned a British flag. In Córdoba anti-British demonstrations were held in the streets. In Buenos Aires shots from a fast-moving car hit the British embassy, where the duke of Edinburgh was staying during a three-week visit to Argentina in celebration of Argentina's declaration of independence. No one was hurt, but rumors quickly spread that an attempt would be made to kidnap the duke and hold him hostage until the Malvinas were returned to Argentina. Civic and labor groups met in special meetings and/or issued circulars supporting the hijackers' acts. In Río Gallegos, the Argentine port closest to the Malvinas, Miguel L. Fitzgerald, a private pilot who had flown alone to the Malvinas in 1964, prepared to fly there again with a group of newsmen and photographers but was stopped by local authorities.

At the United Nations General Assembly Nicanor Costa Méndez, the Argentine foreign minister, announced that the hijackers would be brought to trial because only the Argentine government had the responsibility of defending Argentine sovereignty over the Falklands. This statement, he said, provided further categorical proof that Argentina was most serious in defending its sovereignty over its territory, such as the Malvinas, and it would continue to do so. These rights Argentina would continue to reaffirm with all the energy and authority possible, in international organizations and bilateral negotiations with the United Kingdom.

Argentina suggested to Britain that it would send a ship to get the passengers and the hijackers. Britain accepted the offer, although it suggested in turn that it could send a frigate from South Africa to the Malvinas. Argentina apologized for the attack on the British embassy and the other anti-British incidents and promised that the culprits would be punished and safety measures strengthened.

The Soviet Union suggested that the commando raid was a plot of the United States Central Intelligence Agency to prevent improvement in Argentine-British relations and to ingratiate the United States with the nationalist groups of Argentina, especially the young anticommunist Tacuara group. It also suggested that the attack on the British Embassy was CIA-inspired.

The Argentine government sent the naval transport *Bahía Buen Suceso* to Stanley to bring back the commandos and the passengers of the hijacked plane. The crew remained to bring back the plane later, with the aid of fuel and new batteries brought by the ship. Several hundred people came to the wharf to say farewell to the Argentines. The ship sailed on the night of October 1 and arrived at Ushuaia, the capital and main port of the province of Tierra del Fuego, on October 3. The passengers were taken off the ship quickly and placed on planes to go home, mostly to Río Gallegos, where the plane had been going before it was hijacked. The commandos remained on board ship under heavy guard until they were taken off to be tried. Pleas came from all over Argentina to free the prisoners because they had tried to vindicate Argentine sovereignty over the Malvinas. Perhaps afraid of this public outcry of sympathy for the hijackers, the courts finally gave them lenient sentences, in most cases six months in jail. Big headlines appeared in both British and Argentine newspapers with detailed accounts of the hijacking. The incident should have placed Britain on guard.

8

Britain and Argentina
Try Bilateral Negotiation

First Visit of a High British Official
to the Islands

Resolution 2065 of the United Nations had urged Britain and Argentina to negotiate a peaceful settlement of the Falklands/Malvinas question as soon as possible. In accordance with the terms of the resolution bilateral discussions began almost immediately in London. The conversations were secret, but it soon became known that during the talks Argentina offered full protection to the islanders should it take over the islands, as well as easy communication and transportation between the islands and the mainland of Argentina.

Toward the end of 1968, in order to explain the situation to the islanders and to discuss with them the possible future transfer of the islands to Argentina, Lord Chalfont, minister of state for Latin American affairs in the British Foreign Office, sailed to the Malvinas in the frigate *Endurance* after having accompanied the queen on an official visit to Chile and Brazil. It was the first time a high-ranking British official had visited the islands. British newspapers dedicated more space to the visit of Chalfont to the Malvinas than they had to the visit of the queen to two far more important areas in South America. Before returning to England, Chalfont also paid a short "courtesy" visit to Buenos Aires, where he met the Argentine foreign minister, Nicanor Costa Méndez. Both governments announced that although the Falklands/Malvinas question had been discussed, it had been discussed within the framework of the secret negotiations in London.

Chalfont's visit to the Malvinas and Buenos Aires brought forth a burst of speculations within both countries. These speculations went so far as to insist that an agreement had been reached between the two countries and that the Malvinas would be returned to Argentina. There were strong reasons to believe that this was true.

First, the British Foreign Office had announced on November 23, 1968, that most of the chief differences with respect to the Malvinas had been settled, but that a report that a treaty would be signed to that effect was pure speculation. Both sides, the Foreign Office spokesman said, had promised to give a final report to the United Nations around December 15 before the General Assembly adjourned. The spokesman also said that it was well known that the greatest differences between London and Buenos Aires had been solved, and added that the rumor about an agreement or treaty was possibly due to Lord Chalfont's visit to the Falklands.

Second, in a secret meeting with the six members of the executive council of the Falklands, which was reported to have been stormy, Chalfont had tried to explain to them what cession to Argentina would mean in benefits for the islanders. Of this the islanders wanted to hear nothing. It appeared, so the report went, that the strongest objections came from the two nonelective members of the council, representing the sheep industry. Chalfont had warned the council that Britain could no longer maintain sufficient naval forces in the islands to protect them, that it could no longer help the islands financially because of the world decline in wool prices, that it had to consider the interests of the large British community in Argentina, and that the islanders would be better off under Argentina. Perhaps because of this statement, rumors quickly swept through the islands that if the islanders did not change their attitude, in five years Britain would apply economic sanctions against them to force them to accept Argentine rule. During the discussion, one of the councillors told Chalfont that he had seen a memorandum several months earlier according to which the islands were to be given to Argentina, and only a date for the cession remained to be fixed. If this were true, Britain and Argentina had very likely come to an agreement. This councillor challenged Chalfont to explain why, if the islanders were British and their interests would be considered as Chalfont had so frequently stated, it would be necessary to discuss the matter with Argentina.

Third, the five correspondents of British newspapers who accompanied Chalfont on his visit to the South Atlantic were agreed that some kind of understanding had been reached between the two countries (a "position of agreement") and that Chalfont had been sent to the islands to get the inhabitants to accept it. They also agreed that he had his task cut out for him.

Fourth, on November 25, at precisely the time Chalfont was in the Malvinas, Britain informed the United Nations that within a few years the status of the territories still under British jurisdiction would be clarified. In a special reference to the Falklands Britain stated that it and Argentina were continuing negotiations in accordance with Resolution 2065 of the General Assembly. The Argentine representative also made special mention of Resolution 2065 at the same time. Why should both Argentina and Britain at this precise time bring up Resolution 2065 unless they were at least close to an agreement?

Fifth, on the day after his secret meeting with the executive council of the islands, Chalfont, in a speech to the sheep raisers' association, told the islanders that the negotiations were only one phase of a process and that the "position of agreement" so frequently mentioned was not a treaty. Even if it were made public, Chalfont said, it would in no manner change the sovereignty of the islands against the interests of the inhabitants. But the negotiations had to continue, for if they failed, Argentina might reclaim the islands in other ways that in his opinion might create greater uncertainty and would make life less agreeable for the islanders and much less secure. (Was this another sample of British understatement, another attempt to soften up the islanders, or was it a prophecy?) He ended by saying that the Argentines would get nowhere until a climate was reached in which the islanders desired a change of sovereignty. Was this an attempt to get the Argentines to establish better communications with the islands?

Sixth, observers at the Fifth Antarctic Consultative Conference being held in Paris at this time pointed out that even if Britain returned the Falklands to Argentina, it would not have to give up the Antarctic possessions. They noted that in March 1962, Britain, perhaps looking forward to divesting itself of the Falklands, had created a separate colony, the British Antarctic Territory, detached from and no longer to be ruled from Stanley. In this way Britain secured its Antarctic regions in accordance with the Antarctic Treaty of 1959, signed by Britain, Argentina, Chile, and nine other countries. Because these regions (the South Orkneys, the South Shetlands, and Graham Land) fell under the jurisdiction of the Treaty of 1959, Britain could limit the territorial problem with Argentina to the Falklands, presumably making it easier to solve.

It seems that some sort of agreement or "position of agreement" had been made or was on the verge of being made, for on November 27, 1968, Chalfont got the executive council of the islands to accept, although grudgingly, the Anglo-Argentine "position of agreement" that was to be made public during the middle of December. It had taken Chalfont four days to get the islanders to accept it. The five British correspondents accompanying him, it seems, were to prepare the British public for acceptance of the agreement.

During Chalfont's visit to the Falklands an Argentine plane landed on a street in Stanley, bearing Héctor Ricardo García, owner and manager of *La Crónica* of Buenos Aires, and his newsman Juan Carlos Nava. The pilot was the ubiquitous Miguel L. Fitzgerald, the Argentine flyer who had flown to the islands before, and during Operation Cóndor had tried to take newsmen to the islands but had been stopped. They said they had come to interview the islanders about Chalfont's visit. The plane was damaged upon landing, and the three Argentines were promptly taken into custody as illegal immigrants by a group of marines from the *Endurance*. They stated later that they had received severe but correct treatment. All their television and photographic equipment had been confiscated, as well as all their film. Chalfont asked that they be permitted to sail with him to Río Gallegos on the *Endurance*. When they reached Río Gallegos their cameras were returned to them, but not their film, which was to be returned later via diplomatic channels. The newsmen thanked Lord Chalfont for having obtained their release and for taking them back to Argentina. They believed they had been arrested to prevent them from interviewing Chalfont and the islanders.

Why Lord Chalfont's Mission Failed

Why was the supposed "position of agreement" (also called an "agreement of position" in the newspapers) not made public by the middle of December 1968, as had been announced? As usual, speculation brought forth various reasons, but the truth probably lies in a combination of them.

First, on December 2, 1968, Alginate Industries Limited, through its general manager, Ralph Merton, announced (curiously and/or appropriately at this time) that the islands had large quantities of marine algae which, processed into chemical products, could revolutionize the economy of the islands by bringing in 12 million pounds annually. Merton suggested that when the algae supply in the northern hemisphere ran out, Britain could have recourse to the only large supply left in the world, in the Falkland Islands. He expected his company to begin the mechanical collection of the algae in five years.

Second, an interesting but perhaps counterproductive news conference was held between the British newsmen who had accompanied Chalfont to Argentina and Ambassador Ezequiel F. Pereyra, in charge of the Malvinas section of the Argentine Foreign Ministry. Pereyra, after stating that the Argentine government's feeling toward the inhabitants of the Malvinas assured them of complete security, noted that 140 settlers in the Malvinas had British passports and 800 had Commonwealth passports, but that the latter were forbidden to emigrate to the United Kingdom. On the other hand, there were 20,000 people in Argentina with British passports, and it would make little difference if a few more came to Argentina. He pointed out that a Welsh community had existed in Patagonia for over a century, living peacefully and without problems and still keeping their customs and language. In fact, when the film "How Green Was My Valley" was made, those involved in the filming went to that Argentine region to see what a Welsh community was like.

A change of sovereignty would not affect property ownership, and the form of government would possibly be along the lines of the Argentine *municipalidad*, a form of government in which the natives would have a voice and that would work with and for the community. Economically, the islands would be provided with oil and gas directly from the oil fields at Comodoro Rivadavia, instead of imported coal from the United Kingdom. Also, probably tourism would be fostered and a large international hotel constructed on the islands. And there would be other ways to better the economic situation of the islands.

Asked if Argentines were interested in going to the islands, he answered that the government had received letters from Argentines interested in going there, even one from a nun who wanted to establish a school there. He noted that many people who went from England to the Malvinas later moved to Argentina, where they were like any other citizens, working, studying, and investing in properties. He said that of the approximately 2,000 people in the islands the majority had not been born there but had gone by contract to work there, and therefore this was not a problem of self-determination but simply a question of sovereignty. In any case, if the transfer of sovereignty were made, Argentina would certainly look out for the interests of the people in the islands so that they would not suffer from the transition.

Asked what Argentina would do if the transfer did not take place and the dispute over sovereignty persisted for another ten years, Pereyra replied that the English did not understand how the Argentines envisaged the Malvinas, the fundamental problem of Argentine existence.

But at the moment, he said, the question was the self-determination of the inhabitants of the islands. In that regard you had to consider the isolation of the islands and the character of the people there. But at first the population there had been Argentine, fully and legally established there. It had been uprooted by force in 1833, taken to Montevideo, and replaced by British subjects. The principle of self-determination should have been applied then. However, Resolution 1514 of the United Nations embraced two principles: self-determination and territorial integrity. It was this latter principle that applied to the Malvinas. They were a part of the territory of Argentina geologically and physically, as well as historically, according to Pereyra.

Third, early in 1968 the "Falklands Lobby" was organized to counteract any attempt to return the Falklands to Argentina. Its name was the Falkland Islands Emergency Committee (the term Emergency was dropped in 1973). It consisted mainly of members of Parliament, islanders, Falkland Islands Company officials, and one Falkland Islands landowner. In March 1968, the *Times* published a letter from four islanders headed by A. G. Barton, the retired manager of the Falkland Islands Company in Stanley, saying that Britain was about to hand over the islands to Argentina, which would force the islanders to "submit to a foreign language, law, customs, and culture" (The *Sunday Times* of London Insight Team 1982: p. 46).

The lobby contained some members of Parliament who were vehemently opposed to the cession of the islands. A barrage of questions was thrown at Chalfont, who had difficulty fielding them. The debate brought forth sensational accounts in the conservative newspapers, with the *Daily Telegraph* headlining "The Islands That Britain May Give Away," and the *Daily Express* trumpeting that the islands' coat of arms was "the shield of freedom." The coat of arms depicts a sheep (The *Sunday Times* of London Insight Team, 1982: p. 47).

Fourth, and the immediate reason for the failure of the negotiations, was the strong opposition in Parliament organized by the Falkland Islands Committee. With the return of Chalfont to London on December 2, 1968, discussions of his trip began in Parliament. In spite of Chalfont's declaration upon landing at the airport that he had not discussed the future of the islands with the Argentines during his short stay in Buenos Aires, that sovereignty should not be ceded to Argentina without the express wishes of the islanders, and that he had not stated that the economy of the islands would improve under Argentine rule, and indeed that the announcement of Alginate Industries had pleased him immensely, the opposition attacked him and his colleagues viciously the next day. Led by Edward Heath, Conservative leader in the House of Commons, and the former Conservative prime minister, Sir Alec Douglas-Home, the opposition launched an all-out attack on the Labour government of Prime Minister Harold Wilson, on the basis of Chalfont's report to Parliament.

Labourites pointed out that the negotiations had begun at the request of the United Nations, that Chalfont had not tried to sway the islanders to accept Argentine rule but had told them that Britain would not oppose their becoming Argentine if they so wished, that the House of Commons would in the future perhaps have to confront a transfer of the islands to Argentina (a statement that caused a tumult in Conservative ranks, with cries demanding the breaking off of all negotiations with Argentina immediately), and that there was still much to be discussed with Argentine negotiators.

The Conservatives, seeing here a good pretext for a Parliamentary fight that would bring them public support, kept up the battle for several days, not letting the government rest from denying charge after charge. They openly charged government leaders with lying about handing the islanders over to a foreign country. The violent, acrimonious attacks on the Labourites even compelled Foreign Minister Michael Stewart to cut short an official visit to India and return home to defend the government's position. Stewart tried to assure the Conservatives that his government was very conscious of the close ties between the islands and Great Britain and of their loyalty to the crown. For that reason it had insisted on the importance of the wishes of the islanders. The executive council of the islands, he declared, had accepted that Britain had been acting in good faith in its conversations with Argentina and that whatever agreement might be reached, there would be no transfer of sovereignty against the wishes of the islanders. Stewart's use of the term *wishes* was to prove a critical turning point in the negotiations over the islands.

Douglas-Home, the former Conservative prime minister, demanded that the question of sovereignly not figure in future negotiations with Argentina. Stewart replied that he could not assure it, causing a tumultuous outcry from the Conservative benches. Stewart insisted that assurances given the islanders securely established their position but that in spite of this basic disagreement, the two governments must try to reach an agreement if at all possible.

Other Conservatives wanted to be assured that future negotiations would discuss only such topics as commerce and the establishment of communications between Argentina and the islands. Stewart repeated his promise that sovereignty would be transferred only under the conditions already announced. Heath insisted that the Labourites wanted to continue negotiations in order to find a means whereby they could transfer sovereignty to Argentina, after which the transfer would be presented to the islanders to see if they were satisfied. Stewart retorted that the government's wish was to eradicate the difficulties existing between the islanders and Argentina and to follow the instructions of the United Nations and eliminate disputes over the islands in that organization. To do this it would be necessary to discuss the question of sovereignty. He accused Heath of deliberately twisting everything he had said. When asked what good purpose would be served by continuing negotiations with Argentina, Stewart replied that although the British government should maintain its position, an agreement with Argentina could bring beneficial results to the islanders and better their relations with Latin America in general. All along Stewart had repeated that no pressure had been put on the islanders to accept Argentine sovereignty.

An international side effect of the Falklands negotiations was the rejection by the British government of a proposed cession of the Channel Islands to France at this time (December 4, 1968), when a member of the House of Lords suggested that if sovereignty over the Falkland Islands were transferred to Argentina, it would not be long before the Channel Islands were given to France. To this Chalfont replied that the government had no such intentions.

In the midst of this agitated, sometimes violent and vituperative debate, a note of humor presented itself when a Labourite rose and suggested that the Conservatives who were so interested in the well-being of the islands might do well to spend six months there, because upon their return they might have different points of view. This incident, occurring amid shouts of hilarity, demonstrates how little the British population knew or cared about the islands, although in Parliament they were used for political purposes.

The "position of agreement" was not presented to the United Nations. Parliament refused to accept it on the basis that it was not the policy of the British government to transfer the sovereignty over the Falkland Islands against the wishes of their inhabitants. In December 1968, José María Ruda, Argentine ambassador to the United Nations, stated in a debate over colonialism that in spite of some progress in the negotiations between Argentina and Britain, Argentina could not accept Britain's contention that the wishes of the islanders superseded Argentina's sovereignty over the islands. Lord Caradon, head of the British delegation to the United Nations, replied that Britain was sovereign in the Falklands and that that sovereignty would not be ceded against the wishes of the islanders. Ruda insisted that the wishes of the islanders could never supersede the national unity and integrity of the territory under dispute: that is, that the Malvinas had always been and still were a legal part of Argentina.

However, in spite of obvious differences and conflicting views the two countries, through their foreign ministers, announced that negotiations would continue. The Argentine and British ambassadors to the United Nations so informed Secretary-General U Thant on December 19, 1968. To the chagrin of the British government the Argentine ambassador to the United Nations had announced three days earlier that Britain had not been disposed at that moment to put an official mark on the agreement that the two countries had reached, but that new conversations were to begin in London soon.

An Agreement on Communications and Transportation

Since Lord Chalfont's trip to the Malvinas and Buenos Aires there had been suggestions on both sides to improve intercourse between the islands and the Argentine mainland for the good of the islands, which, even many British subjects agreed, were far too isolated because of British neglect. Even Lord Chalfont supported these suggestions in principle. The islanders had no newspaper and depended solely on the radio for outside news. They lacked adequate educational opportunities and medical services. In general they led an isolated existence. Improving ties with Argentina, it was thought, would bring them closer to the outside world and provide better and more rapid medical services, educational advantages, cultural opportunities, and the like. There were those who even thought it might be more advantageous to market the islands' wool crop through Uruguay or Argentina. For obvious reasons Argentina was willing to help in establishing more adequate contacts with the islands.

But it was not until November 21, 1969, that the two countries agreed to hold special conversations for the purpose of providing forms of free movement and communication between the Malvinas and the Argentine mainland in both directions. On April 1, 1970, talks began in both London and Buenos Aires. On July 14, 1970, the British Foreign Office received some Argentine proposals for the establishment of free communication between the two areas but refused to reply to them. Finally, a year later, representatives from the two countries met in Buenos Aires from June 21 to June 30, 1971, and on July 1 initialed a joint declaration for the execution of measures leading to the establishment of communications between the islands and the Argentine mainland. These measures included telecommunications, postal correspondence, legal papers needed for traveling, ship schedules, air travel (Argentina agreed to build a temporary airstrip on the islands and opened it in 1971, but Britain did not build the permanent airstrip, as agreed upon, until 1974), and the like.

Islanders were invited to suggest forms of communication and transportation they desired. Argentina offered to establish weekly flights between Stanley and Comodoro Rivadavia on the Patagonian coast. It offered to transport mail, cargo, and passengers, using hydroplanes until an adequate airstrip could be built. It also offered technical aid in agriculture and medical services as well as educational and cultural exchange, all fields in which Argentina was far advanced and in which the islands were almost completely deficient. Argentine officials were careful to point out that they did not wish to inundate the islands educationally or culturally or in any other way.

The Argentines leaned over backward to win the good will of the islanders. The air fare between Stanley and Comodoro Rivadavia (a distance of 960 kilometers) would be only five pounds, with the Argentine government subsidizing any additional expense over that amount. Although Britain agreed to establish a regular maritime passenger, mail, and cargo service, Argentina suggested that the *Darwin* of the Falkland Islands Company, which made the sea voyage of 1,900 kilometers (1,140 miles) between the islands and Montevideo, Uruguay, only once a month but whose services were to be discontinued at the end of the year for economic reasons, could make trips between Stanley and Argentine ports. Moreover, it suggested that its naval transport, the *Bahía Buen Suceso*, could stop over at Stanley on its regular monthly trips between Ushuaia and Comodoro Rivadavia.

In addition, Argentina was willing to make the paper work easy. It provided for a travel document, printed in both Spanish and English, which guaranteed freedom of movement within Argentina for residents of the islands and served as the only documentation necessary for Argentine residents traveling in the islands. The document would not carry fingerprints or indicate the nationality of the bearer. It would state the name of the place in the islands where the bearer was born, but not the British name of the islands. In this way Argentina would not have "Falkland Islands" on an official Argentine document. Surprisingly enough, the British representatives agreed to this. The document would have no expiration date, and in addition to letting the bearer travel throughout Argentina, it permitted him to reside permanently in the country and to bring in any articles and baggage free of duty, and his automobile temporarily. If he planned to become a permanent resident of Argentina, all his goods would be allowed to enter Argentina free of charge. The British government agreed that all normal baggage of Argentines wishing to travel in the Falklands would be free of customs duties and that Argentines desiring to become residents of the islands could bring in duty free all their personal effects, one automobile, and their home furnishings for one time only.

Argentina was also willing to take measures to exempt native-born islanders from military service in Argentina if they desired to live there. When asked why Argentina intended to discriminate against islanders traveling with British passports, the Argentine delegates said that it was exactly for that reason: that they were *British* passports. But they assured the British delegates that no islanders traveling with British passports would have their passports confiscated upon reaching Argentina. Beginning in 1972, Argentina would also offer fifteen scholarships to islanders wishing to attend school in Argentina. Only two students a year were given scholarships to continue their studies in Britain, although if they had the money, they might be admitted to British schools in Montevideo (Crosby 1981: p. 69).

The joint declaration included a statement that it would be approved by the governments of the two countries and presented to the United Nations in accordance with that body's Resolution 2065. A special consultative committee of representatives from the Argentine Ministry of Foreign Relations, the British embassy in Buenos Aires, and the Malvinas was established to deal with any questions arising from the provisions of the agreement. Another meeting was to be held in Stanley in 1972. A special provision stated that if either government decided to declare the agreement null and void, it would have to notify the other government six months before the decision went into effect.

At the end of the conversations, the chief of the British delegation stated that he was accustomed to long and difficult negotiations but had never participated in such courteous and cooperative sessions as the ones just terminated. He thanked the Argentine delegation for the cordial and generous hospitality given the British negotiators during their stay in Buenos Aires. It appears that Argentina obtained what it had long desired: a foothold in the Malvinas, or at least a chance to show the islanders that Argentines were not ogres.

Whether the Argentines had outwitted the British is very questionable. The agreement must be considered as something that many Britons had also desired, including Lord Chalfont. Parliament and British papers did not clamor against any special concessions made to Argentina as they had upon Chalfont's return from the Malvinas. There was no lobbying against the agreement by the Falkland Islands Committee, as far as is known. Also, apparently, the Falklands Islands Company did not complain; was this because it had been relieved of heavy expense in sending the *Darwin* to Montevideo once a month?

It is true that Argentina lived some anxious moments when, immediately after the initialing of the agreement, London newspapers reported that the British Foreign Office had announced that Argentina had renounced its claims to sovereignty over the Falklands. The Argentine Ministry of Foreign Relations immediately denied the news account and stated that Argentina affirmed categorically its sovereignty over the

Malvinas. Why was the news account given out? Why, if it had not been given out by the British Foreign Office, was it printed? Or was it a ploy of that office to see what the reaction of Argentina would be? Or did someone in the office really believe that the new agreement actually included Argentina's giving up its claims to the Malvinas, when in fact it seemed to indicate just the opposite?

Whatever the reason, the news account did not deter the two governments from officially signing the agreement. On August 5, 1971, the Argentine minister of foreign relations and the British chargé d'affaires in Buenos Aires signed the agreement initialed on July 1. It was called a "joint declaration" and included a statement that neither nation by signing it renounced its claim to sovereignty over the Falkland Islands (Las Islas Malvinas). Either side could renounce the agreement by giving six months notice. On August 12, the two countries informed the United Nations of the agreement.

Upon presenting his formal report to Secretary-General U Thant, the Argentine ambassador to the United Nations, Carlos Ortiz de Rozas, called attention to the fact that, although both countries considered the agreement very satisfactory, it in no way constituted a definitive solution of the dispute over sovereignty over the Malvinas. Regarding this question the two countries would continue to negotiate until a final decision was reached. Ortiz de Rozas pointed out that the agreement showed how, in a climate of mutual understanding and trust, two countries with a long tradition of friendship could and should solve their problems within the framework of the Charter of the United Nations. He added that he was convinced that in the not too distant future the Malvinas would be returned to Argentina by means of an agreement satisfactory to both countries. Glowing words, but probably justified at the time. As had been planned, Argentina and Great Britain held another round of conversations to implement the establishment of communications between Argentina and the islands in Stanley in November 1972. The event coincided with the inauguration of the temporary airstrip built by the Argentine air force. Other minor details were ironed out concerning the opening of communications between the islands and the Argentine mainland.

It appeared as if Argentina and Great Britain had entered a period of good relations. The Conservative government of the United Kingdom seemed to be happy with the establishment of communications between the islands and the Argentine mainland. This was in fact a great relief because of the growing isolation of the Falklands with the suspension of the monthly trip of the *Darwin* between Stanley and Montevideo. It seems that the British government thought that the agreement was all that was needed to solve the problem between Argentina and the United Kingdom. British officials did not seem to understand or did not want to understand the Argentine position: The agreement on communications was to be only the beginning of further negotiations concerning sovereignty. Britain thought the communications agreement was the principal problem and had been solved; Argentina thought of it only as a separate gesture, a side issue to the main problem, the question of sovereignty over the islands.

9

Negotiations Become More Difficult

Britain Delays Negotiations and Argentina Becomes Impatient

In April 1973, Argentine Foreign Minister Eduardo McLoughlin, before the Third Extraordinary Assembly of the Organization of American States, strongly condemned the remnants of colonialism in the New World, emphasizing the case of the Malvinas. Argentina's legal claim to the islands, he said, conditioned Argentina's relations with other countries whenever this claim might be affected. He accused Great Britain of dilatory tactics and attempts to negate the meaning of the negotiations originating out of United Nations Resolution 2065 to decide the sovereignty of the islands.

In the same month, in a meeting at the British Foreign Office in London, Britain refused to negotiate the question of sovereignty, and the conference broke up immediately. Britain's stand continued to be that it would never give up the islands without the consent of the inhabitants. The British account of the meeting described it as useful and positive, a description used frequently of later meetings, even when nothing "useful" or "positive" had been decided upon. In this meeting a few minor matters concerning the air service between Stanley and Comodoro Rivadavia were also discussed. But during the meetings in early May 1973, communications were not even discussed; this suggests that only the question of sovereignty came up. The British Foreign Office issued no statement about these meetings in May except to say that the conversations would continue in the future.

In August 1973, Argentina informed the United Nations that negotiations over the Malvinas had been virtually paralyzed because of the attitude of the British government. It accused the British of pretending that the discussions concerning communications took the place of discussions over sovereignty, a substitution Argentina could never accept. It went so far as to accuse the British of trying to belittle the true nature of the negotiations, negating the terminology and real concepts that they had formerly accepted and thus circumventing Resolution 2065.

This they did, Argentina contended, by thrusting aside the spirit of cooperation so necessary to a just solution of the problem. In fact, it declared, the British attitude was delaying the whole process of decolonization. Argentina, on the other hand, in all these negotiations had shown innumerable proofs of patience, in spite of the legitimate impatience and emotional fervor the Argentine people felt in regard to the recovery of what they considered a part of their national territory. Argentina asked the United Nations to urge Britain to accelerate negotiations regarding sovereignty over the islands.

On August 21, 1973, the United Nations special committee dealing with decolonization voted unanimously in favor of an acceleration of the negotiations. The committee's resolution stated that eight years had passed since Resolution 2065 had been adopted, and nothing had been done to solve the problem. Therefore, it urged the two countries to continue the negotiations without delay and to inform the secretary-general and the General Assembly of the results of the negotiations as soon as possible, and not later than the twenty-ninth period of sessions. Eight years had gone by since the adoption of Resolution 2065, and nine more were to elapse before Argentina, losing its patience with Great Britain, unfortunately thought it had to take matters into its own hands and invade the islands.

England answered Argentina's accusations by saying that it was ready to continue conversations, and that it hoped that relations between the islands and Argentina would continue to progress on a firmer basis. It seems that Argentina was right in accusing Britain of trying to substitute discussions over communications for the real question: sovereignty over the islands.

In October 1973, the foreign minister of Argentina, Alberto J. Vignes, made a long speech on decolonization to the General Assembly of the United Nations, in which he made special reference to the Malvinas. In spite of the blocks Britain had placed in the road to decolonization, he said, Argentina would not change its policy toward the inhabitants of the islands, which was one of respect for their interests. Argentina would continue to negotiate, but he warned that this procedure could not be prolonged indefinitely and thus serve as a means of maintaining the status quo. If the negative attitude of the United Kingdom led to a dead end, the Argentine goverment would have to reexamine its policy. In that case the United Nations would have to decide how far the intentions of Resolution 2065 had been deflected because of the lack of a true spirit of cooperation in one of the parties to the negotiations.

Britain informed the secretary-general of the United Nations on October 24, 1973, that it was prepared shortly to renew discussions with Argentina dealing with the question of the Falklands, but that Britain had no doubts about its sovereignty over the islands. It was happy that the Argentine foreign minister had said that Argentina was ready to continue along the road of negotiation. Britain also refused to believe that the Argentine Republic desired a solution at the cost of contravening the expressed wishes of the inhabitants of the islands. Here again, it must be emphasized, Britain used the term *wishes* of the inhabitants, where Argentina always used the term *interests*.

Argentina's reply to Britain, given in a long representation to the secretary-general of the United Nations on November 5, 1973, was that the question revolved around Resolution 2065, which in 1965 had asked Great Britain and Argentina to proceed without delay to the negotiations recommended by the special committee for the purpose of finding a peaceful solution to the problem, taking into account the interests of the people of the Malvinas. Argentina noted that the resolution did not enjoin taking into account the wishes of the people of the islands. Nor did it say anything about the right of self-determination. These were not casual provisions, according to Argentina, but, on the contrary, were provisions on which the General Assembly had wisely fixed the bases for a logical solution of a problem that presented peculiar characteristics, with no parallels or analogies with other colonial questions that still existed in the world.

Argentina repeated that it was ready to renew negotiations on the sovereignty of the islands. However, the question of communications between the islands and the Argentine mainland was a concurrent question and not a part of the negotiations concerning sovereignty. It must not and could not condition or delay, still less be substituted for, the question of negotiations over the sovereignty of the islands. On November 21, 1973, Carlos Ortiz de Rozas, the Argentine ambassador to the United Nations, during a debate in the General Assembly on decolonization, requested that negotiations between Britain and Argentina over the Falklands be reopened.

In spite of Argentina's insistence that sovereignty should be discussed in the conversations between the two countries and Britain's refusal to do so, the Argentine government and the authorities of the islands seemed to cooperate in a friendly manner. In November 1973, a large delegation went to Stanley to commemorate the first anniversary of the inauguration of the aluminum airstrip built by the Argentine air force. The delegation consisted of various members of the air force, including the chief of staff; of the Argentine Ministry of Foreign Affairs; of the Argentine national petroleum administration; of the national highway administration; of the naval transport system; and of the British embassy in Buenos Aires. The governor of the Falklands attended the ceremonies at the airstrip in ceremonial garb.

Two receptions were held, one given by Líneas Aéreas del Estado (LADE), a branch of the Argentine Air force that had built the airstrip and was in charge of the air service between the islands and the Argentine mainland, and the other by the governor of the islands, held in his residence. Argentina pointed out at the time that for almost two years it had had an established air service to the islands, first by way of amphibious planes and then by land after the airstrip was completed; that it had taken over providing the islands with oil and gas; and that it had provided medical services for the islanders. It hoped that more could be done for them in the line of roads, education, and naval transport. Argentine newspapers noted that in spite of delays in the cooperation promised by Great Britain for improving the lot of the islanders, Argentina's efforts to help them had been warmly received and appreciated, as exemplified by the ever increasing numbers of islanders visiting the mainland and by the introduction of Spanish as the second language in the islands' schools.

In December 1973, the General Assembly of the United Nations passed Resolution 3160, urging Argentina and the United Kingdom to renew without delay the negotiations over the Falkland Islands. The resolution made special note of Argentina's attempts over several years to get the question solved. The resolution was passed by a vote of ninety-nine votes in favor, none against, and fourteen abstentions, including those of the United States and Great Britain. Again nothing was done. Britain insisted that it could not negotiate against the wishes of the islanders. Argentina insisted that it could, because Resolution 2065 had not mentioned the wishes of the islanders but only their interests, which Argentina was willing to enhance and protect, as it had already amply proved.

Perón's return to the presidency in late 1973 brought a return of jingoistic appeal to the masses, with emphasis on nationalism and passionate patriotism. Perón's followers in congress demanded the return of the Malvinas. Street demonstrations did the same. When in June 1974, the United Kingdom proposed an Anglo-Argentine condominium control over the Falklands, Argentina rejected it offhand on the basis that Argentine sovereignty over the islands was not negotiable and could never be shared with another country.

Yet Argentina continued to help the islanders. In August 1974, the Argentine mission at the United Nations announced an agreement with Britain to permit Argentina to expand the fuel plant in the Malvinas and other measures to improve commercial relations between the two areas. In September Britain's foreign minister, James Callaghan, praised the good will shown by Argentina in getting the islands' population to visit Argentina and get to know it better.

However, in October 1974, Ambassador Ivor Richard, chief of the British mission to the United Nations, repeated the British thesis that all negotiations regarding sovereignty over the islands would have to be dealt with in accordance with the wishes of the islanders. He hoped that the contacts established between the two countries could be carried forward in accordance with those wishes. This insistence on the islanders' wishes went contrary to Argentina's argument that the wishes of the islanders would mean self-determination, a rule that Argentina had rejected as applied to the Malvinas, as had the General Assembly of the United Nations and that body's special committee on decolonization. Argentina immediately rejected Ivor Richard's presentation, stating that it proved that the only solution of the sovereignty problem was the return of the islands to Argentina.

Oil Troubles the Water
and Argentina Becomes More Impatient

At this time the question of exploitation of the islands' natural resources was receiving more and more attention. At the end of November 1974, two members of the Argentine senate demanded that Argentina issue a proclamation that the Malvinas and the continental shelf were legally Argentine. The reason for this was a declaration by Michael Clark Hutchison, a member of the British Parliament and also of the Falkland Islands Committee, that Great Britain would postpone any decision concerning the islands until the results of petroleum exploration there could be analyzed. It is true that oil companies from Canada and the United States had requested permission to explore for oil in the islands. But to this day no oil deposits have been found there. In fact, Professor Donald H. Griffiths, a geophysicist in the Department of Geology of the University of Birmingham, England, stated at the time that it was foolish to believe that there were any massive petroleum resources in the area. So far, Professor Griffiths's appraisal, which has been supported by other petroleum engineers and geologists, has proved to be correct. The nearest oil discovered in this area has been along the Argentine continental shelf.

The talk of oil brought a new Argentine declaration to the United Nations. On December 13, 1974, the Argentine delegate to the United Nations, Ambassador Fernando Fernández Escalante, reaffirmed Argentine sovereignty over the Malvinas and asked that they be returned to Argentina. He asked it in the name of Argentine territorial integrity. According to the rules of international law, Fernández Escalante continued, the natural resources of the islands belonged to the people settled there by Vernet, who had been illegally removed by force. Therefore those natural resources belonged to the country of which the islands had been a part at the time the population had been removed from it, that is, Argentina. Since this was an inalienable right, all the natural resources of the islands should be held in reserve until the question of the return of the islands to Argentina was settled. Argentina, he said, hoped that the negotiations with the United Kingdom would come to a happy end as soon as possible so that justice could be restored.

The diplomatic situation became more difficult very quickly. Argentina's demand that sovereignty be discussed in negotiations and its insistence that the only solution to the problem was the return of the Malvinas to Argentina seemed to make the British government more adamant in rejecting this solution and demanding more strongly that the wishes of the islanders be taken into account. This the Argentines considered a weak excuse for holding on to the islands, especially because rumors now began to spread that there might be huge deposits of petroleum in the region—deposits as large as those of Kuwait, in fact. This put a different light on the question. On January 3, 1975, the Argentine foreign minister, Alberto J. Vignes, told a group of foreign correspondents that although in the case of the Malvinas the only solution was the restitution of Argentine territory usurped by a foreign power, Argentina had decided to follow the road of negotiations in keeping with the pacifist tradition of the country in trying to solve international controversies. This is true, for Argentines are proud of their use of arbitration in settling international problems. In 1878, by accepting U.S. arbitration, Argentina lost land to Paraguay, and in 1891 to Brazil. In 1902, by accepting a British arbitration award, it lost land to Chile.

After another declaration by the British Foreign Office that the islands were British and therefore Britain could exploit any resources on the continental shelf of the archipelago, several members of the Argentine congress demanded that the president of Argentina, María Estela Martínez de Perón, who as vice president had succeeded to the presidency upon the death of her husband on July 1, 1974, take drastic measures to prevent further encroachments by Britain. Members of the *peronista* majority in congress led the assault, some of them even suggesting that it was time to occupy the islands, diplomacy having failed because of British contradictions and lies. One deputy, Fausto Mombelli of the southern province of Chubut, said that Argentina must take over the Malvinas to avoid the interminable diplomatic discussions that led nowhere; indecisiveness would bring only remorse. On March 20, 1975, the foreign minister stated that Argentina recognized no right of a foreign government to claim title to or exercise exploration rights or to exploit minerals or oil in the Malvinas.

A little later an unusual incident occurred to fan Argentine ardor to get back the Malvinas. In accordance with the communications agreement of 1971, the Argentine Office of Sports and Tourism had been promoting cruises to the Antarctic and the Malvinas. No incident had occurred on the first five cruises, but on the sixth the cruise ship, the *Regina Prima*, was not allowed to land its 500 passengers at Stanley because the captain refused to raise the Union Jack on the ship's mast while it was docked in Stanley. He had express orders not to do it, because Argentine officials considered the islands Argentine. On the previous five cruises the Union Jack had not been raised. Perhaps because of an oversight, the British officials had said nothing. But this time they did. Following his orders, the captain refused to raise the flag and sailed the ship home. When it returned to Buenos Aires, there was a huge crowd to welcome it. As it docked a navy band struck up the national anthem, which the crowd sang, and then there were several patriotic speeches by government officials.

Ever vigilant about its rights to the islands, Argentina a little later protested to the United States when the latter placed the islands on a list of areas scheduled, as English colonies, to receive preferential tariff treatment by the United States. After being advised by the Argentine ambassador in Washington, Alejandro Orfila, that under international law this could not be done because the islands were an area in dispute, the United States removed them from the list and called the occurrence a bureaucratic mistake that would be corrected immediately.

To confuse the matter of sovereignty even more, the question of the Falklands came up in a peculiar way in September 1975, at the annual congress of the Interparliamentary Union in London attended by members of parliaments of seventy nations. The Argentine delegation of seven presented a resolution to the group asking that it consider the Falklands not as a colony but as a territory occupied by Great Britain. An Argentine senator, Luis León, declared that through negotiations better relations and communications had been established between Argentina and the islands in accordance with resolutions of the United Nations, but that Britain had refused to help resolve the vital question of the sovereignty of the islands.

A group of islanders then came into the meeting hall and shouted that they feared an Argentine invasion. Perhaps as an explanation of this unusual action, a British delegate, Lord Newall, told newsmen that in a closed meeting of the congress's committee on projects, Senator León had hinted that Argentina might have to appeal to force to recuperate the islands. Newall said he regretted the threat, and called it ridiculous and pathetic.

In a previous debate before the parliamentarians León had accused the British of international piracy and had stated that if Argentina's patience ran out, it might have to tell the United Nations and the world that its dignity could no longer support the situation. The committee on projects did pass a resolution expressing its firm desire that the United Nations seek a rapid solution to the problem, in keeping with the norms and principles of international law and the resolutions of the United Nations.

At the same time that they were reporting these events at the meeting in London, Argentine newspapers, possibly with inward glee, were reporting a *Washington Post* account of the mass removal by force (they called it *secuestro en masa*—massive kidnapping) of the population of the British island of Diego García in the Indian Ocean to other islands. According to news reports, in this case the principle of self-determination of the inhabitants of the islands had not been taken into account by Britain. Yet Britain wanted to use self-determination as an excuse for not returning the Malvinas to Argentina. The island of Diego García was later leased to the United States as a naval base.

All these incidents, widely reported in Argentina, may well have been the first hints of what could happen later. Should Britain have taken more notice of them? By doing so, could it have avoided the invasion of the Malvinas by Argentina in April 1982? León's statement in London demonstrates the impatience of the Argentines, who had been negotiating with the British since 1965, and after seemingly obtaining some concessions in the way of better communications with the Falklanders, had been thwarted in taking the negotiations a step further and discussing the question of sovereignty. Did Argentina's patience finally run out?

The Shackleton Mission Heightens the Conflict

Argentina's fears that no solution would be reached were aroused even more in October 1975, when reports reached Buenos Aires that Britain was sending out a mission to investigate the possibilities of exploiting the natural resources of the Falklands. According to the reports, the Labour government of Britain was confident that Argentina would cooperate in any program for the exploitation of the marine resources around the islands. In the meantime the Labour government would stall Canadian and U.S. interests that wanted to obtain options in that region. The mission, under the direction of Lord Shackleton, whose father had been an Antarctic expert who died and was buried on the island of South Georgia, was to investigate the resources of the colony and its dependencies: wool production, agriculture, the necessity of diversification, fishing potential, and the possibilities of developing mineral and oil production.

On October 22, 1975, the Argentine Ministry of Foreign Affairs declared that it had given no official permission to the Shackleton undertaking because the question of the Malvinas was in process of negotiation as recommended by the United Nations, and therefore both sides should abstain from unilaterally undertaking any new action. However, the foreign minister did not want to interpret Britain's action as provocative.

At this time Argentina acquired a champion in England in the person of Professor Glyn Williams, director of the Department of Social Theory of the University of North Wales, who in a letter to the *Times* (London) of October 27, 1975, took issue with it over the question of the sovereignty of the Falklands. He pointed out that half of the islands' population of about 2,000 were employed by the Falklands Islands Company. This company exercised strong pressure on Parliament through a handful of conservatives who did not want the islands returned to Argentina. He accused this group of spreading false rumors against Argentina and against the Argentine senator, Hipólito Solari Yrigoyen, who as a negotiator for Argentina had been in England for some time and had publicly declared the Shackleton mission in conflict with Resolutions 2065 and 3160 of the United Nations. Williams thought that under Argentine rule the Falklanders would improve their lot, for if thousands of British subjects and Anglo-Argentines lived happily in Argentina, why could not about 800 people in the islands not employed by the company be happy living under Argentine rule? He might have added that through the years many Falklanders had migrated to Australia, New Zealand, South Africa, Great Britain, Chile, and even Argentina.

That a change of pace was taking place is shown in the statement made at the end of 1975 by the Argentine ambassador to the United Nations, Carlos Ortiz de Rozas, that the limits of Argentina's impatience should not be misjudged when it dealt with an obstinate and unjustified refusal to negotiate. Was this another inkling of what was to come in April 1982? The Shackleton mission rankled the Argentine government. On January 4, 1976, the president, Mrs. Perón, had a three-hour meeting with the commanders of the armed forces and the ministers of the interior, foreign relations, and defense. After the meeting the foreign minister announced officially to the Argentine people that the government, together with the armed forces and other governmental institutions that made up the Argentine state, shared the people's zeal for the protection of the dignity and rights of their nation and would act without haste but with all persistence, prudence, and energy necessary to obtain justice for the nation (*La Nación* [Buenos Aires], January 5, 1976).

Now things began to move rapidly. On January 16 the Juridical Committee of the OAS unanimously passed a formal declaration (1) that Argentina had unquestionable rights to the Malvinas and that the fundamental question to solve was the procedure whereby they would be returned; (2) that the Shackleton mission denoted a unilateral innovation on the part of Great Britain and therefore contravened Resolution 2065 and 3160 of the United Nations; (3) that the presence of foreign naval vessels in waters adjacent to American states was a menace to the peace and security of the continent as well as a flagrant violation of international law regarding nonintervention; and (4) that all these actions implied a hostile effort to silence the claims of the Argentine government and to obstruct the progress of the negotiations recommended by the General Assembly of the United Nations. The committee noted that the United Nations resolutions contemplated an agreement between the two governments to hasten the negotiations to establish a legitimate sovereignty over the islands. This was a juridical signpost both governments must heed. Therefore, Britain's unilateral breaking of the negotiations indicated a violation not only of the resolutions but also of the spirit of the contracted agreement.

On January 17, 1976, Derek Rosslyn Ashe, the British ambassador in Argentina, presented a note from British Foreign Minister L. James Callaghan to Foreign Minister Raúl A. Quijano of Argentina. In it Britain requested a continuation of the economic cooperation between the two countries to help the Falklands but deemed the dispute over sovereignty unproductive. As a result Quijano promptly ordered the Argentine ambassador to London, who at the moment was in Buenos Aires, not to return to Britain for the time being. To Ashe, Quijano gave a reply to Callaghan's note asking that, in view of the situation, Ashe be withdrawn. The reasons given by Argentina for the withdrawal of its ambassador were the sending of the Shackleton mission and the British attitude in regard to the question of sovereignty.

According to the British government the Shackleton mission had been sent to do scientific, economic, social, and geological studies in the islands. Some commentators in Britain surmised that the expedition was sent to calm conservative opinion in Britain by proving that the islands had little economic potential and that it was foolish to enter new colonial ventures with little hope for financial gain. However that may be, the Argentines did not see the mission in that light. To them it was an insult added to previous refusals to discuss the question of sovereignty.

In February a serious incident took place that could have led to armed confrontations between the two countries. In December 1975, the chief of the Argentine naval staff had warned the British naval attaché in Buenos Aires that the RRS *Shackleton,* a supposedly unarmed British ship connected with the Shackleton mission (although at the time the British government denied it) and doing geophysical and geological studies in the area of the Malvinas, would be taken into custody if it were found without Argentine permission within the 200-mile limit of Argentine coastal waters. The 200-mile wide continental shelf of the Argentine coast included in Argentine eyes the waters surrounding the Malvinas. On February 4, 1976, the Argentine destroyer *Almirante Storni* intercepted the *Shackleton* seventy-eight miles south of the Malvinas.

The Argentine naval commander asked the captain of the *Shackleton* to heave to in order to let his crew inspect the cargo, but the British ship continued its voyage. The Argentine vessel then fired two shots over the *Shackleton's* bow, but it still refused to stop. It radioed that it had explosives on board for scientific purposes. To avoid loss of life the Argentine vessel ceased firing but ordered the *Shackleton* to steam to Ushuaia, the southernmost port of Argentina. Instead the *Shackleton* headed for Stanley, followed by the *Almirante Storni*, which it soon lost in a heavy fog. The *Shackleton* returned safely to Stanley. Argentine newspapers later learned that the governor of the islands, Neville French, had ordered the *Shackleton's* commander to return to Stanley, but also not to let any personnel of the Argentine destroyer board the ship and not to put the ship in any danger.

Argentina made a strong protest against what it considered an invasion of its coastal waters without its permission, pointing out that Britain had been warned not to let the *Shackleton* do this. The protest accused the British government of breaking Argentine law in studying the Argentine continental shelf without permission of the Argentine government. Argentina demanded that the persons responsible for this act be punished and that no similar incidents occur in the future. Britain also presented a strong protest to the Argentine government against the interception of the *Shackleton* and demanded that the *Almirante Storni* cease harassing the *Shackleton.* The note also stated tht Britain would be pleased to receive an explanation of the incident. Nothing developed from either protest.

Britain later said that the interception of the *Shackleton* had been planned for several weeks by the commanders of the armed forces of Argentina, but not by the government of Mrs. Perón. Admiral Emilio Eduardo Massera, the commander-in-chief of the Argentine navy, had ordered the firing but with special care that it not cause casualties or sink the ship. According to the British Joint Intelligence Committee, the event might have been part of a program of harassment by the Argentine military forces to compel the British government to negotiate, but the committee believed that the military commanders opposed an all-out invasion of the Malvinas (Franks 1983: pp. 11–12).

In May 1976, after Mrs. Perón had been overthrown by the armed forces and Lieutenant General Jorge Rafael Videla had become president, Argentina accused Britain of assuming a hostile attitude in regard to the problem of the Malvinas but reiterated that Argentina was willing to seek a pacific and definitive solution of the problem by means of negotiation as recommended by United Nations resolutions. The Argentine note countered one sent by Britain to the United Nations Commission on Decolonization in which Britain rejected the declaration of the Juridical Committee of the Organization of American States supporting the Argentine position.

The Argentine note was polite but firm, accusing Britain of adopting a negative attitude toward the negotiations, disregarding the resolutions of the international body, and unilaterally creating dangerous situations without regard for the repeated declarations of the Argentine government. The note then referred to the unfriendly act of Britain in despatching to the Malvinas the mission headed by Lord Shackleton to study the possibilities for economic exploitation of the islands in spite of the express opposition of Argentina.

In response to the Shackleton report's suggestion that eventually Argentina would have to cooperate in the exploitation of the natural resources of the archipelago, the Argentine foreign minister stated that the essential element in solving the Malvinas problem was the question of sovereignty.

A little later (September 1976) the United Nations Commission on Decolonization resolved by seventeen votes in favor, none opposed, and five abstentions that it recognized Argentina's attempt to facilitate the decolonization of the Malvinas, and again urged the two countries to accelerate negotiations over the sovereignty of the islands. Britain protested against the resolution, again on the basis that the principle of self-determination should apply, an argument that Argentina had always rejected. In December the General Assembly of the United Nations followed suit by passing a resolution thanking Argentina for its continuous efforts to facilitate decolonization and for promoting the well-being of the inhabitants of the islands. Again the United Nations asked the two countries to accelerate negotiations and to report to the Secretary General as soon as possible. The resolution passed by a vote of 102 to 1 (the negative vote was from the United Kingdom), with thirty-two abstentions.

In the same month a helicopter from the H.M.S. *Endurance* discovered an Argentine settlement on Southern Thule, in the South Sandwich Islands. Britain requested an explanation from Argentina. Argentina replied that the settlement was a scientific investigations center and was in Argentine jurisdiction. It also expressed the hope that nothing would cloud the auspicious prospects for negotiations. On January 19, 1976, Britain protested formally to Argentina against the establishment of the scientific station on Southern Thule without prior British permission, an act violating British sovereignty. However, the presence of Argentines on Southern Thule was not made public by the British government until May 1978. It also did nothing about the station, which was still there when the conflict over some Argentines in South Georgia erupted. According to British intelligence reports at the time, Argentina had expected British opposition to be stronger. If Britain had attacked the station, then Argentina would have attacked the British Antarctic Survey station on South Georgia. British intelligence also believed that at this time there was a contingency plan for a joint air force and navy invasion of the Falklands by Argentina at the same time that a campaign was begun in the United Nations to have Britain turn over the islands. But in February 1977 British intelligence declared that the Argentine navy's contingency plans had been shelved.

Anglo-Argentine Relations Continue Downhill

Early in February 1977, Britain decided that the time had arrived to see whether broad issues bearing on the future of the islands could be discussed with Argentina and the islanders. However, in any discussion Britain would defend its sovereignty over the islands and would guarantee that any proposals would be acceptable to the islanders. There would have to be full consultation with them at all times. At the same time, the government said that the recommendations for the islands in the Shackleton report would be too expensive to carry out, especially the amplification of the airport.

Later in February talks were to be held in Buenos Aires. Britain's Joint Intelligence Committee believed that if the talks broke down, Argentina might decide on armed action against British shipping or against the Falkland Islands. As a precaution, therefore, during the talks a British naval task force of six warships, three support ships, and a submarine would be in the Atlantic on its way from Gibraltar to the Caribbean.

On February 22 and 23, in Buenos Aires, Edward Rowlands, minister of state of the Foreign and Commonwealth Office, and Gualter O. Allara, a subsecretary in the Argentine Ministry of Foreign Relations, met to discuss all aspects of the future of the Falkland Islands, South Georgia Island, and the South Sandwich Islands. They were also supposed to establish terms of reference for future discussions, to be held in Rome in July. The two negotiators agreed to hold further talks concerning political relations, including the question of sovereignty, in relation to the Falklands, South Georgia, and the South Sandwich Islands, and concerning economic cooperation to help the islands in the future.

It appears that this was the first time Britain had displayed concern about the welfare of the islanders. Was this concern due to Shackleton's report, which had painted a grim picture of the economic future of the islands? The London *Times* admitted that the islands' future was bleak, but severely criticized the government for including the question of sovereignty in forthcoming discussions. The *Times* pointed out that the islands depended on Argentina for their fuel, communications, and medical assistance, but insisted that that did not mean the negotiations should include discussions of the sovereignty question, and strongly insisted that the Falklands were British.

No one in Britain seemed to ask the reason for the economic difficulties of the islands, or why the British government or, better still, the Falkland Islands Company had done little for them during so many years except to take huge profits out of them, as Lord Shackleton had reported. When Rowlands visited the Falklands briefly on his way to Buenos Aires he talked with a group of islanders of whom one had a small Argentine flag pinned to his jacket. In meetings with the two island councils Rowlands was told that they would "cooperate in working out terms of reference for formal negotiations covering political relations, including sovereignty, and economic cooperation, provided that the talks were covered by the 'sovereignty umbrella' and that the Islanders were fully consulted" (Franks 1983: p. 16).

Before the next round of talks, Dr. David Owen, the British foreign secretary, presented a paper to the Defence Committee stating that serious negotiations with Argentina had to be undertaken because the Falklands were militarily indefensible without the expenditure of huge sums needed elsewhere. The committee thought that Britain would be forced to fall back on a type of leaseback solution linked with a program of economic cooperation. Under the leaseback proposal, Britain would return the islands to Argentina, recognizing Argentine sovereignty over them, and then lease them back from Argentina immediately for a determined period and pay rent for them. This would at least give Argentina a "symbolic sovereignty" over the islands.

Dr. Owen and the committee thought that negotiations should be kept open to allow time to educate the English public and the islanders. The government believed it had to retain sovereignty as long as possible, even to the point of making concessions regarding the dependencies and the maritime resources in the region, until finally it had to recognize that only a leaseback program would satisfy the Argentines (Frank 1983: p. 17).

In the Rome conversations of July 13 to 15, Allara again represented Argentina and Hugh A. Cortazzi represented Britain. Again nothing was done, because when the Argentine delegate broached the subject of sovereignty, the British delegate said he was not authorized to discuss the point. Yet when they left the meeting the diplomats said that the discussions had been "positive."

Before the next round of talks it appeared that the Argentine position was hardening. Britain received reports that the Argentine government believed that Britain was using delaying tactics and that it should therefore take a hard line in the conversations. In September and October 1977, the Argentine navy had taken captive seven Soviet and two Bulgarian fishing vessels in Falklands waters, and had fired on one of the ships. Admiral Massera had ordered the sinking of the vessels if necessary. Massera had also said that vessels of other flags would be similarly treated if caught fishing in Argentine waters. The Argentine naval attaché in Britain was to inform the British government of this order. In the meantime, the British chargé d'affaires in Buenos Aires was battered with notes from the Argentine government asking that work groups be established and some evidence shown of interest in working out a solution. There was no doubt that the Argentines were disgusted with the lack of progress in the negotiations.

In November 1977, the Joint Intelligence Committee assessed the situation as one in which anything could happen but was unlikely to happen. It considered an invasion of the islands by private citizens (later to be supported by the Argentine armed forces) or directly by Argentine armed forces as unlikely but not to be discounted. The committee considered direct military intervention by the Argentine government very possible if negotiations broke down or if Argentina felt there was no need to continue to negotiate because nothing was being done to transfer sovereignty to Argentina. Britain decided on a military presence in the area at the time of the December talks, consisting of a nuclear-powered submarine in the vicinity of the islands and two frigates about a thousand miles away. These, it was noted, could not repel a large attack force but could deal with limited attacks. These plans were to be kept secret (Franks 1983: p. 18).

At the New York talks between Allara and Rowlands (December 13–15, 1977), it was decided to separate the talks into two sections, one to discuss sovereignty and the other to discuss economic cooperation. Britain withdrew its naval force, but considered deploying it again for the next round of discussions in Lima in February 1978. The British cabinet decided not to, considering the Argentine threat no longer serious.

This scenario repeated itself in Lima (February 15–17, 1978) when the British delegation refused to discuss the question of sovereignty although Argentina presented some suggestions for future economic cooperation in the area. The British delegation proposed Anglo-Argentine cooperation in scientific activities in the dependencies, but Argentina pointed out that the Malvinas and their so-called dependencies were a part of the continental shelf. Because the shelf rights belonged to Argentina, they were outside the scope of the negotiations.

In discussions in Geneva in December 1978, Britain again rejected negotiations on the question of sovereignty but agreed to a convention for scientific cooperation in the South Sandwich Islands and in South Georgia, which it later refused to ratify because the islanders objected to it. Why Britain permitted the islanders to veto this treaty when the South Sandwich Islands and South Georgia were no longer dependencies of the Falklands, as Dr. Owen had stated previously, is a question hard to answer.

In the March 1979 round of conversations the Argentines were told of this veto. Again, at this meeting, nothing was done.

Perhaps because of these delays and to focus the Argentines' minds on the importance of the Malvinas question, the Argentine government proclaimed a Week of the Malvinas to celebrate the establishment of the first Argentine government in the islands on June 10, 1829. In vain, Argentine historians pointed out that the day should also be celebrated for June 10, 1770, when a Spanish force sent from Buenos Aires dislodged the British garrison at Port Egmont. Already a House of Las Malvinas existed, as did school districts and streets named after the islands. By 1975 there had been so many organizations all over the country working for the restitution of the islands to Argentina that a "Coordination of Entities for the Restitution of the Malvinas" had been organized. In 1979, these clubs and institutions held special programs and celebrations. June 10 was declared a national holiday, flags were flown, and government buildings were lighted up. Many Argentines now began to speak of the restitution of the islands by the time the sesquicentennial of their seizure by the British arrived on January 2, 1983.

10

Margaret Thatcher Takes Over

The Year 1979 Begins Auspiciously

The year 1979 brought a new government to Britain under the leadership of Margaret Thatcher, whose Conservative Party was voted into power in May 1979. While Argentines were celebrating the Week of the Malvinas, the new British government was quietly discussing the options open to it in regard to the Falklands: first, break off negotiations and prepare to defend the islands against Argentine attacks ("Fortress Falklands"); second, return the islands and resettle the islanders in other places (considered politically and morally unacceptable); third, continue negotiations to gain time but with no intentions of solving the problem; and, fourth, continue negotiations in good faith to find a solution that would satisfy both the islanders and Parliament (Franks 1983: p. 20).

Nicholas Ridley, the new subsecretary of the Foreign and Commonwealth Office, discussed these options with Lord Carrington, the foreign minister. It was decided to send Ridley to the islands and to Argentina before making a decision. In the islands the councillors told Ridley that they preferred a long freeze on negotiations and opposed the idea of a leaseback. In Buenos Aires, Ridley and Carlos Cavándoli, a subsecretary of the Argentine Ministry of Foreign Relations, agreed to reinstate diplomatic relations between the two countries on the ambassadorial level. But in regard to negotiations, Argentina demanded that conversations be renewed at a far more active pace, that an agreement of scientific cooperation signed the previous year in Geneva be fully carried out, that the interests of the islanders be taken into consideration but that they not be a third party to the negotiations, and that the question of sovereignty be a part of any negotiations in the future.

In September 1979, in presenting the various options to Thatcher and the Defense Committee, Carrington supported some form of leaseback as most acceptable for the government and the islanders and asked to have it approved as the basis for upcoming discussions in New York with Brigadier Carlos Pastor, the Argentine minister of foreign relations. There he would suggest that the discussions be continued later in the year. Thatcher declared that she did not want any decision on principle taken hastily or without first discussing it with the Defense Committee.

In the New York meetings in late September 1979, Pastor suggested that the discussion be accelerated by having ambassadors meet weekly, junior ministers biannually, and foreign ministers annually. He also said he recognized that for Britain the Falklands were of secondary importance whereas for Argentina they were of prime importance. Carrington could only answer that he was in no position to offer a solution while he had to contend with other urgent international problems.

In October Carrington again circularized Thatcher and the Defense Committee, warning that the idea of "Fortress Falklands" or even the option of continuing talks without discussing sovereignty carried a risk of invasion by the Argentines. He felt that there was a real threat of an Argentine invasion of the islands if no real progress were made toward a negotiated settlement. He suggested that talks at the ministerial level be resumed, but Thatcher said she was too busy with the question of Rhodesia to discuss the matter. Ridley, as a result, declined an Argentine invitation to a round of informal talks.

It was at this time (October 1979) that General Leopoldo Fortunato Galtieri, commander in chief of the Argentine army, who later, as president of the country, was to order the invasion of the Falklands, visited the radio and meteorological station at the military base of Esperanza in the Argentine Antarctic. There he spoke by radio to the Argentine people, praising the army for having established a permanent base in the area for scientific investigations that in peace would help to make Argentina a great nation. For this purpose the armed forces would persist in their efforts to populate and develop the zone until the communities there could support themselves. Esperanza with its military base had forty men, women, and children. According to Galtieri, the fact that Argentina had had a base here for three quarters of a century was sufficient proof of Argentina's desire for a permanent scientific-military base in the Antarctic. He added that Argentina had established a weather station in the South Orkney Islands on February 22, 1904, the oldest base in the Antarctic, and it was still functioning.

In the meantime the 1971 agreements for the establishment of communications and trade between the islands and continental Argentina seemed to be bearing fruit. The temporary airstrip built by the Argentine air force and inaugurated in 1972 had been replaced by the British government with a larger airstrip, and flights had been increased to twice weekly. The Argentine airline (LADE) had offices in Stanley. Naval Transports, an arm of the Argentine navy, brought supplies to the islands: lumber from Ushuaia and oil and bottled gas from Comodoro Rivadavia. These supplies had made it possible for the islanders to use gas ranges, hot water heaters, and stoves made on the mainland, and gas had almost completely replaced peat in the homes. It is not known what happened to those islanders who made their living by digging peat. School teachers from Argentina were busy teaching Spanish in both elementary and secondary schools and also to adults. Argentina was also providing the islanders with medical services, with some patients being flown to Argentine hospitals for attention they could not get in the islands.

All of these activities were under the supervision of the Comisión Consultiva para el Desarrollo de las Comunicaciones con las Islas Malvinas, established in Argentina under the agreements of 1971, with agents in Buenos Aires and Stanley. As Argentina frequently pointed out, these services were never interrupted, and for that reason Argentina had been congratulated by the United Nations, whose desire had been that Argentina and Great Britain work out their problem as soon as possible. But these services were under constant attack from the anti-Argentine Falkland Islands Committee in London. Since 1968 it had kept up a campaign in Parliament and in the press against Argentina's presence in the islands and against any further negotiations, alleging that Argentine activities in the islands were a blind for Argentina's ultimate retrieval of them.

In spite of these obstacles, it appeared that by early 1980 the two governments were ready to renew negotiations. Ambassador Anthony James Wilson, who had arrived with the recent renewal of relations on an ambassadorial level, announced in a speech at Tucumán that the problem was not unsolvable, because the two countries had similar points of view, as in the case of Iran and Afghanistan, and that in order to reach a solution only greater comprehension and patience were needed. At the end of January, Carrington suggested to Thatcher and the Defense Committee that exploratory talks be undertaken soon, because to continue to stall would be risky. In April 1980, meetings were held in New York between an Argentine delegation headed by Cavándoli and a British delegation headed by Ridley, who was accompanied by a councillor from the islands. During the talks Argentina restated its claim to sovereignty, but it was agreed that differences of opinion on this subject should not hinder discussion of possible cooperation in development of the resources of the South Atlantic area.

Perhaps because of this statement, rumors began to fly in Britain and in the islands about an agreement between the two countries to exploit possible oil resources in the islands—rumors the Argentine government strongly denied. The rumors were probably supported by the fact that at the moment Argentina was drilling for oil on its continental shelf between Río Gallegos (the nearest port to the Malvinas) and Tierra del Fuego, with contracts having been given to Shell, Esso, and Total to do the drilling. British papers at the same time had been printing stories that the oil resources in the vicinity of the islands might amount to nine times those found in the North Sea. The rumors included an agreement to be made in exchange for a fishing treaty.

All these rumors were lent some plausibility when in June 1980, José Martínez de Hoz, the Argentine economic minister, told the *Times* (London) that while negotiations regarding sovereignty were under way, it might be well for Britain and Argentina to work out plans for joint drilling for oil at some distance from the coast of Argentina and joint fishing rights in the Malvinas area. He added that he wanted Britain to associate itself with Argentina in the latter's economic development. The dispute over the islands had adversely affected British investments in Argentina, where Britain was now the second-ranked investor; however, he said, there were indications that investments as well as commerce between the two countries would increase. Nothing came of these suggestions, in spite of the fact that they were thrown out by one of the most important members of the Argentine government. Were they made to soften up the British attitude?

At the same time, the British ambassador to Brazil, while meeting newsmen in that country to explain his statement deploring the Brazilain president's public assertion that Argentina owned the Malvinas, was asked about the question of oil in the islands. He answered that no oil had been discovered there but that explorations had been made, the results of which were in the hands of the British National Oil Company and the Yacimientos Petrolíferos Fiscales (YPF), the government-owned oil company of Argentina.

In July 1980, Carrington and the Defense Committee reached an agreement on a proposed leaseback solution, and in November Ridley went to the islands to sound out the islanders on the project. He found them divided on it: A considerable minority were against it, while the majority were undecided. When Ridley visited Argentina on his way to the islands, he found Cavándoli demanding a quick renewal of talks, to which Ridley replied that the islanders would have to accept further talks. It was at this time that Brian G. Frow, the director of the Falkland Islands Office in London, said that Britain was proposing to end the 150-year-old occupation of the islands by handing them over to Argentina. Did he have inside information about the purpose of Ridley's trip, or was he trying to stir up opposition to relinquishing the islands? By now the British attitude was bringing strong reaction from the Argentines against it. The word in Buenos Aires was that the islanders were running the British Empire: About 1,500 people were telling the British government what to do, and this attitude was an insult to Argentina as well as to Britain.

The Leaseback Concept Is Suggested and Rejected

Ridley's report to Parliament got a hostile reception, especially when he spoke of suggesting to the islanders a twenty-five-year lease, even though he insisted that the proposal had the support of the majority of the islanders. He felt that in that time Britain could develop the economy of the islands to the maximum, as well as the maritime resources (oil and fishing) around the islands. Because of this statement foreign diplomats in London suggested that Britain might extract all it could from the islands and their waters during its lease and then return them to Argentina.

It appears that some islanders were not pleased with Ridley's proposals. At the end of the year vandals contaminated the fuel tanks in the warehouse of the Argentine oil company, making the fuel unusable. They also painted over the sign of the airline company. LADE had to reduce passenger service on its flights to bring in more fuel oil. On January 6, 1981, the joint councils of the Falkland Islands passed a resolution that contradicted Ridley's report to Parliament. It stated that the two councils did not agree with Ridley's ideas, but that Her Majesty's government should continue its negotiations with Argentina, in which negotiations the councils should be represented. It also stated that the British delegation should try to freeze the question of sovereignty for a determined period of time.

When the Argentine government was handed this resolution by the British ambassador to Buenos Aires, it answered that the matter was an internal problem of the United Kingdom, and that it did not negotiate the question of the Malvinas with anyone but the government of the United Kingdom. For that reason the islanders' vote was a problem that did not concern Argentina. Argentina would continue the negotiations in the same spirit in which it had been pursuing them, in accordance with the resolutions of the General Assembly of the United Nations.

Carrington and the Defense Committee could not accept a freeze on negotiations, which would be unacceptable to the Argentines. They decided to keep the negotiations open and without pressure permit the islanders to see the advantages of a realistic settlement based on leaseback, and to continue early talks as suggested by Argentina.

At the same time that the Argentines were resenting the islanders' attempt to dictate to the British government, they received further discomforting news: Britain was planning to move inhabitants from the island of St. Helena to the Malvinas. Argentine periodicals pointed out that such action would contravene United Nations resolutions by bringing a new factor into the negotiations, a policy Argentina had always rejected on legal grounds. They also pointed out that residents of St. Helena, accustomed to living in a tropical climate, would be most uncomfortable in the Malvinas. Nothing came of the project, if it ever existed. The news story was not denied, and Argentines seem to have believed it, as the Argentine goverment protested strongly against it.

Further negotiations in New York in February 1981 came to nought when Argentina rejected outright an attempt to freeze discussion of the dispute. When the islanders announced that they had had representatives at the discussions in New York and that they had taken part in the discussions, Argentina publicly declared that no islanders had been present during the discussions. It also denied that an agreement had been made to freeze all negotiations until a study of a leaseback type of solution could be made. Such an agreement would have meant a virtual freezing of the sovereignty question for many years. However, in the meantime, Britain could have tried to bring public opinion around to relinquishing the islands.

The British ambassador to Argentina denied that his government had suggested a freezing of negotiations except for the question of sovereignty. He said, correctly, that the question was very complex: Argentina had historical and juridical reasons for wanting the islands returned, and Britain had juridical reasons for keeping them. Moreover, ten years of economic, social, and scientific and educational cooperation had not been enough. For that reason, he said, it was thought that it might be better to continue the cooperation for a longer period before broaching the question of sovereignty. Argentina, on the other hand, rejected any proposal that did not consider the question of sovereignty.

The Argentine insistence that no islanders had been present at the February meetings does not jibe with Carrington's report. He said that although the meetings seemed a failure, they were educational for the Argentines and islanders present. He added that if the islanders insisted on maintaining the status quo, it would be necessary to prepare for a possible worsening of relations with Argentina, with the subsequent necessity of supplying the islands should Argentina withdraw its services, and perhaps even to prepare to defend the islands in case of Argentine attacks.

In May 1981 Anthony Williams, the British ambassador in Argentina, urged further discussions during the year, including the subject of sovereignty, to prevent a decline in relations with Argentina. His government replied that it was not under any illusions concerning Argentina's impatience or even possible armed confrontation if Britain refused to negotiate the question of sovereignty seriously. However, negotiations could not be undertaken without the consent of the islanders, because the government was on record that the islanders' wishes were paramount and because Parliament had very strong views on this. Therefore any situation that might arise, for example the use of force by Argentina, would have to be dealt with as it arose, and always in the context of the islanders' wishes being paramount.

An indication of Argentine impatience was shown on Army Day (May 29, 1981) in Argentina, when General Galtieri, the head of the Argentine army (later, when Argentina invaded the islands, president of Argentina) made a speech in which he stated that by historical inheritance and legal right the Malvinas were Argentine. Therefore Argentina could never permit others to search for and exploit the wealth of that territory. After a century and a half, he said, the problem of the Malvinas was becoming more and more unbearable.

Early in June 1981, Ambassador Williams warned his government that ground had been lost since the February talks and that it might be difficult to rely on continued Argentine understanding. He also took a dig at the islanders, saying that they did not understand the realities of the situation. If some form of leaseback were the only solution possible, it would be well to start an educational campaign in Britain by emphasizing what the cost of any alternative might be. He also warned his government that Argentina might use Britain as a scapegoat for its internal troubles, and this possibility might become more dangerous by the end of the year. British willingness to achieve a negotiated settlement would help in getting Argentines to believe that Britain was not trying to fool them.

At the end of June 1981, a very important meeting was held in the Foreign and Commonwealth Office, attended by Ridley; Sir Michael Palliser, permanent undersecretary of state; D. M. Day, deputy undersecretary of state; Ambassador Williams, who had sent his views in earlier; R. M. Hunt, governor of the Falklands; J. B. Ure, superintending undersecretary of state for the South American department; and Robin Fearn, head of the South American department.

Ure stated that on a recent visit to Argentina he had found the Argentine government well-inclined to the leaseback idea. But he had been informed that the military leaders were less patient and might want more rapid progress in negotiations. He believed much still had to be done in the islands and in Great Britain to educate the people about the danger if nothing were done to settle the Falklands problem. He suggested that the government assure the islanders that they would be accepted in the British Isles, formulate a plan to resettle those who did not want to remain in the islands, develop a plan to distribute land there with more speed, and proceed with some kind of economic development of the islands. He sounded a word of alarm by suggesting that if these measures were unacceptable, the government should think seriously about the defense of the islands. The meeting also discussed the situation within Argentina and in the islands. The governor of the islands, Hunt, said that the islanders wanted to have nothing to do with the Argentines and therefore opposed any leaseback project. The meeting concluded that Britain should play for time, that the new legislative council of the islands soon to be elected should be persuaded to allow talks to be continued, that an educational campaign should be recommended, and that both civil and military contingency measures should be drawn up.

On July 9, 1981, the British Joint Intelligence Committee presented its views on what might happen if Argentine patience ran out. The committee believed that Argentina would first use diplomatic and economic measures against Britain, especially in view of its improving relations with the United States and Brazil. For example, it might disrupt air and sea communications and stop fuel and food supplies as well as medical help. But it might also occupy one of the uninhabited dependencies, as it had done with Southern Thule in 1976, or perhaps even one of the Falkland Islands far removed from Stanley. The committee discounted Argentina's disruption of British shipping. From this memo it is clear that the British government was well aware of Argentina's discontent with the way Britain was proceeding in regard to the negotiations.

The Joint Defense Committee, however, believed that Argentina still preferred peaceful means to settle the problem of the islands, although it was as determined as ever to get them back. Argentina's actions would depend on whether it believed that the British government was genuinely interested in a transfer of sovereignty. The committee also noted that Argentina was very impatient with the attitude of the islanders, and with the use of this attitude by the British government to delay negotiations. The committee did not rule out military action on a small scale by Argentina if it thought there was no hope for a peaceful solution of the conflict. In this case Argentina might act without warning, and if it did, might undertake an attack on British shipping and even an invasion of the islands. This report shows that the British government was well advised, at least eight months before the invasion of the Malvinas by Argentine armed forces, of the possibility of Argentine armed action against the islands.

Ridley agreed with this diagnosis in a note to Carrington of July 20, 1981, in which he said that no alternative to some leaseback plan would stand a chance of solving the difficulty. Yet the islanders would never accept leaseback. Even the new members of the legislative council of the islands soon to be elected would be of no help, because they would oppose any such plan. They would oppose, in fact, any plan to transfer sovereignty to Argentina. Ridley told Carrington that Argentina's patience was running out and that it would take armed action, possibly by early 1982, if it believed that Britain could not or would not negotiate seriously. He dismissed stalling, and suggested that Britain might (1) start negotiations on a leaseback plan, with the proviso that the islanders and Parliament would have to agree on the results; (2) begin an educational campaign on the islands and in Britain showing the advantages of a sovereignty decision; or (3) let Argentina know that Britain would not discuss sovereignty, and prepare for any contingency. He preferred the second possibility, because leaseback could not be discussed without contravening the islanders' wishes, and respecting the islanders' wishes was part of a long-held policy of the government.

The British government's fear of Argentine impatience was well borne out when a week later the new foreign minister of Argentina, Emilio Camilión, handed the British ambassador to Argentina a note in which Argentina's position was firmly set out. Camilión insisted that negotiations to resolve the manner of returning to Argentina the Malvinas, South Georgia, and the South Sandwich Islands should be resolutely pursued. He called British occupation of the islands an anachronism, as unacceptable as it was indefensible. To this unjust situation could be added the incongruency of Britain's failure to develop the resources of the islands, so indispensable for a world in need of energy and food.

He then went on to say that although the opening of the islands to intercourse with Argentina had fulfilled the objective of bettering the life of the islanders, it had not had the hoped-for success in contributing to mutual knowledge and understanding or in helping to bring negotiations to a successful resolution. Because of the isolation, a great ignorance about Argentina existed in the islands. This ignorance was a great obstacle to negotiations, because now it was not the interests but the wishes of the islanders that were being presented as an argument against further negotiations. Yet the question in dispute was not between Argentina and the islanders but between Argentina and Great Britain.

Even now, in late 1981, Camilión continued, the islands were suffering from a continuing economic deterioration. The population was decreasing without any possibility of reversal. The whole situation was very irrational, and no one could seriously maintain that the status quo should be prolonged. Hence, the Argentine government believed that negotiations should be energetically conducted and for that reason was giving them priority in its foreign policy. Emphasizing the urgency of the problem, the note called for a global, rather than fragmentary, solution. For that purpose Camilión presented the following points, on which Argentina based its position:

1. That the reaffirmation of Argentina's traditional position in regard to the Malvinas, South Georgia, and the South Sandwich Islands presupposed the recognition of Argentine sovereignty over them as the essential point in the solution of the problem.
2. That the Argentine government renewed its promise to respect the interests of the inhabitants of the islands.
3. That the preservation of the said interests should take into account their way of life and their traditions.
4. That if the United Kingdom really tried to negotiate in an acceptable manner, Argentina would continue to furnish the islanders with the services they had been receiving since 1971. These services, which could be enlarged, demanded from Britain evidence of its desire to promote the negotiations constructively so that they would not end in sterile exercises.
5. That because these negotiations had been taking place within the framework of the United Nations, Argentina was willing for that world organization to establish safeguards for the interests of the islanders.
6. That Argentina was willing to establish practical formulas to protect the interests of those who might hope to benefit from the development of the island's natural resources.

The document ended with a statement that Argentina was determined to continue the negotiations in a realistic spirit, but warned that it did not believe that it could continue hoping for a solution indefinitely. Negotiations had to continue firmly and with a desire to reach an agreement. This was almost an open accusation that Britain was stalling, as it was. Camilión reminded Britain that there was a national Argentine sensibility about the Malvinas that on the one hand was open to negotiation and on the other believed that it was impossible to delay any further this question affecting the territorial integrity and national dignity of Argentina. Was this intended as a warning to Britain?

Britain Gives Up the Initiative

The fall of 1981 saw an important change in the British attitude. Ridley's suggestion to Carrington calling for a vigorous educational campaign in the islands and in Britain had been accepted by Carrington in July, but on September 7, 1981, he rejected it at a meeting with Ridley and other officials. The British Foreign and Commonwealth Office here gave up the initiative, which Britain had tried to keep throughout the negotiations. From now on it had no policy except to wait and see what happened, and to take contingency measures—a term used frequently in British government circles in those days.

Almost a year later, Carrington said that his decision against an educational campaign had been based on objections from his colleagues, who thought the policy would be counterproductive. (He failed to explain how an educational program of this type could have been counterproductive.) Fearn, in a personal letter to the British ambassador in Buenos Aires, said that the decision was taken because of domestic political constraints that at the time prevented putting pressure on the islanders with an educational campaign or in any other way. In a word, the islanders made the decision so fateful for the British Empire.

Williams, the ambassador in Argentina, protested vehemently in a letter written to Fearn on October 2, 1981, saying that he understood that from now on there would be no policy regarding the islands at all except for a sort of Micawberism. As there was not even the slightest hope that the islanders would accept a transfer of sovereignty, the Argentines would probably decide negotiations were a waste of time. He added that talking for the sake of talking was something the Argentines conceded to the British but not vice versa. He ended with a suggestion that must have been difficult for him to write: If the British no longer could negotiate sincerely about sovereignty, then they should so inform the Argentines and face the consequences (Franks 1983: pp. 29–30).

Carrington's decision not to pursue a public education campaign meant that Britain henceforth had no policy at all—it had given up the initiative in negotiations. Formerly, it had presented suggestions and policies to be followed. Now there would be none of these. In a note to the prime minister and other members of the Defense Committee, Carrington referred to Camilión's note and to the upcoming meeting with Camilión in New York. He would tell Camilión that Britain could not coerce the islanders and that it would appreciate having Argentina make constructive proposals regarding negotiation. This he did in New York. Britain had surrendered its former policy of making "constructive" proposals for future negotiations. It now left matters in the hands of the Argentines.

Who was behind this sudden change? At the time there were all kinds of hints and intimations. Some said it was pressure from members of Parliament, others pressure from the pro-Falklands lobby. Others laid it directly at the door of Margaret Thatcher, which seems the most likely. Carrington would certainly not do anything as rash as this without the approval or suggestion of his boss. Whoever took the decision to make no further suggestions for negotiations and let Argentina carry the ball from now on made a tragic mistake. In all this Williams, the British ambassador in Argentina, seems to have been a shining light of hope and good sense: Why beat about the bush?—tell the Argentines you do not want to negotiate and take the consequences. But honesty is not a diplomatic trait.

When Carrington and Camilión met in New York in late September 1981, things went as Carrington had suggested to his chief, Thatcher. He told Camilión that although Britain desired negotiations and would continue to try to convince the islanders of the desirability of an accommodation with Argentina, it could not force them to accept one. Therefore Britain preferred that Argentina present suggestions for talks to be resumed. Britain gave up the initiative, and permitted Argentina to run the show. Camilión emphasized that the main question was sovereignty. This question would have to be negotiated with Britain and not with the islanders. Argentina would accept no veto of the islanders in regard to the resumption of negotiations. The Argentine press noticed the change in climate, stating that Britain had agreed for the first time that the present status could not be maintained. Camilión and Argentina were optimistic. But now things would go from bad to worse.

Britain, hoping to stall as usual, took heart from a statement made by Camilión to the British ambassador on October 14, 1981. Camilión said that future negotiations would have to be methodically catalogued and each issue discussed piecemeal, although the final results would have to be concluded globally. Then he said that negotiations no doubt would have to be long and difficult. He should never have said this, because the Foreign and Commonwealth Office took this to mean that no early solution was possible and that Argentina desired no confrontation—another bad mistake. Again, although realizing that the main question was still sovereignty, Britain was happy just looking forward to protracted negotiations, even though for many months now, the Defense Committee and other officials had warned that Argentine patience might run out at any moment and armed confrontation might be the result.

Legislative council elections in the islands on October 14, 1981, resulted, as had been expected, in a hardening of the islanders' attitude against negotiations on sovereignty. Brian Frow, the director of the

Falkland Islands Office in London, declared that the islanders' attitude toward Argentina had stiffened. He added that they did not want to be Argentine and that negotiations had come to the end of the road. The candidates for office in the islands were overwhelmingly in favor of breaking off negotiations. Frow said they rejected any form of leaseback, but he also said that they were restive because of the lack of support from London for their desire to remain British subjects and had suggested that Britain was more interested in increasing its trade with South America than in protecting their interests.

On December 2, 1981, Carrington sent a memorandum to Thatcher and members of the Defense Committee in which he discussed his meeting with Camilión and the results of the Falkland elections. He felt that the attitudes of the Argentines and the islanders could not be reconciled, and that in the next meetings with the Argentines, the latter would be left to take the initiative. He was not optimistic about the outcome of the talks. He hoped only that they would not be completely stalemated. In case they were and Argentina withdrew its services to the islands, Britain would have to provide alternative services, using sea rather than air communication, the initial cost of which would be about six million pounds. More and more would be heard from now on about contingency plans, civil and also military. British officials had mentioned them in passing, but now they appeared to become more and more important.

Contingency Planning Becomes More Important

Since early 1981, the Foreign and Commonwealth Office, responsible for civil contingency plans for the islands, had been studying what could be done should Argentina withdraw its services to the islands. The attitude of the islanders and the growing impatience of the Argentines over the lack of cooperation from the British in solving the sovereignty question did not help. Even if the Argentines only withdrew their services to the islanders, it would require an annual expenditure of about six million pounds to replace those services, something the economy-minded Thatcher government did no want to think about. But contingencies had to be faced.

The desire to cut down expenses also played a role that was to influence future relations with Argentina. In order to effect a cut in government expenses, H.M.S. *Endurance* was slated to be scrapped in March 1982. The *Endurance* is an ice-breaker used as a patrol ship of the British navy. It had been stationed in Stanley since 1967 for protection of the islands and for patrolling the dependencies in the South Atlantic, and had taken all important visiting British officials since Lord Chalfont from Patagonia to the islands. One of the ship's helicopters discovered the Argentine military personnel who had landed secretly on Southern Thule, one of the South Sandwich Islands, in December 1976. The presence of the *Endurance* in waters off South Georgia, when it was supposedly ready to be scrapped, provoked the escalation of the South Georgia incident that led to the war.

Although for several years the *Endurance* had appeared on the list of ships to be retired from service in the economy program of the British government, the foreign secretaries, supported by the prime ministers, had been able to prevent this retirement and keep the ship in Stanley. However, when in 1981 the name of the *Endurance* again appeared on the list of ships to be scrapped, Thatcher supported Secretary of Defense John Nott's economy program, and the ship was condemned in spite of pleas from Carrington and Ridley, a petition signed by 150 members of Parliament, and a protest from the islanders.

The ship's defenders argued that it would be well to keep the *Endurance* while the dispute with Argentina continued, but more important, that its retirement might give Argentina the impression that Britain was no longer interested in defending the islands—as in fact happened, as is shown by articles to that effect appearing in the Argentine press. So the *Endurance* was to be scrapped in March 1982.

Related to the *Endurance* controversy was the attempt to close, also for economy reasons, the British Antarctic Survey at Grytviken on South Georgia. Here the islanders also protested, and in this case they obtained a reprieve by raising the necessary funds to keep the base open through the sale of the islands' postage stamps, which have always found a ready philatelic market.

Throughout 1981 both civil and military contingency plans were discussed by the British government. The Foreign and Commonwealth Office was in charge of civil contingencies for the islands should Argentina withdraw its services. By September the office had decided that air service would be impractical, because the only country from which air service to Stanley could be established without changing the runway was Chile. To use either Uruguay or Brazil would entail an extremely costly extension of the runway. Moreover, it was probable that no South American country would permit the providing of alternative air services, in which case the runway would have to be extended even more and at a higher cost in order to accommodate larger aircraft from South Africa. Here is the first known British admission that other Latin American nations supported Argentina in its dispute over the Malvinas. Also, more expenses would have to be incurred for general airport modernization, and Argentina would doubtless not permit planes to be diverted to its territory in case they ran into trouble. But sea transportation would also be very expensive, and would take much more time to transport freight and people.

Military contingencies also presented problems. A paper completed and approved by the British chiefs of staff on September 14, 1981, suggested that Argentina had one of the most efficient armed forces in South America, whereas Britain had only forty-two marines in the islands and H.M.S. *Endurance*, due to be retired in March 1982. The weather in the region and the lack of airport facilities would rule out any significant air support. Britain would therefore have to rely on naval support. It would take time to assemble the necessary naval reinforcements, and surface ships would take about twenty days to reach the islands. All of this could be done only at enormous expense and to the detriment of other military commitments.

The paper then examined the possible actions of Argentina. It could harass or attack British shipping, occupy one or more of the uninhabited islands, take over the Grytviken station on South Georgia, try a small-scale military operation against the islands, or try a large-scale military operation against them. To counteract a large-scale invasion would call for a large force including an *Invincible*-type carrier, four destroyers or frigates, a nuclear-powered submarine, supply ships, and enough manpower to reinforce the garrison. This would be very expensive. (When the war came in April 1982, the force deployed was even greater and more expensive, employing almost all the British naval resources.) The paper noted also that the force it described might not be able to retake the islands should Argentine forces be occupying them when it arrived. To do so would require naval, land, and air forces on a massive scale, and the whole undertaking would be formidable.

The New York Talks of February 1982 Lead Nowhere

When Leopoldo Fortunato Galtieri became president of Argentina on December 22, 1981, he retained his position as commander-in-chief of the army. Because Admiral Jorge Isaac Anaya, head of the naval forces and a member of the ruling three-man junta, was a personal friend of Galtieri and had always been hawkish on the question of the Malvinas, Argentines prophesied a rapid solution to the question. As foreign minister Galtieri chose Dr. Nicanor Costa Méndez, also considered inflexible on the question.

But Ambassador Williams on January 1, 1982, wrote that he considered the new cabinet an improvement over the previous one and that the past year had been very difficult. However, Fearn believed that unless the islanders changed their attitude 1982 would be even more difficult, as it would be harder than ever to make the Argentines seek a solution by negotiation. In general, the British government felt that the Argentine position had not changed with the new government and that a more forceful attitude might be expected from it.

On January 19, 1982, the governor of the islands, Rex Hunt, sent in his annual report for 1981. In it he said that the islanders' relations with both Britain and Argentina had deteriorated over the past year and that island opinion against any type of leaseback had stiffened. The islanders had had their suspicions aroused against the mother country because of, among other reasons, Britain's refusal to grant them

British citizenship, the announcement of the withdrawal of the *Endurance*, and the expected financial cuts for the British Antarctic Survey base. The islanders were miffed at the Argentines for many reasons, but Hunt especially mentioned the reduction of air service (paid for by Argentina!) and six flights made over the islands by the Argentine air force. He said that the islanders would never accept Argentine sovereignty. Commenting on the report, Foreign Office officials accepted the idea that leaseback was dead and noted that the islanders had accepted the Fortress Falklands policy. With the death of leaseback, they also noted, it appeared that no other way was left to prevent a confrontation (Franks 1983: pp. 35–36).

But to the governor the British government explained that confrontation was not necessarily military conflict, and that it would be warned of a collapse of the negotiations. It would be hard for the government to find the money to pay for the defense of the islands. The islanders should be assured that the government was committed to act according to their wishes, but they should not make the mistake of minimizing the limits of its ability to do so, and if there were no negotiated settlement, the islanders' future could only go downhill.

On January 27, Costa Méndez sent a note to Ambassador Williams reaffirming that an absolute condition for a solution of the dispute was British recognition of Argentine sovereignty over the Malvinas, South Georgia, and the South Sandwich Islands. No matter how much time might elapse, Argentina would never abandon its claims to these areas. He asked for serious negotiations for the purpose of deciding on this recognition within a reasonable time, declaring that there had been no progress in all these years and there could be no further delays. The Argentine government again referred to the United Nations resolutions that called for deferring to the interests of the islanders, not their wishes, and noted that the dispute was between Britain and Argentina and the islanders were not included. To settle the dispute rapidly and peacefully, it proposed the establishment of a permanent negotiating commission to meet the first week in each month in alternate capitals, the commission to last for one year, with the possibility of dissolving it without prior notice.

The Foreign Office considered the note worded in tough language but not different from others heretofore received except for the proposal of a permanent negotiating commission and a timetable for one year. It sent a note to Williams for the Argentine government (delivered February 8, 1982) in which it stated that there was no doubt about British sovereignty over the Malvinas, the dependencies, and their maritime zones and continental shelves. Therefore it did not accept the premise that negotiations were for the purpose of recognizing Argentine sovereignty over those areas. However, the British government was willing to continue negotiating later that month in New York for the purpose of coming to an early and peaceful solution of the problem acceptable to the governments of Britain and Argentina and to the people of the Falkland Islands.

While awaiting the above answer, Williams sent his government another note on February 3, in which he stated that he had heard that Anaya, perhaps with the consent of Galtieri, had taken over the negotiations and had decided that there should be a definite period allowed to see whether negotiations succeeded. Williams believed that the period projected by Anaya might end on January 3, 1983, the sesquicentennial of the British occupation of the Malvinas. The Argentine press seemed to feel the same way. During the month of February, before the meeting in New York, many articles appeared in the Argentine press relating to the Malvinas. All of them echoed the new Argentine position on the negotiations with respect to demands for a timetable for the solution of the various problems as well as the transfer of sovereignty. All of them designated 1982 as the key year for the return of the Malvinas, because January 2, 1983, would mark the one hundred and fiftieth anniversary of the invasion of the islands by Britain.

Referring to coming meetings in New York, Carrington advised Thatcher and the Defense Committee that he favored setting up several committees or working groups to discuss different aspects of the dispute as a means of prolonging the discussions, because a rupture might be dangerous, but he opposed deadlines. He also felt it would be difficult to control the islanders, who wanted to hear nothing about sovereignty. Yet this was the most essential point for the Argentines. The British delegation in New York would make clear from the beginning that any agreement reached on the future of the negotiations would have to be approved by the two governments. Thatcher answered that the Argentines should be told that the wishes of the islanders were paramount.

At the talks of February 26 and 27, the two groups established a permanent negotiating commission to speed up the comprehensive solution of the dispute. Ministers would preside over the meetings, establish the agenda, and direct the work of the commission. The commission could include islanders. Its work would be to consider all elements in the dispute, discuss them in depth, and make recommendations for their solution, with the aim of bringing about an overall agreement. The life of the commission would be one year, but either side could terminate it at any time. The work of the commission would not prejudice the sovereignty position of either government. Meetings would be held alternately in the capitals of the two countries and be chaired by the host minister. The British delegation had steadfastly refused Argentina's request for monthly meetings beginning on April 1, 1982. Argentina had also demanded a response to its proposals within a month.

In the joint announcement by the two sides on March 1, 1982, nothing was said about the details of the meeting. The announcement merely stated that the meetings had been cordial and positive, that the two sides had decided to find a solution for the dispute over sovereignty, and that they had considered a proposal by Argentina regarding procedures to make more progress in this regard. Both sides had agreed to inform their governments about the discussions. The day the announcement was made (March 1, 1982), the Argentine minister of foreign affairs issued a statement describing the proposals. The British government took this statement as a breach of confidence, because the delegates had agreed that their discussions would not be made public before the respective governments had been notified of their decisions. However, the Argentine government had merely stated the terms of its own proposals, and had not said anything about the results of the talks. The statement was as follows:

> At the meeting held in New York on 26 and 27 February, the representatives of Argentina and Great Britain considered an Argentine proposal to establish a system of monthly meetings with a pre-established agenda, pre-arranged meeting place, and led by top-level officials. The aim of such meetings will be genuinely to speed up to the maximum the negotiations in train to achieve recognition of Argentine sovereignty over the Malvinas, South Georgia and the South Sandwich Islands, and by this means to achieve substantial results within a time which at this advanced stage of the discussions will necessarily have to be short.
>
> Argentina has negotiated with Great Britain over the solution of the sovereignty dispute over the Islands with patience, loyalty and good faith for over 15 years, within the framework indicated by the relevant United Nations resolutions. The new system constitutes an effective step for the early solution of the dispute. However, should this not occur, Argentina reserves [the right] to terminate the working of this mechanism and to choose freely the procedure which best accords with her interests. (Franks 1983: p. 41)

Although Argentina does not appear to have disclosed prematurely the results of the New York meetings, one can easily see why the British government thought it had. Worse still, the statement implied that Argentina would no longer let the British government get by with stalling and delaying tactics. Making this statement public brought a protest dated March 3, 1982, from Richard Luce, who had replaced Ridley as subsecretary of the Foreign and Commonwealth Office, to Enrique Ros, who held a similar position in the Argentine foreign ministry. He said that the proposals agreed upon in New York were supposed to have remained confidential until the respective governments had been consulted, and that now, with the Argentine government's public announcement and the resulting press comments, it would be more difficult to continue negotiations. He also did not like the threatening tone of the announcement. He was assured that no threats were meant.

However, the Argentine press was full of threats, one paper even discussing the possibility of a direct seizure of the islands, which the United States might not oppose if it were offered naval bases there.

The *Buenos Aires Herald* went so far as to say that Britain had no other recourse but to hand over the islands. No wonder the British government protested the release of the Argentine communiqué.

When Williams saw Costa Méndez on March 5, the latter denied that Argentina in any way wanted to threaten Britain, but he expressed dissatisfaction with the lack of progress in the negotiations and insisted on the need for monthly meetings. He also insisted that Argentina was not imposing deadlines but was trying to establish a program for the negotiations, including recourses established by the United Nations.

As a result of a meeting held by officials of the Foreign and Commonwealth Office on March 5, it was decided that Carrington should send a personal note to Costa Méndez, a draft of which was sent to the islands for consideration by the councillors. It said that Carrington was pleased with the progress made in New York in setting up procedures for further negotiations to settle the future of the islands, and that this progress showed the Argentine government's desire for a peaceful solution of that difficult problem, a solution that would be acceptable to the two governments and the people of the islands. Carrington requested agreement on two essential points: that the commission should explore every angle to solve the dispute, and that the negotiations could not be continued in an atmosphere of threats about what would happen should they break down. The draft was approved by the island councillors, who insisted that no negotiations could be held on the question of transfer of sovereignty. They informed the British government that it should convince Argentina that Britain had a better claim to the islands and that the islanders wanted to remain British. By the time the draft of Carrington's letter had been circulated to various members of the government, it was too late to send it: The conflict over the island of South Georgia had erupted.

11

The Falklands Break into World Headlines

The South Georgia Question Emerges

The island of South Georgia lies in the South Atlantic about 1,300 miles east of Cape Horn and some 800 miles southeast of the Malvinas. Its form is that of a slight arch from northwest to southeast. It is covered with glaciers, icy peaks, and snowfields and has several deep and sheltered bays. It measures 105 miles in length and has a maximum width of eighteen miles. The coasts of the island remain free of ice the year around. In the past it was a very important whaling center. The British Antarctic Survey has a base for scientific and meteorological studies at Grytviken on the bay of the same name. The population of the island consists of seals, sea lions, reindeer (introduced by the British), about thirty species of birds, including millions of penguins, and, of course, the members of the British Antarctic Survey.

At Leith, on Stromness Bay about twenty-five miles from Grytviken, there are installations of a whaling station abandoned in the 1960s. They were owned by Christian Salvesen Limited of Edinburgh, which offered them for sale for the removal of scrap metal. In Buenos Aires Constantino Sergio Davidoff, a scrap metal dealer, became interested in the Leith station for its huge sheds, winches, floating docks, etc., containing an estimated 30,000 tons of metal offered by Salvesen for $200,000. With the market price of scrap metal at around $375 a ton, it was a very profitable deal for Davidoff and his associates, a company called Georgias del Sur S.A.

On September 19, 1979, a contract was signed between Davidoff and Salvesen that transferred all the equipment and installations of four abandoned whaling stations on South Georgia to Davidoff. The contract was notarized by Ian Roger Frame of London, and Salvesen notified the authorities on the Falkland Islands of this action on August 27, 1980. By the contract Davidoff's company could remove everything it wanted from the stations until March 31, 1983, but it could not interfere with navigation, it could not molest or cause trouble to third parties, it could not destroy the flora or fauna of the islands, it could not introduce flora or fauna into the islands, and it could not involve the seller in any illegal acts.

Trouble began with the first visit of Davidoff to Leith in December 1981, to inspect and photograph the installations, and reached unexpected proportions with the landing in Leith of Argentine workmen on March 19, 1982. The question at issue goes back to the initiation of the United Nations program of decolonization, which required a list of colonies from all colonial powers. Britain listed the Falkland Islands and Dependencies as one of its colonies.

The 1971 communications agreement between the Falklands and the Argentine mainland included provision for a special document allowing travel between the Malvinas and Argentina, the so-called white card, a temporary document accepted by both sides. But now Britain claimed that South Georgia and the South Sandwich Islands were separated from the Falklands and constituted a new colony governed directly from Britain but administered for the sake of convenience by the government of the Falklands. In accordance with this new arrangement no one could disembark in South Georgia without first requesting permission at Grytviken and having his or her passport stamped by the commandant of that base, in whom was invested complete authority in the island from magistrate to postmaster.

From the viewpoint of the Argentines the workers who went to the island to dismantle the scrap metal were there legally, because they all had white cards. From the viewpoint of the government of the islands they were interlopers, because they had not requested permission at Grytviken and had not shown the commandant their passports. This is the background of the problem. It appears unimportant and lacking in gravity, except for the fact that by now British officials in Stanley and in London had an obsession about the possibility that Argentina might provoke difficulties and harass Britain by occupying outlying islands. As has been noted, British officials in London had spoken frequently of the possibility that Argentina might lose its patience because of British delaying tactics and take stronger measures to retrieve the islands. British officials for several months had suggested making "contingency plans," and even Prime Minister Thatcher had ordered that they be made.

From the viewpoint of these officials, there was reason to fear that attempts like "Operation Cóndor" might again be made by private citizens or Argentine armed forces to take one or several of the islands. The Argentine military government, in power since 1976, had frequently shown its impatience at the long drawn out negotiations that since 1965 had led to nothing. Then there were the inevitable rumors, like the one in 1977 that declared that military activity was increasing in southern Argentina. What if the military preparations were meant for an invasion of the Falklands? And what if Britain tried to oust any invaders and Argentina declared that it would come to their aid? It was reported that, just in case, Britain had sent two frigates and a submarine to the area, this at a time when economy measures had top priority in Britain. No one seemed to know with certainty whether they were ever sent, perhaps because the measure was top secret.

But this is not the only puzzle in regard to the problem of South Georgia. On this theme there are still many questions to be answered. For example, when were the dependencies separated from the Falklands? Did the separation occur *after* the commencement of the negotiations between Britain and Argentina ordered by the United Nations in 1965? Was Argentina informed of this change in government? Did the change take place when the Malvinas were already considered a territory in litigation, and if so, would such a change be legal? And how is it possible, if these islands were a new, separate colony, that Britain's attempt to close the base at Grytviken for economic reasons was averted by funds obtained by the government of the Falklands from the sale of postage stamps?

Moreover, if Britain was so zealous about the sovereignty of these islands, why, when in 1977 it discovered an Argentine military installation on Southern Thule, said to have scientific purposes, did it content itself with protesting, and not try to dislodge the installation or even publicize the incident until 1978? The Argentine group remained on Southern Thule until the end of the war, when it was forced to abandon the installations.

The Falkland Government Tries to Halt Davidoff's Undertaking

From these questions, it is easy to see why so many discrepancies and so much confusion are to be found in the different versions of the South Georgia incident. The incident began when Davidoff, who had been in occasional contact with the British embassy in Buenos Aires in 1980 and 1981, left Buenos Aires on the icebreaker *Almirante Irizar,* reaching Leith on December 20, 1981. He had notified the embassy of his trip in a letter that arrived after his departure. Perhaps unaware of the regulations, he did not stop at Grytviken but went directly to Leith, inspected the installations, and returned to Argentina.

Supposedly the British knew nothing about this visit until a party from the base at Grytviken found signs that someone had been at Leith. Yet on December 31, Governor Hunt of the Falkland Islands informed the Foreign and Commonwealth Office of the unauthorized presence of the icebreaker *Almirante Irizar* in Stromness Bay. He had been told about it by the base commander at Grytviken, or so he said. Did the British embassy in Buenos Aires fail to inform Hunt?

Hunt also said that in accordance with legislation concerning the dependencies it was required to obtain clearance at Grytviken and that *Davidoff knew this.* How did Hunt know he did? The only answer seems to be that as the British embassy in Buenos Aires was in frequent contact with Hunt he must have found out about Davidoff's visit from that source. Or if the British Antarctic Survey people actually saw the ship and read its name, they were watching the Davidoff party from close but hidden sight, and did not want to show themselves to Davidoff and his men. Someone evidently was lying. Hunt recommended that proceedings be instigated against Davidoff and a strong protest be made to the Argentine government.

Hunt was instructed by London not to start anything that could have undesirable consequences. If Davidoff requested entry at Grytviken it should be given him. If he landed without clearance, he should be ordered to leave immediately but without threats. If he refused to comply, Hunt should request further instructions.

On January 4, 1982, the British ambassador was ordered to present a strong protest to the Argentine government against the violation of British sovereignty over South Georgia and to state that any further attempts to land people there without authorization would give Britain the right to take any action that might be necessary to stop them. The note was handed to the Argentine government on February 3; until then the Argentine government knew nothing about Davidoff's trip. On February 18, the Argentine government rejected the protest.

On February 23, Davidoff went to the British embassy where he was informed of what had happened. He apologized for having caused so many problems and said he was planning to return to South Georgia to start dismantling the installations. He asked that he be told in detail of the procedures he would have to follow in order not to provoke more difficulties. The ambassador asked the governor of the islands for advice but did not receive an answer until March 11, after the workers had left. Why did Hunt wait so long to answer?

On March 9, Davidoff sent the British embassy a formal notice that forty-one people were going to South Georgia on March 11 on the *Bahía Buen Suceso*, an Argentine naval supply ship, and would remain there for four months. He offered to transport supplies to the British Antarctic Survey and to make medical services available to them. The ambassador reported this to London and to the governor of the islands and asked Davidoff for more details about the workers and the ship. On March 16, Christian Salvesen Ltd. informed the Foreign and Commonwealth Office and the governor that it had granted Davidoff an extension of his contract to March 31, 1984. On March 29, the Argentine press published an account of the contracting company, Georgias del Sur S.A., that coincides with the above information and includes a list of the workers and other information sent to the British embassy on March 9. There were thirty-nine workers on the list.

One thing is certain. Before the landing at Leith on March 19 everybody concerned had been or should have been informed about the landing: the embassy, Governor Hunt, the Foreign and Commonwealth Office, and the branch of the Argentine government in charge of issuing the white cards. Hunt said that Davidoff knew that he had to request permission to land, but did he? Why did he fail to do it? Did he, perhaps, in spite of what Hunt said, fail to receive complete instructions? Or, if he did, was he afraid that he might not be given permission? Did he, perhaps, omit the request on orders from someone in the Argentine government, or did he resent having to comply with that little formality in Grytviken?

Another curious thing is that although there are two reports of the landing at Leith, one with a surprising number of details and the other in low key, in neither one of the two does Davidoff appear. He was not on South Georgia during this period. As might have been expected, the movement of information within the Stanley–Buenos Aires–London triangle was intense, and while Stanley proposed every kind of drastic measure, the embassy in Buenos Aires advised remaining calm.

Hunt believed that the Argentine navy was using Davidoff, and that even if he requested authorization at Grytviken, it should be denied him. He advised the commandant at Grytviken to order the Argentines to leave immediately, and he suggested that the *Endurance* be sent to eject them if they did not obey the order to leave. These suggestions were approved by the Foreign and Commonwealth Office. At the request of his government the British ambassador protested the landing to the Argentine government, saying in his note that if the Argentine group were not withdrawn immediately, Britain would have to take whatever action seemed necessary. But he himself recommended restraint to his government until it was clear whether or not the incident was a deliberate challenge authorized by high-level Argentine officials. Orders were given to the *Endurance* commander to go to South Georgia with nine marines, but the governor was ordered to keep the mission secret to avoid the appearance that Britain was trying to escalate the incident.

On March 21, the Argentine government told the British ambassador that the workers were leaving South Georgia that day and hoped that the significance of the incident would not be exaggerated. It also explained that the group was in no way official, included no service personnel, and carried no arms. The Argentine chargé d'affaires in London notified the Foreign and Commonwealth Office that the *Bahía Buen Suceso* and the workers had left on March 21 and that the ship was a naval supply ship under commercial charter to Davidoff. On March 21, the base commander at Grytviken reported that most of the Argentines wore civilian cloth and carried no firearms, but that shots had been heard and reindeer killed, which was against the law.

On March 21, also, the governor sent a personal telegram to Carrington insisting that Davidoff was dangerous, that he was really not a scrap dealer, and that his contract should be revoked immediately. He said that Davidoff had broken his contract on purpose (but did not say how he knew this), and that if Britain acted leniently, Argentina would continue illegal landings until it finally invaded the Falklands themselves.

The night of March 20–21, an incident in Stanley provoked an exchange of notes between the two governments. The Argentine flag at the offices of LADE was replaced with the Union Jack and "tit for tat, you buggers" was written with toothpaste on a desk. The next night "UK OK" was written on the windows.

Grytviken reported on March 22 that some Argentines remained at Leith, and that a French yacht, the *Cinq Gars Pour*, disobeying orders from Grytviken, had gone to Leith and its crew was fraternizing with the Argentines. The governor of the Falklands again insisted that the *Endurance* be sent to eject the Argentines immediately. But the Argentine government asked the British chargé d'affaires in Buenos Aires that Britain not use force in South Georgia because it might inflame Argentine public opinion. There were only a few men left at Leith, he was told. The commander of the *Endurance*, on the other hand, sent a message that the Argentine navy and Davidoff were in collusion, because he had heard a message from naval headquarters in Buenos Aires congratulating the *Bahía Buen Suceso* for a job well done and ordering it to return home as soon as possible. The *Endurance* was ordered to continue to South Georgia.

In the meantime Foreign Minister Costa Méndez declared that he was still expecting a reply from Britain concerning measures accepted in the February 26–27 talks and hoped they were positive, or Argentina would have to return to the United Nations for a solution. But on March 23 the Foreign Office said that the Thatcher government had decided to send the *Endurance* to expel the small group of Argentines still remaining on the islands. Costa Méndez expressed surprise at this action, which was adopted before all diplomatic possibilities to solve the problem had been exhausted. He said that Britain's proposed action might provoke a strong reply, and that the *Bahía Buen Suceso* might return to pick up the men still at Leith.

The British ambassador informed his government that, seen from Buenos Aires, the reaction of Britain to Davidoff's trivial and low-level misbehavior could do lasting harm to the whole state of bilateral negotiations. As a result the Foreign Office ordered the *Endurance* to Grytviken to await orders there. Everything seemed to be settled when on March 23, Carrington sent Costa Méndez a personal note accepting the sending of the *Bahía Buen Suceso* as long as it was done immediately. Otherwise Davidoff's workers would have to be evacuated by other means. Carrington also reminded Costa Méndez that a right political climate would have to be maintained to solve the dispute peacefully by negotiations. It appears that Costa Méndez meant well but was restricted by public opinion and the governing junta. He thanked the ambassador for Carrington's message and said he would talk that evening with the commanders-in-chief. Perhaps the workers could be removed in another ship.

Carrington had not reported to Prime Minister Thatcher and the Defense Committee on the Falklands since February 15. He finally did so on March 24, over a month later! And this time he had to admit that the dispute had reached a point where a confrontation might occur at any moment. In this meeting he also presented the message to Costa Méndez that had been drafted after the meeting of February 26–27 but never sent. Why he presented it at this time is not known. It merely stated that negotiations should be continued, they should be genuine, and they should not be undertaken amid threats of retaliatory actions should they break down. Carrington suggested to Thatcher that contingency plans be formed to replace air and sea services to the Falklands and that the defense minister prepare a military contingency paper (which was never finished).

At this time British intelligence circulated among British government officials the information that Admiral Anaya, the commander-in-chief of the Argentine navy, was behind the hawkish element in the government. Costa Méndez admitted to the British ambassador that he was having difficulty in taking action to have the workmen removed because Anaya was opposing any removal under a threat of force from Britain. Costa Méndez was trying to get Davidoff to remove the men. The British military attaché in Buenos Aires felt that if Britain attempted to remove the men by force, Argentina would reply with force, perhaps even with a rescue operation should the workmen be taken to Stanley. He said that this would be just what the hawks in the Argentine government wanted, because such action would escalate into an occupation of the Falklands. He warned that the threat to Stanley should be taken into account before any rash action was undertaken.

Argentina Challenges Britain in South Georgia

On March 24 the Argentine navy ordered the *Bahía Paraíso* to South Georgia. It was already at sea, perhaps already prepared for this occasion, because it arrived on the evening of March 25. It is a new naval auxiliary vessel, but the Foreign and Commonwealth Office thought it was an unarmed, scientific ship. Its arrival at Leith caused a flutter of notes, dispatches, conversations, and suggestions among the members of the Foreign Office, the British ambassador in Buenos Aires, Costa Méndez, Governor Hunt, and the commander of the *Endurance*.

The British officials were in a state of alarm. The ministry of defense warned Carrington that Argentine ships were at sea to prevent the *Endurance* from evacuating the workers and that unless the problem could be settled by diplomatic action, there was a real danger of a military confrontation that Britain could not win. The British ambassador in Buenos Aires was told that he should get Costa Méndez to persuade his colleagues to find a way out of the impasse and that Britain did not want to escalate the trouble, although it was committed to defend British sovereignty in South Georgia.

The ambassador felt that Costa Méndez was entirely subject to the will of the governing junta, but that he was trying to avoid confrontation through diplomatic efforts. Costa Méndez, he said, thought that any action Argentina might now take would appear to be made under threat of force, because the British press had made much of the sending of the *Endurance* to expel the Argentines from South Georgia. He asked whether the expulsion order might be reconsidered provided Davidoff sent his men to Grytviken to have their white cards stamped. The ambassador recommended this solution to his government, and it was grudgingly accepted by the governor of the islands the next day. The ambassador was directed to tell Costa Méndez that although Britain was publicly committed to the withdrawal of the Argentines from South Georgia, it would, as a gesture of good will, grant them permission to return to Leith if they went to Grytviken.

That night Costa Méndez, after having been informed of this reply, said that he could not make a decision without consulting the president. He would do it that evening, but the president would have to consult with the other members of the junta. The decision of the junta was not made until late the night of March 26. The *Bahía Paraíso*, carrying troops, arrived at Leith late the afternoon of March 25, and spent the twenty-sixth unloading supplies. The next day, leaving the troops on land, it left to patrol the waters beyond the three-mile limit. There the *Endurance* kept watch on it.

On March 27 Ambassador Williams reported to his government that he felt that Costa Méndez had not been honest with him, because he had not spoken to him after meeting with the junta as he had promised. Instead he had given a statement to the press that the men at Leith would be given all necessary protection. He could not get an interview with Costa Méndez, and an undersecretary could not help him, but a message would be given to the British government later that day. Williams felt that the junta was still not agreed about what to do and that the navy was the most determined to force confrontation, whereas the army and air force were less belligerent.

On March 28, Ambassador Williams reported the following note from Costa Méndez to the British government:

> The events which have taken place on the Isla San Pedro [the Argentine name for South Georgia] are being followed by my Government with close attention. I am convinced that both the British Government and Your Excellency share our concern and this is why I am sending this message with the object of dispelling any misunderstanding about my Government's motives.
>
> The activities of the group of workers disembarked at Leith are of a private and peaceful character based on the undisputed fact that they were known in advance by Her Britannic Majesty's Government and in any case on the fact that they are being carried out on territory subject to the special regime agreed [upon] in 1971 between the Argentine and Great Britain. It is moreover within Your Excellency's knowledge that these territories are considered by the Argentine Republic as her own and that the sovereignty dispute about them has been recognized by the United

Nations in its relevant Resolutions. Your Excellency's Government has accepted the existence of the sovereignty dispute.

However the British government has reacted in terms which constitute a virtual ultimatum backed by the threat of military action in the form of the despatch of the naval warship *Endurance* and a requirement for the peremptorily immediate evacuation of the Argentine workers from the island. These actions have been taken without regard to the special characteristics mentioned above. The reaction to which I refer thus constitutes a disproportionate and provocative response aggravated for having received wide diffusion in the press which has had a negative effect on developments and which is not the responsibility of the Argentine Government. In this connection I cannot but refer to the comments published in the British press many of which have had an aggravating effect and in any case do not contribute to the maintenance of the desirable climate for the conduct of negotiations.

In the light of this attitude my Government can only adopt those measures which prudence and its rights demand. In this context the Argentine workers must remain there since they have been given the necessary documentation to do so. . . .

To resolve the present situation I consider it necessary that Your Excellency's Government should display, as does the Argentine Government, the political will to negotiate not only the current problem which concerns us but also the sovereignty dispute bearing in mind that so long as this continues our relations will be open to similar disturbances and crises.

Your Excellency can be sure of counting upon the co-operation and goodwill of my Government to achieve a satisfactory solution. (Franks 1983: pp. 60–61)

The South Georgia Confrontation Leads to War

Again the Argentine government had taken the initiative, but a tragic one, for this incident led to the war over the islands. Had Argentina after seventeen years of futile negotiation finally decided to end the stalemate? Did the Argentine junta feel that it had to make a display of force to get something done? Both sides refused to negotiate in an atmosphere of threats. Was this a convenient excuse for Britain not to negotiate at all? The *Endurance* and the *Bahía Paraíso* were facing each other in the same waters. Thatcher was ordering contingency plans for ships to sail from Gibraltar while Argentina was preparing its navy in southern Argentina and cancelling leave for the armed forces.

On the night of March 28, Thatcher telephoned Carrington that he should respond effectively to the Argentine threat, and Carrington sent Secretary of State Alexander M. Haig a message requesting that the United States act as mediator. Haig tendered the good offices of the United States to the ambassadors of Argentina and Great Britain in Washington. Argentina replied through the U.S. ambassador in Buenos Aires that the United States should help in mediating the whole Malvinas problem and that it was not interested only in South Georgia. Did this mean that Argentina was intent on war or a display of warring threats to make Britain negotiate the sovereignty of the islands as some people think? Yet British intelligence did not think that such an intention was behind the occupation of Leith by Argentina.

However, Britain took precautionary measures. On March 29, British Secretary of Defense Nott informed Thatcher that a vessel had been sent to reprovision the *Endurance,* as well as a nuclear submarine (sent secretly yet known about by the press almost immediately), both scheduled to arrive in the Falklands around April 13. Another submarine was being readied, and a fleet of seven frigates and destroyers could be sent from Gibraltar, taking three weeks to arrive. But this would not be sufficient, and to assemble one that would be effective would require a week. It would be a matter of public knowledge and would take almost three weeks to arrive at its destination. The navy on the same day ordered that such a fleet be prepared, ready to leave Gibraltar for the South Atlantic if necessary.

The Foreign and Commonwealth Office on that day also expressed the belief that it would be ill-considered to reopen negotiations on the Falklands before having resolved the question of South Georgia, and even then, should the South Georgia incident be considered as the first point to be settled, it would appear as if the British government were acting under pressure. British officials strongly believed that the South Georgia incident had been provoked by Argentina to make Britain discuss the sovereignty of the Malvinas. The foreign office received a report at this same time that Haig was concerned about the South Georgia incident and hoped for restraint from both sides. Haig also said that the United States would not take sides but was willing to use its good offices to bring about a solution. To this Carrington answered that he was displeased with Haig's reply because it put the British on an equal footing with the Argentines!

On March 30, the British government answered Costa Méndez's message of March 28. Britain suggested sending a Foreign Office emissary to renew negotiations as soon as the South Georgia question was settled. It also announced in Parliament that the islands would be defended and that the islanders' wishes were still paramount.

Costa Méndez read the answer to his note the next day and lamented that it was not what he had expected to receive. He also said that declarations in Parliament and press accounts of the sending of warships did not help the situation. In Buenos Aires, at the same time, violent demonstrations were taking place against the economic policies of the government and against Britain for sending warships to the South Atlantic. Did these help persuade the junta to occupy the Malvinas in order to get the Argentine people's minds off the economic problems plaguing Argentina and at the same time fulfill their age-old desire to have the islands returned to them? Any Argentine leader who recuperated the Malvinas would immediately become a hero to the Argentine people.

Yet, even as late as March 31, in Britain the Latin American Current Intelligence Group believed that the landing on South Georgia had not been a plot of the Argentine government, although it felt that the junta had used the landing to force Britain to speed up further negotiations on the question of sovereignty. The trouble lay in the lack of central coordination of Argentine policy. The junta was a question mark. Were the members in agreement? Might it be swayed by the strong public feeling in Argentina about the Malvinas? It had military superiority in the region, and this with confused advice from service advisers might make the junta take unexpected action. Still, the group thought that Argentina's reaction to the incident was an attempt to get the British government to reopen talks and obtain the transfer of sovereignty over the islands. It did not think that at that time the junta would use force unless an attempt were made to remove the Argentines from the island.

Costa Méndez did not help matters at this time by declaring that Argentina would never give in to threats of force and that the Argentines on South Georgia were on Argentine soil. Neither did the newspapers help by announcing that Britain had sent a nuclear-powered submarine to the area as well as a destroyer and a naval auxiliary vessel.

Early on March 31, Nott received intelligence reports that Argentina was planning to invade the Malvinas in the early morning of April 2. Nott met with the prime minister and other members of her government. At 9:00 a.m. Thatcher sent President Reagan a message that intelligence reports indicated that the Argentines were preparing to invade the Falklands, and that Britain could not agree to an occupation of the islands. She asked him to tell President Galtieri that Britain would not escalate the dispute and would not start fighting, and to ask Galtieri to give assurance that he would not order a landing. In the same meeting the naval chief told Thatcher what the size and composition of a naval force to retake the island should be. He was ordered to prepare it just in case it might be needed.

On April 1, the British ambassador reported that in an interview with Costa Méndez the latter said that the question of South Georgia was closed. The sending of a special envoy was unnecessary, because the question was not South Georgia but the transfer of sovereignty. Argentina had been negotiating this question since 1964 and would have accepted an envoy if he were sent to discuss the ways of transferring to Argentina the sovereignty over the Malvinas and their dependencies, which was essentially the cause of all the difficulties. Costa Méndez could not have been more frank.

On the same day, the British government informed the governor of the islands and its ambassadors in New York, Washington, and Buenos Aires that reliable reports indicated that Argentine forces would assemble at Stanley early the next morning. The U.S. ambassador in Buenos Aires met with Galtieri to hand him a note from Haig. Galtieri refused to divulge Argentina's intentions but stated that Britain should discuss the surrender of sovereignty over the Malvinas.

On April 1, British intelligence reports noted that by the end of March Argentine military leaders were ready to use military means to solve the dispute over the islands. Later in the evening of April 1, Thatcher, Carrington, and Nott met and decided that troops should be put on immediate alert for possible deployment to the South Atlantic. The naval force being assembled in British ports was on four hours' notice to sail within the next forty-eight hours to meet ships from Gibraltar to sail south together if it were necessary.

In the meantime President Reagan had been trying to telephone President Galtieri since the night of March 31, when Thatcher had asked him to intercede personally with Galtieri. He did not reach Galtieri until the night of April 1. Reagan offered to send George Bush to try to get a solution, an offer that Galtieri rejected. Reagan urged Galtieri not to invade the Falklands, assuring him that Britain would react violently and an all-out war would break out. He told Galtieri that Thatcher was a proud and hard-headed woman and that she would not only protest but also send the entire fleet and all the men necessary to get back the islands. In case of conflict, Reagan said, the United States would have to support Britain because of political principles and military alliance.

But the junta remembered the two visits of Galtieri to the United States in 1981 on which he was very well received (after the war he said that at that time he had been the favored nephew of Uncle Sam) and the help Argentina was giving the United States in combating communist expansion in Central America. It believed that without the support of the United States, Britain would have to seek a negotiated settlement. In the Security Council of the United Nations, it expected either majority support because of Argentine support for the resolutions of the Committee on Decolonization, or a veto by the Soviet Union or China. Here again the Argentine government miscalculated badly. It received only one vote in the Security Council, and no veto. Argentina also thought it would receive international support for an order to take the Malvinas without spilling British blood. But this restraint did not have the effect the junta had hoped it would. International opinion, fanned by British propaganda, saw the Argentine invasion only as an act of aggression by a government not noted for its protection of human rights.

Argentine troops, 11,000 of them, began to land on the Malvinas early the morning of April 2. There was only one casualty: An Argentine soldier was killed. Not a single islander was hurt.

Mediation Attempts Begin Immediately, But Fail

As a result of the emphasis put on the invasion by the press, radio, and television, two facts dominated world opinion: (1) the lightning-speed of the invasion, which took only a few hours, and (2) the use of aggression to settle an international dispute. That it was a bloodless "aggression" (only one Argentine soldier was killed and no islanders were hurt) was hardly mentioned and was soon forgotten. At the time little or nothing was said of the seventeen years of frustrating negotiations that had preceded the invasion. That the Anglo-Argentine dispute resulted from a process of decolonization sponsored by the United Nations was also forgotten, except by members of the Organization of American States and by Argentina, which had to repeat and repeat it.

Thus, the Falklands achieved world fame as the victim of Argentine aggression, and the world seemed to feel that Argentina had to be punished for its actions. Taking advantage of the natural interest of the news media and the preoccupation in world official circles with the possible consequences of the conflict, British propaganda moved swiftly and with consummate skill to fix in official minds and in public opinion a picture of Britain as the victim, whose honor had been outraged, and to justify its retaliatory plans. The campaign of public "education" was made easier by the general lack of knowledge about the history of the struggle over the islands and about the misinformation used by Britain to justify its actions and later, conveniently, to perpetuate its stalling tactics.

Britain introduced Resolution 502 in the Security Council on April 2. It demanded an immediate cessation of hostilities and the withdrawal of Argentine troops from the Falkland Islands (Islas Malvinas). It also called on the Argentine and British governments to solve their differences by diplomatic means and to respect fully the purposes and principles of the Charter of the United Nations. It will be remembered (although no one seems to have reminded the Security Council at the time) that this last clause expressed exactly what Argentina had been trying to do for seventeen years with little help from Britain. And because of this failure "to respect the purposes and principles of the Charter of the United Nations" many hundreds of young men were to lose their lives in an unnecessary war.

Because the Argentine foreign minister, Costa Méndez, could not arrive for a discussion of the resolution until the next day, a one-day delay was granted to Argentina. After his arrival on April 3, Costa Méndez lost no time in delivering a long speech against the resolution. After sketching the history of the conflict between the two countries, of Argentina's unsuccessful attempts to comply with the United Nations resolutions because of Britain's refusal to negotiate, Costa Méndez asked why, more than twenty years before, Britain had voted against Portugal's retention of Goa on the grounds that retention would deny India the right to its territorial integrity, whereas now it was presenting a resolution denying that same right to Argentina. In the Goa question Portugal's request had been rejected by the Security Council because it was a question of defense and an expression of colonialism. The same would be true now with the Malvinas. Britain's request should be denied, as Portugal's had been.

But Britain's request was not denied. Later Costa Méndez was accused of having talked down to the nonaligned states represented on the council, and of having appeared to demand that they vote against colonialism. It seems also that he did not want to discuss the matter after he had finished his speech. However, probably the council would have voted for the resolution anyway, because it was presented based on the principle of disavowing an act of aggression. British propaganda, taking echo in the United States, had done its work well—the world must condemn aggression wherever found.

On the day of the invasion Britain froze all Argentine assets in the United Kingdom, stopped imports from Argentina, and banned the export of military supplies to Argentina. At the North Atlantic Treaty Organization (NATO) it was surprisingly easy for Britain to convince its partners that sending a force to the Falklands was necessary to stop aggression, even at the cost of weakening NATO's defenses in Europe. Claiming the right to defend itself, Britain invoked Article 51 of the United Nations Charter against aggression. Constantly emphasizing that it was defending its territory against aggressors, it received the approval of NATO. But in Europe the question immediately arose whether there was another reason for NATO's acceptance of Britain's request: Was this an easy way to test the ships and arms of NATO?

Getting the support of the European Economic Community (EEC) was more difficult, but with some maneuvering Thatcher on April 10 obtained its backing for an embargo on military supplies to Argentina. On April 16 the EEC also banned imports from Argentina and supported UN Resolution 502. However, on May 17, Ireland and Italy refused to renew their sanctions against Argentina.

In the Organization of American States, as had been expected, Argentina was more successful. On April 20, in a meeting called by Argentina of the foreign ministers of the American states composing the organization, a resolution was passed by a vote of eighteen in favor and three abstentions calling for a meeting of foreign ministers of the member nations to consider invoking against Britain the Inter-American Treaty of Reciprocal Assistance. Called the Rio Treaty or the TIAR, it had been adopted in Rio de Janeiro in 1946 to defend the Americas against outside aggression. The three countries that abstained were the United States, Colombia, and Trinidad-Tobago. Trinidad-Tobago had recently received its independence from Britain. Colombia explained its abstention by stating that although it supported Argentina's claim to the Malvinas, it believed invocation of the Rio treaty to be premature because all possibilities to mediate the question had not been exhausted.

This was also the opinion of the United States delegate to the OAS meeting, who felt that the action was inopportune under the circumstances of the moment, because Secretary of State Haig at the time was still trying to get a solution of the problem. On April 28, the OAS supported Argentina's claim to sovereignty and condemned the EEC's sanctions against Argentina. But it also urged both sides to return to negotiations to settle the conflict, bearing in mind the interests of the islanders. Here again it supported Argentina, as during the negotiations with Britain, Argentina had always emphasized the *interests* of the islanders as opposed to Britain's emphasis on the *wishes* of the islanders.

From the viewpoint of Argentina, because the Malvinas had been unquestionably Argentine since 1810, the sending of the British fleet to remove the Argentine forces was an act of aggression against Argentina, an American state, and therefore came under the Rio treaty. From the viewpoint of Britain and its supporters, because the islands were British, the aggression came from Argentina and therefore the Rio treaty did not apply.

Argentina received strong support from the other Latin American nations. When on April 30 President Reagan announced support for Britain by the U.S. government, he received strong condemnation from most of the Latin American nations. Only Chile announced that it would maintain neutrality in the conflict, because at the time it and Argentina were in the process of having the question of the ownership of the Beagle Channel at the southern tip of South America arbitrated by the papacy.

In the meantime Secretary of State Haig had been trying to mediate the conflict. Haig was a close friend of Sir Nicholas Henderson, the British ambassador in Washington, a very capable and indefatigable worker for British interests. As early at March 31, Haig met with Henderson and was told that Argentina without a doubt was planning to invade the Falklands and had to be stopped. The anxious calls from British officials to Reagan and Haig that night and the following day emphasized British need for U.S. help.

With the invasion, the need for U.S. action seemed obvious. Haig took over. He convinced the president and the National Security Council that he should head a diplomatic shuttle mission to the two countries to try to prevent open warfare while the British fleet was still steaming toward the Falklands. Haig and his team of eight men flew first to London on April 8. There Haig suggested to Thatcher that both sides withdraw from the islands, the Argentines returning to the mainland and the British fleet standing off the islands, that an interim government be established in the islands, and that negotiations be renewed at a fixed date.

The prime minister opposed all three suggestions and stood adamantly by the points she had made in Parliament a few days before: the withdrawal of the Argentine forces, the return of British rule to the islands, and self determination for the islanders. Haig suggested that the United States supported Resolution 502 and also a peaceful solution of the problem. In principle the United States agreed with Britain, but perhaps there might be a way to permit Argentina to stay in the islands without profiting from its show of force. Thatcher remained adamant.

Upon its arrival in Buenos Aires, the group was joined by General Vernon Walters, the U.S. ambassador-at-large and a personal friend of

President Galtieri. Haig tried to convince the governing junta of Argentina (consisting of Galtieri representing the army, Admiral Jorge Isaac Anaya the navy, and Brigadier Basilio Lami Dozo the air force) that Britain meant business. If the junta insisted on occupying the islands, it would be faced by a superior force and lose the war. It was later reported that Haig also suggested that war could only lead to political unrest and economic ruin for Argentina. If this is true, it is a wonder that the Argentines did not accuse the mediating group of interfering in the internal affairs of their country.

To Haig's insistence that the British were serious and that the United States would support them Galtieri replied that the British would not fight and insisted that Argentina was sovereign in the islands, a principle Argentina could never relinquish. He suggested instead that the British withdraw, that sanctions against Argentina be lifted by the United States and the EEC, and that a date be set for negotiations. The talks, April 9–10, went nowhere, although the Argentine junta accepted the idea of an interim government for the islands if Argentines were allowed to move freely around the islands and to acquire property there.

A downcast team returned to London. Thatcher was as stubborn as the Argentine junta. A true "iron lady," she demanded that the Argentines leave the islands before negotiations could begin. Back in Argentina the team again met the same intransigence, so it decided to return to Washington. Now the arguments continued in Haig's office, with Jeane Kirkpatrick, the U.S. ambassador to the United Nations, and members of the Latin American section of the Department of State arguing for neutrality, and Haig supporting Britain. On April 30 Reagan announced that the United States allied itself with Britain, supporting it with military supplies and imposing economic sanctions on Argentina. He based his action on Argentina's use of armed force to take the islands. After the war Argentines wrote that during the negotiations Haig on three occasions had said that something being suggested would cause political damage to Thatcher. These remarks, together with his assertion that if the problem were not solved, the United States would have to support Britain, made them feel that Haig himself had always supported Britain.

Haig was also involved in another attempt at mediation. Dr. Fernando Belaúnde Terry, the U.S.-educated president of Peru, halfway through the Haig shuttle had proposed a seventy-two-hour truce. It had been accepted by Argentina but rejected by Britain. But Belaúnde was determined to mediate the conflict and prevent open warfare. Haig declared his mission terminated on April 30, and on May 2, at 1:30 A.M. Argentine time, Belaúnde telephoned Galtieri to present him with a peace proposal he had formulated with Haig the day before. The proposal had seven points:

1. Immediate cessation of hostilities.
2. Reciprocal withdrawal of armed forces.

   3. Neutral and temporary administration of the islands.
   4. Recognition by the two governments of differences over the islands' future.
   5. Recognition of the viewpoints and interests of the islanders.
   6. Brazil, Peru, West Germany, and the United States to take part in the negotiations to implement this proposal.
   7. A definitive agreement to be reached by April 30, 1983, to be backed by the four countries named above (Wilson and Gavshon 1983: p. 6; Sopeña 1983: p. 10).

This plan of Belaúnde, accepted by Argentina and barely mentioned in London, is chronologically related to the sinking of the cruiser *General Belgrano* about forty miles outside the 200-mile zone of exclusion around the islands decreed by Britain itself.

Belaúnde had worked with Haig on the negotiations, and perhaps because of this he moved so secretly that even Javier Pérez Cuéllar, the Peruvian secretary-general of the United Nations and friend of Belaúnde, knew nothing of his plans. Belaúnde informed Galtieri of the plan at 1:30 A.M. on May 2, and asked for a reply by 10 A.M. the same day, even if it was only an acceptance in principle, because Haig and Francis Pym, the British foreign minister, were meeting in Washington at that time and there might be a possibility of a solution.

Galtieri replied at 10 A.M. accepting the plan and informing Belaúnde that he was almost certain that the junta would ratify it at a meeting to be held at 7 P.M. Foreign Minister Costa Méndez was to discuss details of the plan with the junta. Along with a few other points, he requested that "aspirations and interests" be substituted for "viewpoints and interests" of the islanders and that Canada replace the United States on the committee of control. Belaúnde accepted these changes. At noon Peruvian and Washington time (2 P.M. Argentine time) Belaúnde, anxious to learn Pym's reaction, called Haig, who answered that at that moment they were leaving for lunch. That afternoon at 4 P.M. Argentine time, the *General Belgrano* was sunk outside the exclusion zone with the loss of 368 lives, over half of the Argentine lives lost in the war.

Desmond Price, former head of the Royal Dutch Shell Company in Argentina, received and brought back to Britain much information from high Argentine officials. It includes detailed accounts of the movements of all Argentine naval vessels at that time together with naval orders and the time they were issued. The Price documents do not always coincide with reports of the British Admiralty (Wilson and Gavshon 1983: p. 6).

Early on May 1, the day after Haig had terminated his negotiations, Britain initiated naval and air attacks on Port Stanley, occupied by Argentine forces. The Argentine commander of the South Atlantic naval force, Admiral Juan José Lombardo, ordered the Argentine fleet to proceed in three groups to a given set of coordinates. As part of the operation, the *General Balgrano* with its two destroyer escorts was given a patrol and support mission with orders to stay south of the exclusion zone at all times. On the same day, at about 6 P.M., reports were received that the bombardment of Stanley had ceased and that the British fleet had been ordered to disperse. In view of these intelligence reports Lombardo ordered the return of all Argentine vessels to their home bases. The order was confirmed at 1:19 A.M. the following day. At 7 A.M. the *General Belgrano* set a course of 290 degrees, but always far from the exclusion zone, and headed for its base, Ushuaia. When it was torpedoed it was only a hundred miles from the Argentine coast and had been navigating away from the exclusion zone for nine hours. The commander of the *Conqueror*, the nuclear submarine that sank the cruiser, later testified that he had been following it for thirty hours (Wilson and Gavshon 1983: p. 6).

There are some serious questions to be asked about the sinking of the *General Belgrano*. Why did the British government wait thirty hours before ordering it sunk when nine hours had passed since it had started on its way to Ushuaia? Who really gave the order to sink it? And was there any connection between the order to sink the *General Belgrano*, the possibility of Argentina's accepting a peace plan, and the lunch of Haig and Pym?

Fortunately, thanks to the peculiarly British political characteristic of seeking the truth no matter whom it may hurt, the British press and parliamentary opposition have persisted in trying to unravel the circumstances of the sinking of the *Belgrano* and to establish Thatcher's responsibility in it. The reticence of the Thatcher government about the events of May 2 has merely sharpened the investigators' desire to learn the truth.

With the sinking of the *General Belgrano* Argentina would hear of no mediation, and on May 7, Belaúnde's government announced the withdrawal of his proposal so as not to endanger its relations with the Argentine governing junta. But another Peruvian, Pérez de Cuéllar, was going to try his hand at mediation as secretary-general of the United Nations. After obtaining the passage of Resolution 502 by the Security Council of the United Nations, the British government, as its officials freely admitted later, tried to have as little to do as possible with that body for fear that it might jeopardize British purposes. Pérez de Cuéllar had acted in low key during the Haig shuttle, but had organized a group of senior officials of the United Nations to study the possibilities of a peaceful settlement. He presented his proposals to both sides, separately, on May 2.

After that he met frequently with Francis Pym, the British foreign minister after the sacking of Lord Carrington; Sir Anthony Parsons, the British ambassador to the United Nations; and Enrique Ros, the Argentine ambassador to that body. Pérez de Cuéllar did not let either side know what the other was proposing, but he carefully made suggestions to keep the negotiations from collapsing. He was the go-between par excellence, straightforward, accurate, helpful, and professional.

The sinking of the *Sheffield* by the Argentines on May 4 perhaps made Pym soften his position somewhat. After all, Argentina's navy was not a one-shot navy (fire a shot and run) as British officials had derisively described it. On May 6, Pym dropped the British insistence on the preeminence of the islanders' wishes, a point that had obstructed negotiations for many years. He demanded, however, that the Argentines drop their insistence on sovereignty over the islands, which had also obstructed the negotiations. On May 11, Ambassador Ros announced that Argentina had dropped its insistence on claiming sovereignty.

Both sides seemed elated by what appeared to be the most important breakthrough so far. Why the negotiations were soon abandoned is unknown. From Argentina came contradictory statements, even from Foreign Minister Costa Méndez. From Britain came skepticism over the plan, fanned by who knows who. Pérez de Cuéllar, nevertheless, maintained his determination to bring the two parties together. From Britain he obtained approval of a United Nations administrator for the islands. By May 14, he believed he had acceptance of the following stipulations: a cease-fire and the withdrawal of both sides under United Nations supervision; negotiations in good faith, to end by December 1982; and an interim government of the islands under United Nations administration with representatives from Argentina and the United Kingdom.

Ambassador Parsons took the proposals to Britain and placed them before Thatcher and the inner cabinet. Some parts of the proposal had been left purposely vague. There were points to be filled in, like the future role of the Falkland Islands Council, troop withdrawals, and the inclusion in the discussions of South Georgia and the South Sandwich Islands. All of these and other matters were discussed in a very long meeting. What happened has not been made public. Thatcher and her cabinet demanded clarity and specifics, which Parsons tried to supply. Some parts Pérez de Cuéllar, as an experienced diplomat, had deliberately left vague. The British wanted them cleared up, but they did accept a United Nations administrator for the islands and no longer insisted on self-determination for the islanders. These changes in themselves were a radical departure for Britain. If they had been accepted by Argentina they might have ultimately speeded up the end of British rule in the Falklands, if not the immediate inception of Argentine rule. Would the Haig mission have succeeded in April if the British had conceded this much then? Is this what the sinking of the *Sheffield* had achieved?

Unfortunately, although some Argentines as well as Americans (like Jeane Kirkpatrick) and Britons at the United Nations thought the proposal a good one, one that Argentina could accept, it was couched in language that did not disclose the true flexibility of the British government. Argentina rejected it, even insisting again that sovereignty would have to be discussed. Pérez de Cuéllar's excellent diplomatic work had been in vain. Parsons was so informed on the night of May 18.

On May 21 the British landed at San Carlos on the northern coast of East Falkland. The counterinvasion had begun. It was to be a short but bloody war ending with the surrender of the Argentine forces on June 14, 1982. It cost the lives of 712 young Argentines and 255 Britons.

12

Epilogue: An Evaluation

The United States and the Falklands/Malvinas Conflict

With the invasion of the islands by Argentina in April 1982, the United States was faced with a dilemma. On the one side was Britain asking for help, the unquestionable ally in a Europe plagued by disagreements and reservations about the policy of containing communism that the Reagan administration had adopted as its first priority in its foreign policy. On the other hand was Argentina, just emerging from a long struggle against terrorist infiltration, whose friendship with the United States had seldom been so strong. Its political stability was needed to extend to the South Atlantic regions the unity of the Western world. Moreover, Argentina's position vis-à-vis the Malvinas was unanimously supported by the other Latin American nations with which the United States was linked by treaties of defense and solidarity. And all of them had denounced colonialism in the New World.

The friendship of Argentina had been secured just recently, for in its fight against terrorism, it had been accused by the United States of widespread violations of human rights, an accusation that led to a virtual shutoff of arms to Argentina through the Humphrey-Kennedy amendment to the law permitting arms to be sold to allies of the United States. The amendment forbade sending arms to countries violating human rights.

This action had made Argentina unable to participate in 1979 in the annual naval maneuvers known as UNITAS, in which South American nations and the United States took part in war games to defend the South Atlantic. The Pentagon, fearing a loss of control over the South Atlantic, began a movement of rapprochement by establishing an air bridge with U.S. bases to supply Argentina with everything necessary to permit it to participate in UNITAS in 1980 and in planning for OCEAN VENTURE in 1981.

Relations between the two countries continued to improve with the election of Reagan, and many visits were exchanged by high officials. General Galtieri, before becoming president of Argentina, had visited the United States three times in 1981, and official cordiality reached a level seldom equaled in the past. Moreover, Argentina supported Reagan's policy in Central America.

There were, therefore, adequate reasons for the United States to remain neutral. It was the only country with sufficient power to bring pressure to bear on both sides to make them see reason and get them to negotiate seriously. But people with vision and guts were missing in Washington. U.S. officials also had little knowledge of the situation, except for a few people in the American Section of the Department of State, who were not heard. Only once was a voice raised in protest, that of Jeane Kirkpatrick, when she said that if Argentina considered the Malvinas Argentine, its invasion could not technically be called an aggression.

Haig's mediation efforts, although perhaps well intentioned, were doomed to failure because they bore the British stamp in that they refused to recognize, or were incapable of understanding, the need to resolve the question of sovereignty. If Argentina did not negotiate about sovereignty, about what could it negotiate?

The failure of Haig's negotiations, for which he blamed the Argentines but which in fact was his own fault as well as Thatcher's, inclined the balance in favor of Britain. And so the United States found itself in the dreadful position of participating in an adventure whose aim was to perpetuate colonialism in the New World with the help of a military force that, by its overwhelming superiority in arms, violated the international principle of proportionality.

But the errors did not end there. By taking the decision to help Britain, the United States rent apart the unity, already fragile, of the American hemisphere. Why did it relegate New World unity to second place? Because NATO and Western Europe were more important to U.S. interests, in the opinion of the U.S. government. Latin America has usually been taken for granted and has occupied second or third place in the political priorities of the United States, in spite of its importance to the commerce, wealth, and security of the United States.

By now the United States has apparently somewhat healed the wounds it inflicted on its relations with the rest of the hemisphere by taking sides in the conflict. Yet this time the wounds have been deep, and ill-feeling against the United States still runs high. Conscious of its disloyalty to Latin America and cognizant of the strong anger against it, especially in Argentina, the United States has set itself to repair the damage.

In a meeting of the General Assembly of the United Nations in November 1982, the Latin-American nations introduced a resolution urging Argentina and Britain to renew negotiations to find a pacific solution to the dispute over the sovereignty of the islands. It was approved by a vote of ninety in favor, twelve against, and several European abstentions. This time a telephone call from Thatcher to Reagan was to no avail. The United States voted in favor of the resolution in the unusual company of the Third World countries and the Soviet bloc. Argentina diplomatically returned to the *status quo ante bellum*.

Even then the U.S. vote was only a partial redress, because during the debate the United States succeeded in getting all reference to the Malvinas as a colony omitted, thereby depriving Argentina of the argument that there is no room for colonies in the New World. The United States also tried but failed to get all reference to sovereignty omitted. It seemed the Reagan administration was still under the British spell.

If the United States could forget its own interests and give the Philippines their independence, permit Puerto Rico to vote on its future government, and return the canal zone to Panama in spite of strong internal protests, why does it insist on defending British sovereignty over the Falkland Islands? Why not instead establish justice by following its best traditions, demonstrated on so many occasions, and unite with the rest of the hemisphere in erasing all trace of colonialism?

Could it be that the U.S. Navy and the British Admiralty have decided that the islands are essential for protecting oil routes around South Africa in case of world conflict? With the eastern coast of Africa unsafe for Western tankers, they would have to cross the South Atlantic to reach South America, where they would be under the protection of friendly navies, ultimately to reach the Caribbean and the North Atlantic. In such a case the Falklands/Malvinas would play a crucial strategic role. Could this have been in the minds of U.S. naval officers courting Argentine admirals before the invasion of the islands by Argentina? If it was, perhaps the invasion and subsequent reconquest by Britain made them change their minds and throw in their lot with the British Admiralty as the more efficient ruler of the Falklands and a stronger ally in case of trouble.

Britain and the Falklands/Malvinas Conflict

The attitude of the United Kingdom during the seventeen years that the Anglo-Argentine negotiations lasted ranged from virtual acceptance of the return of the islands to Argentina to the most intransigent refusal to consider, even in principle, the transfer of sovereignty. From 1965, when the first contacts were made, to 1968, when Britain appeared ready to make some concessions, the negotiations were agreeable. By 1968 the two governments had agreed to the transfer of the islands to Argentina under certain conditions. The secret agreement, however, leaked out, and as a result, in March 1968, the Falkland Islands Emergency Committee was organized to prevent the return of the islands through a campaign to sway the government and public opinion. The committee extended its "educational" campaign to the islands' population by describing it as the victim of a plot and finally even as the conscience of Britain.

The campaign worked. When in December 1968 the proposal to transfer sovereignty was mentioned in parliament, the reaction was violent. It did not relax until Foreign Secretary Michael Stewart promised that nothing would be done against the "wishes" of the islanders. The substitution of the term *wishes* for the term *interests*, which had been agreed to in the United Nations, became a perfect excuse for those who opposed the negotiations to obstruct them, and a stumbling block for others who sincerely wanted to negotiate a solution of the problem. For the Thatcher government the *wishes* of the islanders became paramount.

After 1968, the islanders became the arbiters of the negotiations. They rejected every proposal except those from which they might benefit, such as the agreement on communications with Argentina in 1971–1973. The multiple benefits received by the islands from these agreements would have cost Britain six million pounds annually, and were acknowledged by the United Nations as a most worthy effort in the process of decolonizing the islands.

After the signing of the communications agreements, Britain concentrated its efforts on delaying the negotiations as much as possible, with complete disdain for the U.N. mandate. Yet it worried mildly about the danger of confrontation, knowing full well that Argentina had never given up the idea of getting back the islands.

In July 1981, Nicholas Ridley, minister of state in the Foreign and Commonwealth Office, presented a plan approved by Lord Carrington, the foreign minister, providing for a public education campaign in the islands and in Britain to apprise the people of the facts of the situation and the advantages of a solution to the question of sovereignty. It was rejected by the Thatcher government on the basis that the wishes of the islanders were paramount (Frank 1983: pp. 27–28; The *Sunday Times* of London Insight Team, 1982: p. 56).

At that time, of the approximately 1,800 "natives" on the islands, only 140 had British passports that automatically permitted them to enter the United Kingdom. Others with only commonwealth passports could not. And as late as 1981 800 "natives" were denied British passports for not having had British grandparents. It was not until January 1983, six months after the war in the Malvinas ended, that the British government granted British citizenship to all the inhabitants of the islands.

After Ridley's plan was rejected, the British government, it seems, ran out of ideas and chose to play a delaying game. By doing so it gave up the initiative, inviting Argentina to present a plan for future rounds of negotiations. Argentina presented a tight schedule of meetings and a deadline to end the dispute. The British government delayed answering the Argentine proposal until the incident on South Georgia convinced it that the delaying game had become dangerous, and then decided to offer a compromise solution with complete disregard for the islanders' wishes.

Fearing an invasion of the Falklands, Britain appealed immediately to the United Nations for help, although for ten years it had disregarded that body's mandate to negotiate in earnest. Sir Anthony Parsons, the British ambassador to the United Nations, on April 1, 1982, asked the Security Council for immediate action to prevent the invasion. After the April 2 invasion, he skillfully obtained on April 3 the passage by the Security Council of Resolution 502, calling for the immediate withdrawal of the Argentine troops, the cessation of all warlike activities, and the renewal of negotiations. Argentina did not comply with the resolution. Neither did Britain. Instead, Britain continued preparing the task force begun on March 31. By April 5–6, the task force was on its way to Ascension Island.

But to win the war it was necessary first to win over world opinion. This was done through the media and behind the scenes in the United Nations, at NATO headquarters, in the European Common Market, and in the United States at all levels of government. The campaign was a masterpiece of British effort into which were thrown intelligence, speed, and efficiency. It should be incorporated into manuals of strategy on how to prepare for a victory in an unpopular war.

During Haig's negotiations Thatcher showed herself as intransigent as the Argentine junta. She appeared uninterested in the peace proposals of Peruvian President Belaúnde, although she softened somewhat her attitude toward the plan of Secretary-General Pérez de Cuéllar. Her attitude toward the negotiations may be explained by her conviction that if she wanted to recover the islands (thereby strengthening her political position in Britain), she would have to act quickly, taking advantage of the belligerent mood of Parliament and public opinion before it subsided or changed as it had during the Suez Canal crisis of 1956. If, as some British and Argentine observers believe, the *General Belgrano* was sunk to prevent Argentina from accepting the peace proposals, it had the desired effect.

It is doubtful whether Thatcher would have been swayed (if she ever received it) by a letter written to her and published in *La Nación* of Buenos Aires on April 19, 1982, just when the task force was on its way to the Falklands. It was from the Asociación de Agricultores Británicos (Association of British Husbandmen) and other descendants of Britons in Argentina:

> We, Britons and descendants of British husbandmen in Argentina wish to inform Her Majesty's Government that for years and in some cases for generations we have lived and worked happily under Argentine governments of different political orientations. We have lived in keeping with our traditional British way of life, without obstacles of any kind, and our experience has brought us to believe that the inhabitants of the Malvinas have nothing to lose and much to gain by placing themselves under Argentine sovereignty.

Argentina and the Falklands/Malvinas Conflict

The invasion of the Malvinas signified for the Argentines the recuperation of Argentine territory unsuccessfully demanded for over 149 years, the last seventeen of them in fruitless negotiations with Great Britain. It is not easy to blame Argentina for losing its patience. It had tried since 1965 to follow the mandate of the United Nations by negotiating with Britain only to have its efforts thwarted time and again. For the Argentines time had run out. As a result, for the first time in its history Argentina abandoned its tradition, of which it had been so justly proud, of not, on its own initiative, trying to resolve an international dispute by the use of arms. We must point out that perhaps the invasion would not have occurred had a constitutional civil government been in power at that time. But however understandable Argentina's motives may have been, we must admit that it committed some grave errors.

First, it failed to realize that the world might consider its action as an unadorned, malicious aggression, an action that would permit Britain to get world sympathy.

Second, the Argentine government underestimated Britain's possible reaction to the invasion. If Argentina intended to keep the islands regardless of British reaction, it should have prepared the islands and the country for the eventualities of war. It did not do this, not even after the British task force was on its way.

Third, Argentina assumed that the United States would support it or at least remain neutral if a conflict occurred. Members of the government, mostly military officers, seemed infatuated by the show of friendship bestowed on some of them during visits to Washington, by the cooperation of the Pentagon with the Argentine navy, and by Argentine support of Reagan's policy in Central America. In spite of Haig's warning, they believed the United States would at least remain neutral.

Fourth, the Argentine government did not seem to realize that it was isolated from the mainstream of international politics, without prestige and with a bad reputation for military coups and trampling on human rights. It was the responsibility of Foreign Minister Nicanor Costa Méndez to inform the junta of Argentina's position in the world, but either he did not inform the junta or it did not listen to him. This lack of awareness greatly facilitated Britain's predisposition of world opinion against Argentina. In the minds of many people outside Latin America, Argentina (although more European than the United States in its cultural background) was just another Latin American nation that was always having revolutions and was unable to establish a stable democratic government.

Fifth, perhaps the greatest error of the Argentine government was not to accept the mandate of the United Nations and even use it against Britain. If Argentina had withdrawn its troops in keeping with Resolution

502, it could have beaten Britain at its own game, by accepting the resolution and calling world attention to the real situation: the refusal of Britain to negotiate the ownership of a territory claimed by Argentina for 150 years. Even if Argentina could not have complied with Resolution 502 because it was not assured of a fair solution to the problem, it definitely should have accepted the peace plan of Secretary-General Javier Pérez de Cuéllar. It was a good plan to stop the conflict and reopen negotiations, with a guaranty of supervision by four neutral nations. In rejecting it the Argentine military leaders demonstrated a pride and stubbornness equal to Thatcher's. With its bloodless invasion of the islands, the Argentine government could have called world attention to its discipline as well as its military capacity. With obedience to the mandate of the United Nations, it could have demonstrated its respect for the authority of the highest international tribunal, and thus could have earned the regard of the world while at the same time forcing Britain to negotiate in good faith.

After 149 years of claims and counterclaims, 17 years of fruitless negotiations, and a seventy-four-day war, the Falklands/Malvinas conflict is still unresolved. The Argentine government invaded the islands out of national pride. The British government retaliated to save its national pride by sending a task force of a size—over 100 ships and 25,000 men—seldom seen even in British naval history and obtained the help of half the world's powers in ejecting the Argentines.

Argentina was defeated and humiliated, and its military government fell in disgrace and dishonor. Britain recovered the islands but at a cost it can ill afford. And the sovereignty of the islands remains in dispute.

A Brief Chronology of the Falklands/Malvinas

1501	Amerigo Vespucci sights the islands on his second voyage to the New World.
1520	Esteban Gómez sights the islands and calls them the Islas de Sansón y de los Patos.
Feb. 4, 1540	A lost ship from Francisco de Camargo's expedition sights the islands, remaining there several months.
Aug. 1592	John Davis discovers the islands for Britain.
Jan. 27, 1690	John Strong makes the first British landing on the islands.
July 13, 1713	The Treaty of Utrecht reaffirms Spain's right to control the seas around Spanish dominions.
1749	First diplomatic exchange over the Falklands: Britain proposes to explore them and Spain insists on its exclusive right.
Feb. 10, 1763	The Treaty of Paris again reaffirms Spain's right to close the South Atlantic.
Mar. 17, 1764	Louis Antoine de Bougainville founds Fort St. Louis, the first known settlement on the islands.
Jan. 1765	John Byron takes possession of the Falklands for George III and founds Port Egmont by planting vegetables.
Jan. 8, 1766	John McBride's expedition lands in the Falklands, with instructions to hold Port Egmont and warn off any other settlers.
Apr. 1, 1767	Bougainville returns Fort St. Louis to Spain.
June 4, 1770	Juan Ignacio de Madariaga expels the British from Port Egmont.
Sept. 15, 1771	Francisco de Orduña returns Port Egmont to the British.
May 20, 1774	The British abandon Port Egmont, leaving a lead plate inscribed with their claim of ownership.

179

1777	Charles III orders Port Egmont destroyed.
Oct. 25, 1790	Britain and Spain sign the Nootka Sound Convention forbidding the British to colonize in the South Atlantic.
Jan. 8, 1811	The governor of Montevideo evacuates the Malvinas.
July 9, 1816	Argentina declares independence from Spain.
Nov. 6, 1820	David Jewitt takes possession of the Malvinas for Argentina.
Jan. 1826	Luis Vernet establishes a settlement in the Malvinas.
June 10, 1829	Vernet is appointed governor of the Malvinas.
Aug. 30, 1829	Vernet issues a decree against whaling and sealing in the islands.
Nov. 19, 1831	The *Harriet* arrives in Buenos Aires to stand trial for violating Vernet's decree; a diplomatic dispute ensues between Argentina and the United States.
Dec. 28, 1831	Silas Duncan of the *Lexington* destroys Vernet's colony.
Jan. 2, 1833	John James Onslow seizes the islands for Britain.
1842	The settlement at Port Luis is moved to Port William, later renamed Port Stanley.
June 23, 1843	Queen Victoria issues a letter patent incorporating the islands into the dominions of the crown.
1852	The Falkland Islands Company is chartered.
	Juan Manuel de Rosas is overthrown; Britain and Argentina enter a long period of close relations, with high British investment in Argentina.
June 1943	Juan Domingo Perón comes to power in Argentina and immediately begins to foster anti-British sentiment.
Dec. 14, 1960	UN Resolution 1514 calls for an end to colonialism; Britain lists the Falklands as a colony and Argentina objects.
Dec. 15, 1965	UN Resolution 2065 calls for Argentina and the United Kingdom to negotiate over the islands.
Early 1968	The Falkland Islands Committee is organized to lobby against return of the islands to Argentina.
Nov. 1968	Lord Chalfont persuades the islanders to accept the "position of agreement" with Argentina, scheduled for disclosure in mid-December.
Dec. 1968	Conservatives and some Labourites attack the Labour government in Parliament over the Falklands: the "position of agreement" is scuttled.
July 1, 1971	Argentina and Britain agree on measures to improve communication between the islands and the Argentine mainland.

Apr. 1973	The British refuse to discuss sovereignty; negotiations virtually cease.
Dec. 1973	UN Resolution 3160 urges the renewal of negotiations.
Oct. 1975	Britain sends the Shackleton mission to investigate the islands' economic resources; Argentina responds with anger.
Jan. 1976	Britain and Argentina recall their ambassadors.
1979	Ambassadorial relations are reinstated.
Fall 1981	Britain abandons the initiative in negotiations, suggesting that Argentina make proposals.
Dec. 20, 1981	Argentine scrap dealer C. S. Davidoff visits South Georgia to inspect a purchase, without British permission.
Feb. 3, 1982	The British government protests Davidoff's action to Argentina.
Feb. 26–27, 1982	Argentina and Britain agree to establish a permanent negotiating commission.
Mar. 19, 1982	Davidoff's workers land on South Georgia without British permission; Britain orders the *Endurance* to remove the Argentines.
Mar. 24, 1982	Argentina orders the *Bahía Paraíso* to South Georgia.
Apr. 2, 1982	Argentine troops land on the Malvinas.
Apr. 3, 1982	UN Security Council Resolution 502 calls for an immediate cessation of hostilities and the withdrawal of Argentine troops from the islands.
Apr. 8, 1982	U.S. Secretary of State Haig begins an attempt at mediation.
Apr. 30, 1982	Haig declares his mission terminated; U.S. President Reagan announces U.S. support for Britain and economic sanctions against Argentina.
May 2, 1982	At 1:30 A.M. Peruvian President Belaúnde presents a peace proposal to Argentine President Galtieri. At 10:00 A.M. Galtieri replies with proposed modifications and a preliminary acceptance, to be ratified by the Argentine junta at a meeting scheduled for 7:00 P.M. At 4:00 P.M. Britain sinks the *General Belgrano,* with the loss of 368 lives. The junta rejects Belaúnde's plan.
May 4, 1982	Argentina sinks the *Sheffield.*
May 18, 1982	Britain rejects a peace proposal by UN Secretary-General Pérez de Cuéllar.
May 21, 1982	British forces land on East Falkland.
June 14, 1982	Argentine forces in the islands surrender.

Select Bibliography

Few if any topics as restricted as the Falkland/Malvinas Islands can boast as extensive a bibliography as they do. And yet, except for the Argentines, who have never stopped claiming the islands on historic as well as geographical grounds, few people know much about them, including the Britons, who have occupied the islands for 150 years. It is an exceptional bibliography for such a small and little-known region, as an examination of Margaret Patricia Henwood Laver's *Annotated Bibliography* will show.

For the early history of the islands, during the sixteenth, seventeenth, and eighteenth centuries, the authors have leaned in the main on the distinguished scholarship of Julius Goebel, Jr., and Ricardo R. Caillet-Bois. Unfortunately the 1982 reprint of Goebel's book contains an introduction by J.C.J. Metford (really an article from the July 1968 issue of *International Affairs*) that is a biased pro-English attempt to discredit some of Goebel's erudite conclusions. Readers may want to read Goebel and Metford and compare their findings. Additional helpful material will be found in the works of José Arce, Antonio Gómez Langenheim, Manuel Hidalgo Nieto, and Enrique Ruis Guiñazú et al., and in the book by Ruiz Guiñazú (*Proas de España en el mar magallánico*), all listed in the following bibliography.

The nineteenth-century history of conflict over the islands is covered extensively by many scholarly articles and histories, and even in British, U.S., and Argentine textbooks in history, international law, and political science. The authors have selected the most helpful materials for the bibliography, such as H. S. Ferns's excellent work on British-Argentine relations in the nineteenth century and the extensive collection of documents in the work of José Luis Muñoz Azpiri.

It would be impossible to put into the bibliography all the periodical materials the authors used for the more recent period of conflict and negotiation. Suffice it to say that there were literally mounds of materials collected during extensive stays in Argentina and Spain, of notes from U.S., British, and Canadian periodicals, and of periodicals and books sent to the authors through the years by friends in Latin America. It must be noted that practically everything published in British periodicals on the Malvinas/Falklands is republished verbatim in Argentine periodicals, a most helpful bibliographical crutch. Since April 1982, when the invasion of the Falklands occurred, a flood of materials has hit the Argentine newsstands. One of the better books is Bonifacio del Carril's *La cuestion de las Malvinas*. In Britain the best book that has appeared so far is that of the *Sunday Times* (London) Insight Team, well written and interesting if not completely accurate. For the person who wants more detail, the official Franks report is intriguing, although its conclusions are not always clear.

Arce, José. *Las Malvinas (las pequeñas islas que nos fueron arrebatadas)*. Madrid: Instituto de Cultura Hispánica, 1950.

Boyson, V. F. *The Falkland Islands, with Notes on the Natural History*. Oxford: Clarendon Press, 1924.

Britain and the Falklands Crisis: A Documentary Record. London: Her Majesty's Stationery Office, 1982.

Buenos Aires Herald, November 9, 1982.

Caillet-Bois, Ricardo R. *Una tierra argentina. Las Islas Malvinas. Ensayo basado en una nueva y desconocida documentación*. 2d ed. Buenos Aires: Ediciones Peuser, 1952.

Carril, Bonifacio del. *La cuestión de las Malvinas*. Buenos Aires: Emecé Editores, 1982.

Cawkell, M.B.R.; Maling, D. H.; and Cawkell, E. M. *The Falkland Islands*. London: The Macmillan Company, 1960.

Chambers, B. M. "Can Hawkins's *Maiden Land* be Identified as the Falkland Islands?" *The Geographical Journal* 4 (1901):414–423.

Colección de documentos relativos a la historia de las Islas Malvinas. Vol. 1. Buenos Aires: Frigerio Artes Gráficas, 1957. Vols. 2 and 3 in one volume. Buenos Aires: Guillermo Kraft Ltda., 1961.

Crosby, Ronald K. *El reto de las Malvinas*. Buenos Aires: Plus Ultra, 1981.

Daus, Federico. *Reseña geográfica de las Islas Malvinas*. Buenos Aires: Imprenta de la Universidad, 1955.

Falkland Islands Economic Study 1982. Chairman: The Rt. Hon. Lord Shackleton, KG, PC, OBE. Presented to the Prime Minister. Presented to Parliament by the Prime Minister by Command of Her Majesty September 1982. London: Her Majesty's Stationery Office, 1982.

Ferns, H. S. *Britain and Argentina in the Nineteenth Century*. Oxford: Clarendon Press, 1960.

Fitte, Ernesto J. *La agresión norteamericana a las Islas Malvinas. Crónica documental*. Buenos Aires: Emecé Editores, 1966.

Fitzroy, Robert. *Narrative of the Surveying Voyages of His Majesty's Ships "Adventure" and "Beagle," between the Years 1826 and 1836, Describing Their Examination of the Southern Shore of South America, and the "Beagle's" Circumnavigation of the Globe*. 3 vols. London: H. Colburn, 1839.

Franks, Lord. *Falkland Islands Review. Report of a Committee of Privy Councillors. Chairmen: the Rt. Hon the Lord Franks, OM, GCMG, KCB, CBE. Presented to Parliament by the Prime Minister by Command of Her Majesty January 1983*. London: Her Majesty's Stationery Office, 1983.

Gamba, Virginia. *The S. A. C. File. 4..2..82: The South Atlantic Conflict File, An Argentine View*. Buenos Aires: Committee Pro-Sovereignty of the Malvinas Islands, 1982.

Goebel, Julius, Jr. *The Struggle for the Falkland Islands: A Study in Legal and Diplomatic History*. New Haven: Yale University Press, 1927. Reprinted in 1982 with a preface and introduction by J.C.J. Metford.

Gómez Langenheim, Antonio. *Elementos para la historia de nuestras Islas Malvinas*. 2 vols. Buenos Aires: El Ateneo, 1939.

Groussac, Paul. *Las Islas Malvinas*. Buenos Aires: Talleres Gráficos Argentinos L.J. Rosso, 1936.

Hacke, William, ed. *A collection of original voyages: containing I, Capt. Cowley's voyages* . . . . London: Printed for James Knapton, 1699.

Hawkins, Richard. *The observations of Sir Richard Hawkins, Knight, in his voyage into the South Sea in the year 1593*. Reprinted from the edition of 1622. London: The Hakluyt Society, 1847.

Hidalgo Nieto, Manuel. *La cuestión de las Malvinas. Contribución al estudio de las relaciones hispano-inglesas en el siglo XVIII*. Madrid: Consejo Superior de Investigaciones Científicas, 1947.

Izaguirre, Mario. *Estado actual de las cuestión Malvinas*. Buenos Aires: Centro Naval, Instituto de Publicaciones Navales, 1972.

Jane, John. *The voyages and works of John Davis, the navigator*. Edited with an introduction and notes by Albert Hastings Markham, London: The Hakluyt Society, 1880.

Johnson, Richard. "The Future of the Falkland Islands." *The World Today* 33 (1977):223–231.

Johnson, Samuel. *Thoughts on the Late Transactions Respecting Falkland's Islands*. London: Printed for T. Cadell, 1771.

Jones, Clarence F. "The Economic Activities of the Falkland Islands." *The Geographical Review* 14 (1924):394–403.

La Nación (Buenos Aires), November 11, 1965.

La Nación (Buenos Aires), January 5, 1976.

La Nación (Buenos Aires), April 19, 1982.

La Prensa (Buenos Aires), May 17, 1946.

Laver, Margaret Patricia Henwood. *An Annotated Bibliography of the Falkland Islands and the Falkland Islands Dependencies As Delimited on 3rd March, 1962*. Cape Town: University of Capetown Libraries, 1977.

Leguizamón Pondal, Martiniano. *Toponimia criolla en las Malvinas*. Buenos Aires: Editorial Raigal, 1956.

Moore, Tui de Roy. "In the shadow of gunboats." *International Wildlife* 12 (1982):4–11.

Moreno, Juan Carlos. *Nuestras Malvinas. La Antártida*. Buenos Aires: Cantiello y Cía., 1938.

_____ . *La recuperación de las Malvinas*. Buenos Aires, Plus Ultra, 1973.

Muñoz Azpiri, José Luis. *Historia completa de las Malvinas*. 3 vols. Buenos Aires: Editorial Oriente, 1966.

Observations on the Forcible Occupation of the Malvinas, or Falkland Islands, by the British Government, in 1833. London: Charles Wood and Son, 1833.

Pereyra, Ezequiel Federico. *Las Islas Malvinas, soberanía argentina: antecedentes, gestiones diplomáticas*. Buenos Aires: Secretaría de Estado de Cultura y Educación, 1969.

Pettingill, Olin Sewall, Jr. "Tussock World." *American Birds* 36 (1982):915–921.

_____ . "Natural history of an unlikely battlefield." *Audubon* 84 (1982):52–63.

Quesada, Héctor C. *Las Malvinas son argentinas (Recopilación de antecedentes)*. Buenos Aires: Secretaría de Educación de la Nación, Subsecretaría de Cultura, 1948.

Ratto, Héctor R. *Actividades marítimas en la Patagonia durante los siglos XVII y XVIII*. Buenos Aires: Guillermo Kraft Ltda., 1930.

Ruiz Guiñazú, Enrique; Gandía, Enrique de; Caillet-Bois, Ricardo R.; and Zorraquín Becú, Ricardo. *Los derechos argentinos sobre las Malvinas.* Buenos Aires: Ediciones Peuser, 1964.

Ruiz Guiñazú, Enrique. *Proas de España en el mar magallánico.* Buenos Aires: Ediciones Peuser, 1945.

Shackleton, Lord, "Prospect of the Falkland Islands, with Contributions by R. J. Storey and R. Johnson. I. The Economic Survey. Lord Shackleton." *The Geographical Journal* 143 (1977):1–13.

Sopeña, Germán. "El caso *General Belgrano.* Oscuridades y sospechas que siguen dando que hablar en Inglaterra." *La Prensa* (Buenos Aires), July 14, 1983.

Strange, Ian. "Unmentioned Crisis in the Falklands: Wildlife Survival." *Animal Kingdom* 85 (1982):6–13.

Sunday Times of London Insight Team. *War in the Falklands. 1982. The Full Story.* New York: Harper and Row, 1982.

Torre Revello, José Miguel Andrés. *Bibliografía de las islas Malvinas: obras, mapas y documentación (contribución).* Buenos Aires: Imprenta de la Universidad, 1953.

United Nations, General Assembly, Resolution 1514, December 14, 1960.

United Nations, General Assembly, Resolution 2065, December 15, 1965.

United Nations, Security Council, Resolution 502, April 3, 1982.

Wilson, Andrew, and Gavshon, Arthur. "Secrets of Belgrano revealed by documents." *The Observer* (London), June 5, 1983.

Index